CW00485435

**Centre for Inclusion and
Collaborative Partnerships**

The Open University
Walton Hall
Milton Keynes
United Kingdom
MK7 6AA

Tel +44 (0)1908 332840
Fax +44 (0)1908 332841
cicp-recep@open.ac.uk
www.open.ac.uk/cicp

The Open
University

From Kate Hawkins

With compliments

Lifelong Learning Participation in a Changing
Policy Context

Lifelong Learning Participation in a Changing Policy Context

An Interdisciplinary Theory

Ellen Boeren

Chancellor's Fellow, Moray House School of Education,
University of Edinburgh, UK

LIFELONG LEARNING PARTICIPATION IN A CHANGING POLICY CONTEXT:
AN INTERDISCIPLINARY THEORY
Copyright © Ellen Boeren, 2016

All rights reserved. No reproduction, copy or transmission of this publication may be made without written permission. No portion of this publication may be reproduced, copied or transmitted save with written permission. In accordance with the provisions of the Copyright, Designs and Patents Act 1988, or under the terms of any licence permitting limited copying issued by the Copyright Licensing Agency, Saffron House, 6–10 Kirby Street, London EC1N 8TS.

Any person who does any unauthorized act in relation to this publication may be liable to criminal prosecution and civil claims for damages.

First published 2016 by
PALGRAVE MACMILLAN

The author has asserted her right to be identified as the author of this work in accordance with the Copyright, Designs and Patents Act 1988.

Palgrave Macmillan in the UK is an imprint of Macmillan Publishers Limited, registered in England, company number 785998, of Houndmills, Basingstoke, Hampshire RG21 6XS.

Palgrave Macmillan in the US is a division of Nature America, Inc., One New York Plaza, Suite 4500 New York, NY 10004-1562.

Palgrave Macmillan is the global academic imprint of the above companies and has companies and representatives throughout the world.

Hardback ISBN: 978–1–137–44182–9
E-PUB ISBN: 978–1–137–44184–3
E-PDF ISBN: 978–1–137–44183–6
DOI: 10.1057/9781137441836

Distribution in the UK, Europe and the rest of the world is by Palgrave Macmillan®, a division of Macmillan Publishers Limited, registered in England, company number 785998, of Houndmills, Basingstoke, Hampshire RG21 6XS.

A catalog record for this book is available from the Library of Congress

A catalogue record for the book is available from the British Library

Typeset by MPS Limited, Chennai, India.

Contents

List of Figures and Tables

Figures

Tables

Preface

This book has been written at a time when adult lifelong learning is suffering. While leading international organisations recognise its importance, the system demonstrates major weaknesses in terms of social inequality and ineffectiveness. Previous research, extensively reported in Courtney's (1992) *Why Adults Learn*, shows that participation in lifelong learning seems to be strongly linked to learners' motivations, attitudes and expectations. While current lifelong learning policies tend to focus on the individual responsibilities of adults to survive in the competitive knowledge-based economy, it is now time to devote an entire monograph to demonstrating that participation is in fact a shared responsibility between different players: the individuals, the learning providers and social policy approaches at the level of countries. It is important to publish a fresh approach that moves away from the narrow idea that participation revolves around individual motivation and psychological characteristics of adults. Therefore, it is necessary to consider how elements of sociological literature and the functioning of educational institutions, workplaces and countries contribute to our understanding of 'why adults learn'.

Acknowledgements

This book is the result of researching adult lifelong learning participation over the past ten years. My thanks go first and foremost to my PhD supervisors Ides Nicaise and Herman Baert of the University of Leuven, Belgium. Critical discussions with colleagues from the LLL2010 consortium helped to further improve my research skills. Special thanks needs to be given to my colleague John Holford at Nottingham. It was possible to work on this book as part of my Chancellor's Fellowship at the University of Edinburgh, UK. I therefore owe a big thank you to my colleagues at the Moray House School of Education.

Introduction

I started my academic journey nearly ten years ago, having obtained my Bachelor's and Master's degrees. I then managed to obtain a position at the Flemish Catholic University Leuven (KULeuven – Belgium) to undertake research on lifelong learning participation and motivation as part of the European Sixth Framework project 'LLL2010 – Towards a Lifelong Learning Society in Europe: the Contribution of the Education System'. The project ran from September 2005 to February 2011 and owing to the length of the project, I had the opportunity to complete a PhD during this period.

Throughout this project, my conceptual understanding of participation issues in the field of lifelong learning increased. As part of my PhD, I attempted to widen the scope of existing participation models, mainly developed in the North American context and mainly originating in social psychology. The following projects have given me the opportunity to empirically validate my theoretical work: an interdisciplinary approach to evaluating participation models published in the *International Journal of Lifelong Education*; work on the self-gathered LLL2010 Adult Learners Survey involving 13,000 adult learners in formal education across Europe; and participation in work on datasets like the Eurostat Adult Education Survey and the Labour Force Survey. The final conference of the LLL2010 project was organised in February 2011 in Leuven, Belgium, and I successfully defended my doctoral thesis on the 20th May 2011, also in Leuven.

It is now almost ten years later and I have obtained a permanent position at the University of Edinburgh, UK, following an initial tenure track appointment (Chancellor's Fellowship). During the first three years of my tenure track fellowship, I was fortunate to be given time to continue increasing my knowledge of why adults do or do not participate in lifelong learning activities. After nearly ten years studying the topic, I now feel ready to publish my first monograph on research in the field.

The book consists of nine chapters and follows a systematic approach as it builds up from the individual perspective towards an overarching approach. In the following chapters, I refer to the main streams or dimensions of literature that I would like to consider as separate puzzles contributing to the overall and integrated understanding of adult lifelong learning participation. Being that much has been written in the past in a fragmented way, it has naturally been impossible to discuss every single piece of work forming a part of this field. However, the book will provide the reader with an overview of the major streams to be found in the literature relevant to the topic of adult lifelong learning participation.

The nine chapters have been divided into three major parts. The first part of the book sets out background information in relation to adult lifelong learning participation. The second part explores the participation of different disciplines and works towards an integrative interdisciplinary theory. Part three focuses on scenarios for future research and makes recommendations for policy and practice. The structure of the book is presented in Figure I.1.

Part I 'Background' consists of two chapters.

Chapter 1, 'Adult Lifelong Learning Participation: Definitions and Contexts' sets the scene, focusing on the major aims of contemporary lifelong learning debates, as set out by leading agents, such as the European Commission, the OECD (Organisation for Economic Co-operation and Development) and UNESCO (The United Nations Educational, Scientific and Cultural Organization). This chapter also provides clarity regarding the choice of terminology. The chapter's aim is to demonstrate the importance of adult lifelong learning participation through reflecting on its benefits.

Chapter 2, 'Trends and Barriers in Adult Lifelong Learning Participation', provides an overview of the most recent participation figures across the globe, but also engages in a discussion of the major barriers preventing adults from taking part in lifelong learning activities. Understanding of the types of barriers discussed in the literature is needed to understand the overviews provided in the following chapters.

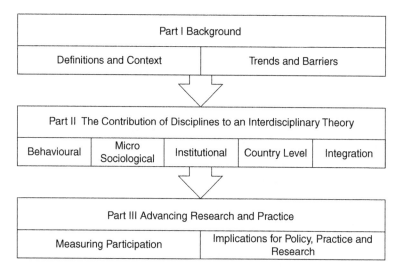

Figure I.1   Overview of chapters

Part II 'The Contribution of Disciplines to an Interdisciplinary Theory' consists of five chapters.

Chapter 3, 'Lifelong Learning Participation: The Behavioural Perspective', explores the question, from a mainly psychological perspective, of why certain adults do and others do not participate in adult lifelong learning activities. The chapter refers to discussion on participation as being the result of an underlying decision-making process, so reflecting on the role of motivation, including psychological constructs such as confidence and attitudes. Finally, the chapter engages in discussion around the changing psychological perspective across the life span and its influence on adult lifelong learning participation.

Chapter 4, 'Lifelong Learning Participation: The Micro Sociological Perspective', also focuses on the role of the individual, but from the perspective of participation in relation to social class and social mobility. This chapter reflects on the notion of cost–benefit analysis as part of adults' underlying decision-making processes, stating why this cost–benefit analysis is different for adults from different socio-economic and socio-demographic groups, then targeting for discussion variables such as age, gender, educational attainment, occupational status and race/ethnicity.

Chapter 5, 'Lifelong Learning Participation: Institutional Barriers', moves the focus from the individual level to the role of educational institutions. As has been explored in the previous chapter, adults will not be able to participate in adult lifelong learning activities if there is no offer available to them. However, educational institutions or training providers can also prevent adults from taking part if they construct high levels of institutional barriers. This chapter will discuss knowledge in regard to the role of course modes in facilitating or preventing access, also tackling lack of access indicators in educational benchmarking and the role of information in raising awareness about lifelong learning opportunities.

Chapter 6, 'Lifelong Learning Participation: Country Level Determinants', takes one step further in my mission to understand participation, introducing the role of the country in education policy. From recent European research it is very clear that participation rates in Scandinavian countries are higher than anywhere else. It is therefore important to go beyond the level of individual responsibility and explore how various social policy aspects in countries encourage or prevent participation. This chapter will discuss different lifelong learning typologies as published in the recent adult lifelong learning literature and will reflect on the role of welfare regimes, to which many of these lifelong learning typologies have been linked.

Chapter 7, 'Lifelong Learning Participation: The Need for Integration', is the outcome of an attempt to integrate aspects of individual, institutional and country levels and to understand adult lifelong learning participation as an interdisciplinary subject that should be studied to explore interactions between different levels. This chapter starts with reflections on general integrative theories, published by authors like Giddens and Lewin. It then focuses on the integrative theories of the major scholars in the field, including Rubenson and Desjardin's work on the 'Bounded Agency Model' and my own Comprehensive Lifelong Learning Participation Model, which I constructed, together with my supervisors, as part of my doctoral research (Rubenson & Desjardins, 2009; Boeren, 2011).

The final Part III 'Advancing Research and Practice' consists of two chapters.

Chapter 8, 'Measuring Adult Lifelong Learning Participation', is written as a critical reflection on the strengths and weaknesses of different surveys organised by the European Commission and UNESCO measuring adult lifelong learning participation: e.g. the Eurostat Adult Education Survey, the Labour Force Survey and PIAAC. This chapter compares the findings of these major surveys while focusing on the limitations of these measurement instruments and presents some alternative scenarios for future data collection.

Finally, Chapter 9, 'Implications for Policy, Practice and Research', is the concluding chapter, focusing on the 'lessons learnt' from this interdisciplinary review of adult lifelong learning participation studies. Here, insights for policy makers and practitioners will be supplemented by the need of an expansive research agenda on the topic.

Part I
Background

1

Adult Lifelong Learning Participation: Definitions and Contexts

This first chapter will introduce the reader to the rationale of why I have written an entire book around the notion of participation in adult lifelong learning activities. I will refer to the importance of lifelong learning and will provide background information regarding the policy context in which participation debates have been shaped over the previous decades. I will do this by referring to the work of leading organisations in the field, such as the European Commission, the OECD and UNESCO.

Why participation

Participation studies in the area of adult lifelong learning are not new. Participation models have been published in the international literature, particularly during the 1970s and 1980s, and an overview and critique of these models can be found in Courtney (1992). However, since the mid-1990s, a renewed interest in participation has taken place, and the scholarly field has since moved on.

Why adult lifelong learning?

First of all, it is important to note that, as opposed to the term lifelong education or alternative terms like 'recurrent education' or 'permanent education', the term 'lifelong learning' is now widely used (Boeren, 2011). Lifelong learning represents learning from cradle to grave, while focusing on learning that can take place both within and outside the education system. It is thus also perceived as being 'life-wide' because it can include learning in a wide range of settings and over a wide range of subjects.

Adult learning in fact refers to learning that takes place in adulthood, mainly after the end of compulsory initial education, including higher education immediately following the end of compulsory education. Indeed, the adult learners' population is often operationalised in different ways, as will be explored in this book. Owing to the dominant use of the term 'lifelong learning' in policy discourses nowadays, I have decided to use the term 'adult lifelong learning participation' throughout this book instead of 'participation in adult education'. More on the trends of changing terms and policy discourses will be explored when discussing the roles of major agencies, such as the European Commission, UNESCO and the OECD.

Types of lifelong learning: formal – non-formal – informal

Learning activities are often classified between formal, non-formal and informal learning. This classification was initially developed by UNESCO, but is nowadays widely used in the field of adult lifelong learning (see UNESCO, 1979, for an overview of adult education terms). In fact, texts will often refer to formal and non-formal education or training, and informal learning, although different interpretations are sometimes given to these terms.

In general, formal learning refers to those learning activities that take place in formalised settings, comparable to the initial schooling system; they are characterised by the possibility of obtaining a recognised certificate, diploma, degree or other qualification. Non-formal learning differs from formal learning insofar as an officially recognised qualification will not be granted upon completion of a non-formal learning activity. While a certificate might be provided, it does not have any civic or legal value. Informal learning is usually defined as learning that takes place in a non-intended and accidental way, such as learning through undertaking activities with family or friends. The European Commission defines informal learning as learning that takes place outside formalised settings, whether it has been the intention of the adult to learn something new or otherwise. In fact, learning happens on a daily basis and is therefore often non-intentional, incidental and random.

With respect to this book, it is important to understand the difference between formal and non-formal learning in comparison to informal learning, as statistics focusing on adult learning usually only measure participation in formal and non-formal activities and do not engage with information in relation to informal learning. For instance, this is what European policy makers do when they refer to participation statistics based on the European Adult Education Survey or the Labour Force Survey; this will be explored in more depth in Chapter 8. The European target of 15 percent of adults participating in adult lifelong learning by 2020 therefore refers to participation in formal and non-formal learning activities, not in informal learning. On the one hand, this measurement has proved to be a shortcoming as a wide range of skills and knowledge is acquired through informal learning, through interaction with others outside educational or training settings. On the other hand, measuring the intensity of informal learning might be more difficult to achieve; one can assume that informal learning takes place in everyday life and is present in a wide range of other activities. The notion of lifelong learning participation as a combined measure of participation in formal and non-formal education and training makes it, at the least, a comprehensible construct with which to work.

So what does the scholarly literature tells us about the different types of activities in which adults can participate? Colley et al. (2003) have provided a deep analysis of the concepts of formal, non-formal and informal learning and made useful reflections on existing theories in the field: e.g. Eraut (2000), the definitions used by the European Commission, the work of Livingstone (2001), Billett (2001), Beckett and Hager (2002), Hodkinson and Hodkinson (2001), Hunt (1986) and Stern et al. (1999). Having conducted the analysis, Colley et al. (2003, p. 39) warn the reader to not oversimplify the distinctions between types of learning because *'in all or nearly all situations where learning takes place, elements of both formal and informal learning are present. But the most significant issue is not the boundaries between these types of learning, but the inter-relationships between dimensions of formality/informality, in particular situations.'*

Nowadays, the debate on formal, non-formal and informal learning indeed concentrates on how these learning forms can be linked to each other, mainly through the recognition of skills and knowledge acquired through non-formal and informal learning within the credential-based formal education and training system. Accreditation of Prior Learning or Accreditation of Prior Experiential Learning has thus become a more prominent item on the agenda of international educational agencies over the past decade. The focus on learning within specific activities is now also viewed as different. In the context of workplace learning, Eraut and Hirsch (2009, p. 25) have distinguished between three types of 'early career learning' which they have labelled as 'work processes with learning as a by-product', e.g. through consultation with colleagues, solving problems or meeting with clients; 'learning activities located within work or learning processes, e.g. learning from feedback, receiving information about work procedures ... and learning processes at or near the workplace'. Participation in lifelong learning activities with the aim of obtaining a qualification would fall into the third category and would count as a formalised type of learning within the workplace. Participation in short courses would also fit into this category and would be formal or non-formal depending on whether or not the course is credential-based. For the purpose of this book, and the trends explored below, it is important to understand that information gathered to monitor benchmarks and indicators tends to reflect participation in formal and non-formal education and training.

Major aims of lifelong learning

Nowadays, it can be argued that there are two major reasons why participation in lifelong learning is perceived as important. It should also be acknowledged that issues surrounding the need to participate have changed during previous decades, a point I will expand upon later in this chapter. The first, and generally acknowledged to be the major reason, is the need to survive in a knowledge-based economy, in which the need to remain competitive in the global market requires a highly skilled workforce, the owners of a strong level of human capital (Holford & Mohorcic-Spolar, 2012). This argument is often backed up by what Boshier (in Holford et al., 1998, p. 4) labelled as 'human resource development in drag'. A second reason is that adults need to live together and society will be a better place to live if there is a higher level of social cohesion and a strong sense of active citizenship. The World Bank (2003) also mentioned the reduction of crime and the increase of charitable giving. Additionally, it is important to mention that participation is also relevant for personal development.

It is believed that participation in lifelong learning activities can help in obtaining these goals. The basic pillars of lifelong learning are often linked to what Delors et al. (1996) expand upon in *Lifelong learning: the treasure within*. Delors et al. (1996) distinguish between 'learning to know', 'learning to do', 'learning to be' and 'learning to live together'. In referring to the two main aims of lifelong learning nowadays, one could argue that 'learning to know' and 'learning to do' have the strongest links with the economic aim of learning. That is, the need to participate in qualification-based and vocationally oriented education and training in order to survive in the competitive knowledge-based society. The social aspects of learning are present in the dimensions 'learning to be' and 'learning to live together' because these are more focused on the need to participate in lifelong learning for both personal growth and increasing levels of social cohesion amongst the members of society.

In the European Commission's work on the European Lifelong Learning Index (ELLI), comparable to the Canadian Composite Learning Index and carried out by the Bertelsman Stiftung, an overview has been created of specific types of learning activities and how these belong to one of the four dimensions (Hoskins et al., 2010). Interestingly, 'adult participation rates in formal education and training' has been fitted into the category 'learning to know', while 'participation in job-related non-formal education and training', 'participation of employees in CVT courses' and 'enterprises providing any other form of training' have been assigned to 'learning to do'. The dimension of 'learning to live together' mainly consists of references to social, cultural and political participation, while 'learning to be' includes a wide and open indicator on 'participation in lifelong learning', measured through 'participation in continuing/further education and training'. It is thus clear that both dimensions of 'economic competitiveness' and 'social cohesion' are present, but with more concrete focus on the first one.

The 2013 OECD Skills Outlook, which reports on the result of the PIAAC project, includes an Survey of Adult Skills of 22 OECD countries and regions and two partner countries, Russia and Cyprus, citing a range of skills that are needed in modern society (OECD, 2013c). Strong emphasis is placed on the need for ICT skills, due to the fact that societies have changed into post-industrial service economies and the effects of globalisation (Bell, 1973). Compared to the 1980s, more employees are now working in the financial or private sector, insurance or estate agencies, while fewer people are found to be working in manufacturing sectors (Gershuny, 2000). This has led to an increase of nearly 20 percent in occupations pursued by highly educated employees. It is thus generally important that the population is able to adapt to new technologies and changes in society, while participation in lifelong learning is perceived to support people in undertaking this challenge.

A stronger theorised conception of these different aims has been constructed by Torres in what he calls the 'rationalities' that explain the underlying dynamics of educational policy related to adult learning (Torres, 2013, p. 35). The 'rationality' of what he labels 'Human Capital Investment' starts from a strong economic viewpoint closely linked to vocational training and productivity and is clearly present nowadays in a wide range of countries across the world. Similarly, 'International Pressures' dominate lifelong learning policy making in order to boost productivity between countries, but also to create insight into social inequalities persisting in many societies.

Training to increase adults' notion of citizenship and to improve people's life chances is labelled by Torres (2013, p. 37) as the rationality of 'Political Socialisation', while he warns that this can go hand in hand with indoctrination practices. The social aims of adult lifelong learning are also present in his rationality of 'Constitutional Mandates', which refers to keywords like citizenship, democracy and welfare, as well as in the rationality of 'Social Movements' in which adult learning has an important function in creating people's identities and in establishing social relations. Finally, Torres (2013) mentions 'Compensatory Legitimation' as a way for governments to increase the gaining of legitimacy and state authority through adult lifelong learning. While this classification of rationalities is a great contribution to the knowledge base on the politics of adult lifelong learning, Torres (2013) agrees that most policies nowadays are based on 'instrumental rationality'. Nowadays, the term 'instrumental' often reflects the cutting of investment while trying to maximise profit. In general, it is possible to recognise tensions between the more social aspects of adult lifelong learning and those related to economic goals, which are mainly underpinned by neoliberalism and capitalism.

The outcomes and benefits of participation

Therefore, participation is perceived as important because of economic and social aims. But what about the outcomes of participation? What is the evidence that these are real?

Through participation, it is believed that both the individual and society are able to profit in two ways (Laal & Salamati, 2012). On the one hand, participation and the generation of new skills and knowledge are likely to result in monetary benefits, both for the individual in terms of a higher salary, and for society as a whole in terms of an increased level of economic production. On the other hand, participation might result in strong non-monetary benefits, including higher levels of well-being and happiness for the individual, and a more peaceful and tolerant society at the structural level. Indeed, these might generate additional indirect financial benefits because of lower costs for healthcare and social services. The different levels of benefits of participation in lifelong learning are also reiterated in the work of Campbell (2012). He published 'Skills for Prosperity' to disseminate research undertaken by LLAKES (The Centre for Learning and Life Chances in Knowledge Economies and Societies), arguing that developing the population's skills can generate positive economic and social benefits when resources are effectively managed and designed. He distinguishes four major beneficiaries (Campbell, 2012, p. 5). Firstly, society as a whole will profit from skill development as higher levels of skills are associated with higher levels of health and increased opportunities to climb the social ladder. Societies with strong skill development tend to have stronger levels of social cohesion between their members. Secondly, the economy will prosper because a highly skilled society tends to boost competitiveness, innovation, productivity and entrepreneurship. Equipping the population with a good level of skills can also reduce the level of economic inactivity. Thirdly, employers can benefit from increased skills levels, which is likely to lead to stronger levels of performance and so boost productivity and profitability. Fourthly, as stated by Campbell (2012), individuals who develop their skills will benefit from higher wages and the ability to carry out high quality jobs will provide them with higher levels of job satisfaction. Moreover, it is also likely to make them more 'marketable' in the labour market, which will increase their chances of sustaining their current job or to moving on to a better one. While these four benefits interact with each other, it is interesting to see how Campbell (2012) not only focuses on health and social cohesion at a society level, but also on the more economic, money-driven benefits at the level of the economy, employers and the individual.

Since benefits and outcomes are meant to tell us something about the effectiveness of participation, they have become a point of focus for a range of scholars in the field. One of the most recent overviews on the benefits to adults engaging in learning was provided by Field in a chapter on impact in the Second International Handbook of Lifelong Learning, edited by Aspin, Chapman, Evans and Bagnall (Aspin et al., 2012). Field (2012) recognises two major streams of impact: (1) economic impact and (2) impact on well-being.

Evidence of positive economic impact is given through reference to leading research in the field, although mainly undertaken in the British context. Field (2012) refers to work by Blundell et al. (1996) demonstrating a rise in earnings for men taking part in training at work. Field also makes reference to work by De Coulon and Vignoles (2008) on the rise in earnings by women who undertook specific training to gain vocational qualifications, then touches on Zhang and Palamenta's findings on the positive correlation between participation and wage effects in a Canadian context (Zhang & Palamenta, 2006), and also includes an examination of a range of British research outcomes claiming a positive relationship between literacy and numeracy skills and higher earnings (McIntosh and Vignoles, 2001; Ananiadou et al., 2003; De Coulon et al., 2007).

Positive effects on both employment and earnings are shown in work by Dorsett et al. (2010). However, insights into the relationship between adult lifelong learning participation and economic benefits do not seem to be consistent. Field (2012) notes that Swedish research by Ekström (2003) and Albrecht et al. (2007) demonstrates that there is no significant relationship between participation and income level. Research conducted by Jenkins et al. (2003) provides evidence to argue that participation in vocational learning activities in adulthood does not always seem to result in higher wages. Also, Torres (2013), based on his work in adult learning, mentions the lack of empirical evidence about the economic impact of basic and literacy education in the developing world. Blanden et al. (2010) wrote about the small benefits of adult lifelong learning and how this argument is being used by governments to lower investment in adult lifelong learning.

Other research on the economic benefits of learning to which I would like to refer relates to ongoing debates in the field of educational sociology, in particular those that question the value of degree level education and whether employment related benefits are still as clear as they used to be. In relation to adult lifelong learning, it is important to understand the value of participation in higher education as a mature student. Berggren (2011, p. 105) concludes that 'Having a degree improved the chances of obtaining a matching profession by three times' but found that this is notably more advantageous for women than for men.

Bernardi and Ballarino (2014) have outlined three possible scenarios related to the match between participation in higher education and the occupational outcomes: (1) the Trade-off scenario, in which the opportunities to enter higher education increase, but in which the value of the titles in terms of occupation decreases; (2) the Worst-off scenario, referring to an equal status-quo in relation to entrance into higher education, combined with a further decrease of occupational value. These first two scenarios refer to deflation of credentials. The third scenario, (3) the Best-off scenario, sees an increase of educational opportunities, without a loss of occupational value, meaning that while more people obtain credits, this does not have a negative impact on occupations. Bernardi and Ballerino (2014) have conducted European comparative analyses on both the European Social Survey and the EU Survey on Income and Living Conditions, concluding that the current situation seems to represent the Trade-off scenario, or even partially the Worst-off scenario. This implies that while equal opportunities in accessing higher education are increasing (Trade-off), this is not necessarily reflected in people obtaining better jobs.

Similar arguments have been explored by Brown et al. (2011) who state that increasing levels of education will not automatically translate into getting the best jobs. Hansen (2012), who critically reviewed their book, *The Global Auction: The Broken Promises of Education, Jobs and Incomes*, states that several explanations for this can be put forward. First of all, the higher education sector is forever expanding, recently in regions like China and India. Highly skilled adults in lower-wage societies are capable of conducting similar high skilled jobs as adults in the West, but are willing to work for lower salaries. Additionally, 'Digital Taylorism' has made typical white collar jobs less complex because of advanced software and technological developments, which leads to these jobs being shifted to lower skill levels. Finally, while the expansion of higher education has been massive, horizontal segregation is still very much present, with a few elite universities fighting for the very best students. In fact, 90 percent of students end up in mainstream higher education, outside the elite system.

Judging by the wide range of discussions, it is clear that more research in this area will have to be undertaken, to which I will also refer in the later chapters of this book. However, Field (2012) argues that despite the small effect sizes and some non-significant research outcomes on the economic impact, the overall picture is rather positive, suggesting that participation in adult lifelong learning participation is likely to have a positive effect on earnings in a significant proportion of lifelong learning situations.

In relation to well-being, Field (2012) argues that research evidence on the positive correlation between participation and well-being seems to have achieved a higher level of consistency. Research evidence for a positive impact on mental health is backed up by reference to research by McGivney (1999), Aldridge and Lavender (2000), Dench and Regan (1999) and James (2004). Feinstein has been active in undertaking research exploring the relationship between participation in adult lifelong learning activities and health, and has published widely in this area (Feinstein and Hammond, 2004; Hammond and Feinstein, 2006; Sabates and Feinstein, 2006).

Another area of well-being to which Field (2012) refers is 'depression'. Schuller et al. (2004) find that participation in adult lifelong learning activities helps people to counter this mental illness. More than ten years ago, they wrote about *The benefits of learning: the impact of education on health, family life and social capital*. In the first chapter, the authors make a distinction between economic benefits and social benefits, while in the following chapters, there is a strong focus on mental health, family life and life in the community. Schuller's work demonstrates the positive links between health and education, claiming that many of these effects are causal, and not just correlational. Sabates and Hammond (2008) published a report on 'The impact of lifelong learning on happiness and well-being' concluding with a focus on benefits in relation to happiness, well-being, self-esteem and self-efficacy. However, both Field (2012) and Sabates and Hammond (2008) warn that participation in learning activities might also put people under pressure to perform well and may cause high levels of stress. Nonetheless, in general, participation in lifelong learning activities and aspects related to well-being seems to be positively correlated. Another European project that has explored the benefits of lifelong learning is BeLL (Benefits of Lifelong Learning). However, it is important to mention that this project has only explored participation in non-formal education outside the vocational system, such as Folk High Schools in the Scandinavian system (Manninen & Merilainen, 2011). More specifically, the project has explored participation in lifelong learning activities in languages, ICT, arts and sports, but also participation in specific activities related to social skills and social cohesion. Basic skills education has also been included. The consortium undertook a survey in ten countries (Czech Republic, England, Finland, Germany, Italy, Romania, Serbia, Slovenia, Spain and Switzerland), collecting responses from 8,646 respondents. During the analysis phase, the team extracted ten benefit factors, which they regrouped into three overarching factors: (1) control of a person's own life, including sub factors on 'locus of control', 'self-efficacy' and 'sense of purpose in life'; (2) attitudes and social capital, referring to 'tolerance', 'social engagement' and 'changes in educational experiences'; and (3) health, family and work, consisting of the sub factors 'health', 'mental well-being', 'work' and 'family'. In their analysis of how these different factors related to each other, Manninen and Merilainen (2011) argue that social capital and educational experiences have helped people to gain a stronger level of control over their own lives. Moreover, it also led to better levels of health and positive effects being felt by family and in working life. It would have been interesting to see whether similar benefits and correlations were found in relation to participation in formal adult lifelong learning activities.

Of course, specific research projects have reported on a diverse range of outcomes; unsurprisingly, both economic and social benefits are often reported alongside each other and it is thus not good practice to see them as separated from each other. Specific examples of how to measure the outcomes of lifelong learning have been provided by the ELLI project, as discussed above (Hoskins et al., 2010). This project has created an indicator for the 'economic and social outcomes of learning' and distinguished between seven core dimensions: (1) earnings and income, (2) productivity, (3) employment, (4) health, (5) life satisfaction and happiness, (6) social cohesion and democracy and (7) sustainability. These factors have been used as aggregated country level indicators. The indicator for health reflected on scores of self-perceived and self-reported health issues by people, but also on life-expectancy statistics. The most extensive measure was the one on 'social cohesion and democracy' consisting of a range of indicators, such as several country level indicators like the Gini-coefficient, the unemployment rate and the deprivation rate, but also of some statistics gathered at the individual level such as political trust, participation in elections and satisfaction with democracy. While a range of seven indicators has been used, it is not difficult to recognise that both the 'economic' and 'social' aims of current lifelong learning policies correlate with each other.

While debates continue about the benefits of adult lifelong learning participation, it is not always easy to assess these benefits. One of the reasons is that many countries lack the availability of longitudinal data. Because of the importance of high quality data to assess participation benefits, this topic will be explored in more depth in Part III of this book.

The changing policy context

Having explored the background of why it is so important to understand why adults do or do not participate in adult lifelong learning activities, I now turn to explaining what I mean by 'the changing policy context' as mentioned in the title of this book.

To go back in time, the notion of participation in the economic sense became stronger from the mid-1990s onwards, when the European Commission developed a strong view on the role of lifelong learning (Griffin, in Jarvis, 2010; Holford & Mohorcic-Spolar, 2012). In earlier decades, the role of UNESCO and OECD was stronger, and tended to focus on social cohesion and active citizenship. The humanistic perspective of adult lifelong learning participation, which was very holistic, democratic and social in nature, has thus shifted towards a strong economic perspective. Discourses around participation should be interpreted through the lens of this changing policy context. While the two aims of lifelong learning are still maintained, it is generally agreed that the economic aim dominates nowadays.

Rubenson (2006), as well as Schuetze (2006), has written about two different generations of lifelong learning policy. The first one ranges from the 1960s to the 1980s during which terms like 'recurrent' and 'lifelong' education were used and the social underpinning of education was at the forefront, being marked by a worldwide crisis in relation to education (Barros, 2012). Lifelong education, previously researched by Yeaxlee (1929) and Lindeman (1926), was put back on the agenda, placing a stronger focus on the need to participate in education across a life span – including after the end of initial schooling. Hence, the emphasis was on the importance of providing equal educational opportunities accessible for all (Barros, 2012).

The leading organisation to put lifelong education back on the agenda was UNESCO. Their 1972 'Faure report', *Learning to be, the world of education today and tomorrow,* has been very influential in this debate. The second 'generation' started in the 1990s and made strong connections between education and work. It has become the dominant view of lifelong learning policy makers in the new Millennium, marked by neoliberal discourses in which lifelong learning has moved away from its 'humanistic' perspective (Rubenson, 2009; Boeren, 2011; Barros, 2012).

While UNESCO provided the dominant focus of the first generation, the OECD and the European Commission's role became more dominant during the second generation. The signing of the Lisbon Treaty in March 2000 and the European Year of Lifelong Learning in 2006, in which members of the European Union agreed to strive towards a participation rate of 12.5 percent of the adult population in at least one lifelong learning activity measured on a four weeks basis, have been crucial to the development of a new lifelong learning policy.

The shift in policy was also underlined by a shift in vocabulary, as the concept of 'adult education' was replaced by the notion of 'lifelong learning' (Biesta, 2006; Milana, 2012). Nowadays, debates about learning and teaching tend to put a stronger emphasis on the role of student centred learning environments while the role of the teacher has moved towards facilitating the learning of students, which can also take place through interaction with others, e.g. in the community (Lave and Wenger, 1991).

Biesta (2006) and Milana (2012) also focus on the logic of the capitalist market economy in the globalised world in which adults are expected to take responsibility for their own learning. This is reiterated by Barros' analysis of the effects of neoliberal lifelong learning policies, in which adult learners become consumers of lifelong learning activities (Barros, 2012). While education refers to a rather 'collective' approach directed by a country's or region's educational policy, the term 'learning' underlines the individual initiative that needs to be undertaken. As will be explored in the next chapters, this shift has also led to lifelong learning participation being analysed through the lens of theories such as human capital theory, rational choice theory and cost benefit approaches (Milana, 2012). Together with the changes in vocabulary, Barros (2012) has also focused on more extensive changes resulting from changing policy purposes, which she labels as a shift from a 'qualification-based model' to a 'competencies-based model'.

Critical engagement among scholars is strongly present. Shifts in education policy have been discussed widely in the literature and are a standard focus of many lifelong learning books' introduction sections or earlier chapters (e.g. Holford & Mohorcic-Spolar, in Riddell et al., 2012). There is universal agreement about lifelong learning that has become a 'guiding principle' for full and broader participation in various life domains (Óhidy, 2008, p. 21). However, the emphasis on 'human capital' came into play during the last few years of the previous century. In this respect, Óhidy (2008) distinguishes between 'two main ideas': (1) democratic education in which there is more space for self-development and liberation and (2) the development of human resources strongly linked to the advancement of the performative knowledge-based society. While the author discusses both 'ideas', the focus on the economic side comes out strongly: '... the lifelong learning concept should not be reduced to satisfying the demands of the labour market and other economic claims ...' (Óhidy, 2008, p. 26). In general, it is indeed hard to ignore the economic focus of lifelong learning in policy discourses.

Torres (2013), as discussed above, in his publication the *Political sociology of adult education*, argues that the policy field has 'lost its transformative and empowering vision and mission ...' (Torres, 2013, p. 20). Nowadays, the main focus is on regulating capitalism. In his description of alternative models of education policy, he refers to human capital theories and 'pragmatic idealism', which he labels as 'incrementalism'. In a human capital model, a concept studied in depth by Nobel Prize winner Becker (1964), the focus is on strengthening economic growth and income, also linked to the positive effects this will have on equity and equality in society. Pragmatic idealism is incremental in nature as well, strongly concerned with practical outcomes. Lifelong learning for adults is mainly perceived as a way to work on 'deficits' and is therefore linked with the notion of compensation, i.e. by offering lifelong learning activities to those adults who did not finish school during their youth. The critical note I want to raise here is that while this might be true in a range of developing countries, this model of working on 'deficits' is overtaken by a model of 'accumulation' of skills and knowledge in the Western world. Incrementalism is distinct from what Torres (2013) calls 'structuralism'. He refers to the 'Pedagogy of the Oppressed and Popular Education', linking back to the work of Freire. Reflections on this model focus on the role of community education and policy planning, starting with need detection within the community instead of a top-down decision-making process. Empowerment of people and an increase in their psychological strengths is one of the core aims of this model. Finally, within a structuralist vision of education, Torres (2013) argues that 'social engineering' is meant to enable social inequalities to disappear. It is a model that is also largely centred on the idea of the 'compensation' of deficits. Apart from analysing different policy models and expanding on the 'instrumental rationality' of adult lifelong learning policy shaped by neoliberalism, Torres (2013, p. 21) also explains why it is difficult to attract high levels of interest from policy makers. His arguments touch upon the complexity and wide range of the sector, the less prestigious nature of adult learning compared to learning in earlier life, a discussion about whether participation leads to benefits at work – as we have seen previously – and the under-theorisation of the field, which leads to an unclear sense of direction about what needs to be done. As will be explored in Chapter 6, because of the differences in lifelong learning participation in different countries across the globe, it is plausible to introduce different policy models. In this regard, I agree with Broek and Hake (2012) that successful policies will need to understand the historical, social and economic contexts of previous policies, as well as the structures and instruments that are available (or might have to be developed) in order for the policy to work.

The problem of participation

While the importance of lifelong learning participation is stated in various policy documents, such as a set of White Papers, discussion notes and reports from the European Commission, UNESCO and OECD, and there are optimistic research findings demonstrating the positive impact of participation, a problem occurs when looking deeper into current participation patterns and statistics – the focus of the following chapter. Participation is a deeply unequal matter and does not only vary between individuals, but also between countries (Boeren, 2011). It is thus clear that not all adults receive similar chances to become an adult learner, and that one's place of abode and personal background are strongly determining factors.

The Matthew effect – referring to Matthew's Bible story about those who already have receiving more – is evident in that those who have a successful educational record have a better opportunity to participate in the labour market than others. If policy makers want everyone to contribute successfully, it is recommended that they invest in stimulating participation among the most disadvantaged groups in society, e.g. by adopting targeted measures (Desjardins, 2015).

In one of its reports, 'Co-Financing Lifelong Learning: Towards a Systematic Approach', the OECD (2004) warns against the negative impact of lifelong learning, precisely because of these patterns of unequal participation. The situation is likely to widen gaps in society instead of narrowing them. Morgan-Klein and Osborne (2007, p. 24) even speak about 'depressing reading' in relation to the consultation of participation statistics. It is therefore important for policy makers and practitioners to make efforts to target underrepresented groups. A detailed review of participation rates in adult lifelong learning activities in the developed world were published 10 years ago, supplemented by a new overview of participation statistics, as extracted from the PIAAC's Survey of Adult Skills (Programme for the International Assessment of Adult Competencies) (Desjardins, 2015). Commissioned by UNESCO, Desjardins et al. (2006) titled their report *Unequal chances to participate in adult learning: international perspectives*. They examined data from the International Adult Literacy Survey (IALS), the Adult Literacy and Lifeskills Survey (ALLS) and the EU Barometer, distinguishing between six different contrast groups in relation to adult lifelong learning participation, thereby setting out the major determinants of participation (see Table 1.1).

It is clear from the contrast groups presented at the following page that those with high levels of skill and education are most likely to participate in adult lifelong learning activities. This observation has

Table 1.1   Schematic overview of participation chances

	Employment	Job	Age	Education/ skills	Participation chances
Group 1	Employed	Blue	45–65	Low	Below average
Group 2	Employed	White	45–65	High	Above average
Group 3	Employed	–	26–45	–	Above average
Group 4	Unemployed/ out-of-labour	–	45–65	Low	Below average
Group 5	Unemployed/ out-of-labour	–	45–65	High	Above average
Group 6	Unemployed/ out-of-labour	–	26–45	–	Above average

Source: Based on findings by Desjardins et al. (2006, pp. 74–75).

also been confirmed by the results of PIAAC (Desjardins, 2015). On average, amongst the countries participating in PIAAC, those with the lowest skill levels have a participation rate of 14.9 percent in terms of job-related adult lifelong learning activities, while those with the highest skill levels have a participation rate of 60.4 percent. For non-job related learning activities, this difference is 6.8 versus 12.5 percent, which represents 25.6 versus 74.2 percent for both job- and non-job related education and training.

Examining Desjardins et al.'s analysis in 2006, it is also interesting to note that younger adults – those in the first half of the 26–65 age group – have higher chances of participation, even if they are unemployed or if their education and skill level is lower. This has also been confirmed by recent analysis of the PIAAC survey; although the reference is to adults aged 35 and younger, when checking for other individual variables *'including gender, education, parents' education, functional literacy, and immigration status'* (Desjardins, 2015, pp. 6–7). Based on the PIAAC results, it is also clear that women, on average, have greater opportunities to participate in adult lifelong learning activities, although in terms of their participation patterns – e.g. in terms of course subjects – they differ from men. The reasons behind these mechanisms will be explored in more depth in Part II of this book.

In order to understand the inequalities in participation, it will also be important to consider the unequal participation rates among countries, to which an entire chapter in this book has been devoted.

Countries failing to invest or under-investing in adult lifelong learning is also a problem as it leads to widening, instead of narrowing gaps in society. While adult lifelong learning is meant to attract a wide variety of adults, it is clear that this does not correspond to the real life situation. In order to provide more adults with opportunities to develop themselves, and to profit from the benefits of lifelong learning, it is important to explore the current position of theories explaining these inequalities.

Before providing more details about participation statistics across the globe, it is necessary to provide some background information on how exactly policy makers and leading agents in the field are trying to stimulate participation in adult lifelong learning. Exploring the role of important players, such as the European Commission, UNESCO and the OECD, it is clear that nowadays rankings, statistics and numerical overviews of participation related topics have become the leading ways to shape policy. Hence the following section focuses on the use of benchmarks and indicators in lifelong learning policy.

The focus on benchmarks and indicators

Reflections on current education policies have referred to the notion of 'governance by numbers' (Grek, 2009; Simola et al., in Ozga et al., p. 96). Nowadays, ranking, statistics and numeric overviews determine state-of-the-art analysis of the education sector. While this approach has been important in Europe since 2000, it is also being used in other parts of the world, e.g. in countries participating in OECD programmes such as PISA and PIAAC. In a 'governing by numbers' approach, the most recent figures in multiple educational domains, including participation in adult lifelong learning activities, are compared between countries and regions in order to stimulate policy making towards achieving particular targets. Several leading influential organisations have set specific benchmarks or indicators in relation to lifelong learning. It is important to provide an overview of the targets that dominate this sector.

European Commission

First of all, in relation to Europe, I would like to refer to *Adult education policy and the European Union: theoretical and methodological perspectives*, edited by Milana and Holford (2014). The book provides a broad overview on the evolution of Europe in relation to lifelong learning. Because of the limited space in this book, I will specifically address aspects relevant to adult lifelong learning participation. A dominant core focus is on the use of statistics.

The growing emphasis on rankings and statistics – think about the various numbers of university rankings being published – has in fact been in fashion in Europe since the beginning of the new millennium (Ioannidou, 2007; Wiseman, 2010). Policy monitoring has become one of the core underpinnings of the European Union's 'Open Method of Co-ordination' (OMC) following the signing of the Lisbon Treaty in March 2000 (Holford & Mohorcic-Spolar, 2012). The OMC is an example of 'soft power' and is thus based on an approach of informing countries instead of directing them in terms of what specific strategies they have to implement (Dehmel, 2006; Lee et al., 2008). Grek describes the situation as follows:

> The new technology of the governance of the European educa-tion space through indicators and benchmarks is not only to be seen as the project of fulfilling Brussels' requirements of achiev-ing specific goals and objectives. Instead, it has to be examined as deeply penetrating consciousness-moulding and thus the serious business of constructing new categories of (educational) thought and action – the project of reinventing a 'new' European identity of competitive advantage and responsible individualism. (Grek, 2008, p. 215)

In the field of education, the European Union strived towards com-mon benchmarks and indicators to be achieved by 2010 (European Commission, 2001). Examples included the goal of 12.5 percent of adults aged 25 and 64 participating in at least one adult learning activity, measured on a four week's basis. Ioannidou (2007) argues that this way of monitoring participation was aimed at the develop-ment and reform of current education policies. In fact, education policy remained the responsibility of the individual Member States.

The European Union is the supranational organisation that is currently active in setting priorities and a common education agenda. However, it does not have the legislative power in the field of education to force countries to undertake certain actions. Therefore, benchmarks and indicators are used as 'soft power' tools in order to fabricate a European educational space (Ozga, 2012). By putting peer pressure on countries, achieved through the collection of statistics and assessments, the EU hopes to contribute to a policy learning process in which countries can explore why their peers are doing better than them.

The 'governing by numbers' approach is closely linked to the overall aims of the European Union to evolve towards the most competitive knowledge-based economy in the world (Grek & Ozga, 2008). Five core benchmarks were formulated in 2000, and reformulated in 2009. The adult lifelong learning participation benchmark, which was set at 12.5 percent in 2000 – to be achieved by 2010 – was raised to 15 percent in 2009 – to be achieved by 2020 (European Commission, 2010). These targets are measured within a four week reference period, calculated through data from the Labour Force Survey. The other four core benchmarks to be achieved by 2020 are: (1) at least 95 percent of children between the age of four years and the age for starting compulsory primary education should participate in early childhood education; (2) the share of early leavers from education and training should be less than 10 percent; (3) the share of low-achieving 15-years olds in reading, mathematics and science should be less than 15 percent; and (4) the share of 30–34-year-olds with tertiary educational attainment should be at least 40 percent.

The benchmark on tertiary education is also relevant for adult learners, being that higher education should also be accessible to mature students. Data from Eurostudent (2009) shows that in many European countries, most students aged 30 and over are part-time students. The Social Dimension of Higher Education has been established in Europe to widen access in the tertiary education sector in order that student numbers are a better representation of society as a whole (European Commission, 2009). It is also important that these older learners succeed in accessing higher education and have positive learning experiences.

The project PL4SD (Peer Learning for the Social Dimension) has been researched by the Social Dimension over the period 2012–2015, hoping to influence policy as well as generating specific actions to widen access to higher education. In fact, as I will explain later in this book, the benchmarks focusing on younger age groups in compulsory education are also relevant for adult lifelong learning. It is generally accepted that higher educated adults participate more in adult lifelong learning activities, i.e. in view of their employment in more knowledge intensive jobs or because they have developed a positive attitude towards learning owing to their previous success. While adult lifelong learning might compensate for earlier deficits, it often functions as a way of accumulating knowledge and skills for those who already possess high levels of these.

OECD

OECD's role in relation to lifelong learning has been discussed by Schuller (in Jarvis, 2010, p. 292). He mentions OECD's involvement in reviewing education policies, but also their presence in the field of skills assessment. Not only the European Commission, but the OECD also works with educational indicators and is a major player in the field of education policy (Henry et al., 2001; Martens & Jakobi, 2010). The OECD publishes regular 'Education at a Glance' reports, providing a detailed overview on OECD's educational indicators. The report is very extensive – the 2014 report had over 500 pages (OECD, 2014). Not only does the report focus on initial education, including higher education, but also on the relationship between educational attainment, labour market participation and earnings, as well as social benefits. In addition, it provides calculations on private investments to participate in education. Country specific indicators are also presented at the level of investments made by governments to stimulate education in their countries. Specific indicators are measured in relation to access to learning opportunities, while a final section deals with the learning environment and the organisation of educational institutions, mainly focusing on the training and development of teachers.

In the 2014 report, Chapter Three, indicator C6 questions 'How many adults participate in education and learning?' Participation rates are compared between adults with different levels of literacy and educational attainment, labour market status and parental education. The report also demonstrates the lack of interest in learning activities amongst a significant proportion of the adult learning population, as reiterated by Desjardins (2015), and reports on the barriers preventing them from (further) learning.

Specific information relating to the OECD Indicator C6 can be found in Figure 1.1. It is clear that a strong focus is placed on the skill levels of adults. Apart from literacy and numeracy skills, it has to be mentioned that ICT skills are important as well.

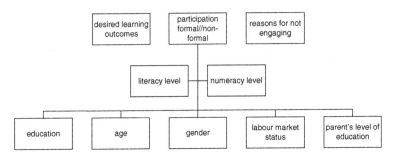

Figure 1.1   Schematic representation of OECD Indicator C6
Source: Own drawing based on Education at a Glance (OECD, 2014).

A specific Working Paper has been published in relation to the monitoring of adult learning policies (Borowsky, 2013). This report represents the work of the 'Working Group on Adult Learning', a group of people who explore the development of new indicators to be included in the 'Education at a Glance' reports. The group is thus also concerned with making recommendations for future data collection and the design of surveys measuring aspects related to adult lifelong learning.

The Working Paper focuses on the importance of indicators in reaching a set of general adult learning goals in relation to 'updating knowledge and raising skills', 'reducing inequalities', 'investment', 'information and guidance', 'usability and certification' and 'quality and organisation of education delivery' (Borowsky, 2013, p. 3). For each of the general sections, a list of in total 18 goals has been formulated, which is supported by the formulation of 44 concrete indicators. Relevant to participation are the indicators 'Participation rate in job-related non-formal education by educational attainment', 'Participation in job-related non-formal education by skills levels', 'participation in formal/non-formal education by workplace aspects', 'Percentage of employed persons with self-reported need for further training to meet work duties by skill level and skill requirement of the job', 'participation rate in all non-formal education and non-formal education for personal reasons', 'rate of unmet non-formal and/or formal education needs by participation in non-formal and/or formal education', 'obstacles to further participation in non-formal education for non-formal education participants', 'obstacles to participation in non-formal education for non-participants in non-formal education', 'rate of participation in all types of learning activities by age group', 'rate of persons who have looked for and found information', 'participation in formal/non-formal education, according to whether individuals have looked for and found information about learning activities', 'adults finding information concerning learning activities by sources of information and by participation in formal/non-formal education', 'participation in non-formal education and informal learning by the existence and type of recognition system', 'participation rate in non-formal education by way of delivery', 'participation rate in formal and/or non-formal education' and 'benefits to participants in non-formal and/or formal education'.

At first sight, the indicators formulated by the OECD are more specific than the general benchmark of 15 percent participation set out by the European Commission. However, the OECD will need to make sure high quality data collection mechanisms will be available to measure these indicators in the best possible way over an extended period of time. Over the years, the OECD has already developed several surveys, of which PISA – the Programme for International Student Assessment – is probably the best known (Engel, 2015). Sellar and Lingard (2014, p. 917) even labelled OECD's PISA as having generated 'new global modes of governance in education'. More specific to the field of adult lifelong learning, PIAAC – the Programme for the International Assessment of Adult Competencies – has been developed and was conducted for the first time in 2011 and 2012.

The next chapters in this book will provide a more in-depth investigation of the role of PIAAC. Apart from the two major surveys built around the measurement of competencies, the OECD has also developed the Teaching and Learning International Survey (TALIS) which measures teachers' working conditions, and the Assessment for Higher Education and Learning Outcomes (AHELO) which will survey higher education students about their outcomes and their job prospects for the future. Results of a feasibility study in relation to AHELO have been published in three volumes (OECD, 2012, 2013a, 2013b). It is thus clear that not only the European Commission, but also the OECD, puts a strong emphasis on the collection of data and the production of reports monitoring the results of separate countries, in order to inform policy makers about the progress they are making.

The role of UNESCO

UNESCO has played an important role in defining and influencing the field of adult lifelong learning and is the driving force behind the CONFINTEA International Adult Education conferences (Ouane, in Jarvis, 2009). The last one took place in 2009 in Belem, Brazil and, as CONFINTEA takes place every 12 years, it is expected that the next one will be organised in 2021. More about work undertaken in relation to CONFINTEA will be presented in the following chapter in discussion of participation trends across the world.

Similar to the work of the European Commission and the OECD, UNESCO has worked on benchmarks and indicators, such as the Education for All goals, as a set of indicators to be achieved by 2015, agreed upon during the 2000 World Education Forum in Dakar (UNESCO, 2000, p. 7 in Ouane (2009) in Jarvis (2009), pp. 308–309). Some of these indicators are indeed relevant for adult lifelong learning participation. However, the Education for All agenda needs to be understood in relation to the Millennium Development Goals, established in 2000 during a UN Summit. Eight goals have been formulated in order to stimulate development across the world, with the second goal directly relating to the provision of primary education for all across the globe. It is not only participation that is important for successfully finishing primary education is regarded as an important goal. In addition, the third Millennium Development Goal has important links with education in relation to gender, being that a specific sub-indicator has been established to monitor the gender distribution of students in primary, secondary and tertiary education (see Table 1.2).

With the period 2000–2015 behind us now, UNESCO has already reflected on the future in the 2015 Education for All Global Monitoring Report (UNESCO, 2015). In the foreword to the report, Irina Bokova, the Director General of UNESCO, rightly points out that some significant progression has been made, e.g. the higher number of children and young people going to school and the higher number of girls attending school. However, severe problems still exist and the poorest children and those living in conflict areas still suffer from a lack of education. There are still a significant number of adults lacking core skills such as numeracy and literacy, and it will therefore be important to continue targeting education in the future.

Table 1.2 UNESCO indicators

Goal 1 Expanding and improving comprehensive early childhood care and education, especially for the most vulnerable and disadvantaged children.

Goal 2 Ensuring that, by 2015, all children, particularly girls, children in difficult circumstances and those belonging to ethnic minorities, have access to and complete free and compulsory primary education of good quality.

Goal 3 Ensuring that the learning needs of all young people and adults are met through equitable access to appropriate learning and life-skills programmes.

Goal 4 Achieving a 50 percent improvement in levels of adult literacy by 2015, especially for women, and equitable access to basic and continuing education for all adults.

Goal 5 Eliminating gender disparities in primary and secondary education by 2005, and achieving gender equality in education by 2015, with a focus on ensuring girls' full and equal access to and achievement in basic education of good quality.

Goal 6 Improving all aspects of the quality of education and ensuring excellence of all so that recognised and measurable learning outcomes are achieved by all, especially in literacy, numeracy and essential life skills.

Source: UNESCO, 2000, p. 7 in Ouane (2009) in Jarvis (2009), pp. 308–309.

In 2012, Burnett and Felsman published a report on the 'post-15 education MDGS' and set out some scenarios for the future based on interviews with representatives from educational ministries in more than 20 countries, from the UN and from the Global Financial Institutions. Unsurprisingly, there was a broad consensus on the need to keep a strong focus on education development post-2015. The report 'The Road to Dignity by 2030: Ending Poverty, Transforming All Lives and Protecting the Planet' mentions the need for education and training. A specific position paper, as well as an initial concept note, in relation to the post-2015 era of Education for All, has also been published in the meantime. It clearly spells out that the education agenda should take a 'lifelong learning approach' (UNESCO, 2014, p. 2), reflecting on the need to learn throughout life, but also on the life-wide nature of lifelong learning. Strong emphasis has been put on this position paper on reducing inequalities in working towards opportunities to access education for all. Gender and marginalised groups have been specifically mentioned here. In relation to adults, literacy and skills for functioning at work and in daily life have been discussed.

It is clear that UNESCO has also reflected on the policy shift from 'lifelong education' to 'lifelong learning'. They decided to change the name of the Hamburg-based 'UNESCO Institute for Education' (UIE) to 'UNESCO Institute for Learning' (UEL), which primarily focuses on informal, non-formal and lifelong learning and which is one of the core institutes of UNESCO Education, together with the International Bureau of Education and the International Institute of Educational Planning (UNESCO, 2006). The changing of the institute's name from 'Education' to 'Learning' has been characterised by a statement expressing an approach to lifelong learning that now takes a holistic view, paying attention to the most vulnerable in society and also to those in developing countries, through partnerships with civil society organisations and NGOs. In this regard, the work of UEL tends to have a strong focus on literacy development and the support of lifelong learning work on the African continent. The entire discourse fits well with the notion of the learning society and the need to integrate elements of active citizenship and cohesion with the need to learn in order to develop a workforce. Work of UEL is published as GRALE: the Global Report on Adult Learning and Education. The second edition was published in 2013 and focused on literacy (UNESCO, 2013).

Successes of policy borrowing and policy learning

One of the aims of working with benchmarks and indicators is therefore to create a sense of peer pressure amongst countries in order that policy makers experience significant demand to undertake actions if their recorded performances, which are publicly available through the publication of progress reports, are poor. In relation to working towards a policy situation that generates better domestic outcomes in each country, discussions are being held about the relative importance of 'policy borrowing' versus 'policy learning' (Raffe, 2011). Policy borrowing refers to the transfer of countries' best practices to others, while policy learning nuances the usefulness of copy and paste approaches while seeking to explore best practices with the aim of analysing what would work in the domestic context of their own country. Policy learning is also employed through an exploration of comparative policy results with the aim of providing a sharper analysis of the domestic problems that each country has to deal with, thus aiming to understand these problems better.

Raffe (2011, pp. 3–4) has formulated six recommendations for optimal policy learning:

(1) Use international experience to enrich policy analysis, not to short-cut it,
(2) Look for good practice not best practice,
(3) Don't study only 'successful' systems,
(4) Use international experience to understand your own system,
(5) Learn from history and
(6) Devise appropriate structures of governance.

Raffe (2011, pp. 3–4)

In general, Raffe (2011) presents good arguments as to why policy learning is preferable to policy borrowing, one that takes necessary historical and cultural elements into account.

The question is whether policy borrowing or policy learning are really effective in terms of changing policies and making systems more functional in achieving targets. Currently, it is clear that many countries have not yet achieved the European benchmark of 15 percent set for 2020, but many countries also failed to reach the target of 12.5 percent by 2010. In fact, the literature on working with surveys is both positive and nuanced about the power of working with numbers to influence and shape new forms of educational policy (Engel, 2015). Survey results can act as agents of change; Engel (2015) mentions a range of examples of research studies that have explored the usefulness and impact of PISA, conducted with 15-year-olds (e.g. Takayama, 2009 for Japan; Ertl, 2006 and Martens & Niemann, 2010 for Germany; Bonal & Tarabini, 2013 for Spain; and Engel & Frizzell, 2015 for Canada and the United States).

The OECD has also published a working paper on 'The policy impact of PISA' (Breakspear, 2012) in which it is argued that the results of PISA have led to changes in policy approaches in the majority of countries taking part in the study. The report demonstrates that the PISA results have informed policy debates extremely well in Japan, England and Denmark. However, Turkey, France, Luxembourg and Finland are listed as countries in which the PISA results have not had a very strong influence on policy debates. It is not surprising that this is the case in Finland being that it is usually represented as the best practice example within the study. All the other countries scored 'very' or 'moderately' on policy influence, with the majority scoring 'very'. In relation to adult lifelong learning, it is of course a question of whether PIAAC will be able to attract the same level of attention and the same level of power and influence as PISA. While PIAAC results are out, it is too early to make critical reflections on its wider impact at this stage.

Benchmarks and indicators as generators of data

The focus on benchmarks and indicators has led to the development of new or the use of existing data collection methods, usually surveys. In the field of adult lifelong learning, the Labour Force Survey, coordinated by Eurostat, has been used to monitor adult lifelong learning participation (Boeren, 2011). Detailed information on the Labour Force Survey will be provided later on in this book, together with a discussion of other surveys, such as the Adult Education Survey and PIAAC.

These surveys are not only useful for monitoring policy and developing new policy strategies. The fact that these surveys are available makes it attractive for researchers in the wider lifelong learning field to conduct projects based on secondary data analysis. In the UK, the Economic and Social Research Council (ESRC) decided to launch a new secondary data analysis scheme in 2012, while many countries nowadays have developed data repositories in which these data are available. As a staff member of a British university, I am able to download a wide range of UK datasets from the UK Data Archive. Comparative data can often be obtained for project purposes. Although secondary data analysis has its advantages and disadvantages, it is a valuable way of exploring new research questions with new methodological and statistical approaches (Smith, 2008).

In the field of adult lifelong learning, most published research is qualitative, not quantitative (Fejes & Nylander, 2014). It is thus also important to invest in skills training in relation to quantitative methodologies for postgraduate researchers. Secondary databases are usually available at a low cost and offer opportunities for the exploration of social, theoretical and methodological issues. Therefore, secondary data analysis should be encouraged. However, it will frequently not provide a full picture of what one is interested in, and should therefore best be combined with other research methods, including qualitative research. The dominant focus on the use of statistics from this side of policy makers needs to be explored by adopting a critical lens; hence the decision to devote a chapter to the strengths and weaknesses of the use of quantitative databases in the field of adult lifelong learning participation.

Conclusions

This chapter has introduced the reader to the importance of studying adult lifelong learning participation. I have focused on the main aims of lifelong learning and on the possible benefits that participation can generate. An overview has been given of the changing policy context and the dominant focus on the use of benchmarks and indicators to stimulate education policy making. Before turning to Part II, exploring the different theoretical insights generating explanations of why certain people do or do not participate in adult lifelong learning, it is important to provide an overview of the current trends of lifelong learning participation across the world.

2

Trends and Barriers in Adult Lifelong Learning Participation

The policy context of participation and the role of agencies in influencing lifelong learning discourses at the global level have been explored in the previous chapter, but what about trends in participation in different continents across the globe? What are the specificities of these regions' policies to stimulate lifelong learning participation and what data is available to provide an overview of current trends? In addition, I aim to explore trends in relation to recent scholarly writings in the field of adult lifelong learning participation.

Trends in the participation literature

Leading lifelong learning journals

Before setting out the statistical trends in lifelong learning participation across the globe, it is important to analyse trends in terms of publication. Who has published research on adult lifelong learning participation in recent decades, and what exactly has been the focus of their research? Owing to Courtney's publication in 1992 – *Why adults learn, towards a theory of participation in adult education* – I have mainly focused on subsequent publications. I began by searching through three of the leading international journals in the field: *Adult Education Quarterly*, *Studies in Continuing Education* and *International Journal of Lifelong Education*. While all three journals are international in nature, they have traditionally been edited by people in different continents, in America, Australia and Europe respectively. My own understanding of adult lifelong learning participation has been influenced by reading these publications, but also by the use of a snowball method. Exploration of articles' reference lists has given me the opportunity to widen my initial scope. As mentioned in the introduction, this book aims to discuss the general themes, instead of discussing every single piece of work separately, for which I do not have the space.

Since 1992, the *International Journal of Lifelong Education* has published 28 articles that contain 'participation' in the title; *Adult Education Quarterly* has published 16; and *Studies in Education* has published five. It should be mentioned that the *International Journal of Lifelong Education* publishes six volumes per year, *Adult Education Quarterly* four and *Studies in Continuing Education* three. Taking the number of annual volumes into account, the *International Journal of Lifelong Education* still seems to publish the highest volume of participation related articles.

The first 'strand' of articles present in the three journals addresses the participation of specific, often underrepresented groups in adult lifelong learning activities on the African and Asian continent. Examples within the *International Journal of Lifelong Education* include: Brown and Duku (2008) on participation politics of parents in South African schools; Mulenga and Liang (2008) about the participation of older Taiwanese adults in the Open University; Walter (2004) on the participation of Thai women in literacy programmes; Albasheer et al. (2008) on participation in relation to teacher education in Jordan; and Maruatona (2006) on lifelong learning and democracy in Africa. The *Adult Education Quarterly* has published articles looking at participation in a literacy programme in Salvador (Prins, 2006) and the participation of women in an English as a Second Language programme in Cambodia (Skilton-Sylvester, 2002).

A second strand relates to participation in vocational education and training. Two out of five articles with 'participation' in the title in *Studies in Continuing Education* deal with vocational elements (Smith, 2012; Kyndt et al., 2013). In *Adult Education Quarterly*, Billett (2002) has published about workplace pedagogy. Kyndt et al. (2011) have also published on career related learning in the *International Journal of Lifelong Education*, but other articles within this strand with participation in the title are not present. In fact, it is plausible that authors researching this field explore other publishing opportunities within specific vocational education and training journals.

Thirdly, lifelong learning journals also publish articles on participation in higher education; one of the foci in recent years has been the participation of mature and underrepresented groups. Thomas (2000) has researched this area extensively and published a paper on widening participation in *Studies in Continuing Education* in 2000. O'Donnell and Tobbell (2007) have explored transitions to higher education for adult students and published the results of their research in *Adult Education Quarterly*. In the *International Journal of Lifelong Education*, I found a number of publications in relation to higher education. Broek and Hake (2012) have explored policies to increase the proportion of adults in higher education. Gorard and Smith (2006) have critically reviewed widening participation evidence in England. Osborne (2003) has reported on a comparative study on widening participation in six countries. Callender (2011) has focused on part-time learners and Jung and Cervero (2002) on the participation of mature learners at undergraduate levels.

I then identified a fourth strand relating to the determinants and predictors of participation in lifelong learning activities, which strongly represents the theme of this book. In *Adult Education Quarterly*, readers are able to find the Bounded Agency Model, published by Rubenson and Desjardins (2009). This model will be explored in greater depth later in this book. Knipprath and De Rick (2015), two of my former colleagues in Leuven, have published an article about 'How social and human capital predict participation in lifelong learning'. The work of Blunt and Yang (2002) will be expanded upon in the next chapter which demonstrates the importance of their work in relation to attitudes as predictors of participation. Finally, Livneh and Livneh (1999) have published work on participation predictors for educators.

While work by Kyndt et al. (2013) has been mentioned in relation to the 'vocational' strand in lifelong learning journals, it should be said that their paper in *Studies in Continuing Education* also focuses on the determinants of participation, specifically for those who are low-qualified. It is therefore also important to include this paper in this fourth strand. In fact, research published in relation to the Asian and African context also usually focuses on understanding why people participate, although within a very specific geographical context.

This is different to, for instance, the work by Rubenson and Desjardins (2009) who propose a new theoretical approach to understanding participation, one based on a broad range of previously published theoretical and empirical information. The same can be said about the papers published by Boeren et al. (2010), based on my PhD work, and by Roosmaa and Saar (2012) who have explored participation barriers in a range of EU countries. The focus in these papers is thus not only on individual determinants of participation, but also on structural factors associated with participation, as is the case with the work of Benavot et al. (1993) who have explored structural factors in relation to basic education.

Moreover, a longitudinal perspective, based on empirical survey data from the US has been introduced by Yang (1998). Understanding of participation determinants in relation to life transitions, as will be explored in Chapter 3, has also been offered by Blaxter and Tight (1995). A sociological interpretation has been undertaken by Babchuk and Courtney (1995), the same Courtney who published the 1992 monograph *Why Adults Learn* (Courtney, 1992).

Books: edited collection and monographs

Over the years, a number of edited collections in the field of lifelong learning have been published, with most of them including a specific chapter on participation studies in the field. Examples include London (2011), who edited *The Oxford Handbook of Lifelong Learning,* and Kasworm et al. (2010), who edited the *Handbook of Adult and Continuing Education,* supported by the American Association for Adult and Continuing Education, of which earlier versions had been published, e.g. by Wilson and Hayes (2000). Jarvis (2010) edited *The Routledge International Handbook of Lifelong Learning.* Chapman et al. (2006) compiled *Lifelong learning, participation and equity* with Springer as part of their lifelong learning book series. Rubenson (2011a) edited *Adult Learning and Education,* published by Elsevier. Several publishers nowadays have book series on lifelong learning and although participation is not the main topic of interest of many of these books, they are helpful in informing us about the contextual characteristics and policies of lifelong learning.

Two edited collections have been published as the final output of the LLL2010 project. I published a chapter in both books based on my involvement in the project. Riddell et al. (2012) edited *Lifelong learning Europe: equity and efficiency in the balance,* disseminating the final results of the project, including separate results for different sub-projects. Secondly, Saar et al. (2013) edited *Lifelong learning in Europe: national patterns and challenges* in which each national team received the opportunity to focus on a specific feature of adult life-long learning within their country. The book *Adult learning in modern societies: an international comparison from a life-course perspective* was edited by Blossfeld et al. (2014) as part of the dissemination process of the EduLife project, another large scale European Framework project. While the themes discussed in edited collections are usually broad and varied, all of these volumes contain a wide range of inputs helping towards further understanding of why adults do or do not participate in adult lifelong learning activities. I will therefore refer to many of them in the following chapters.

In terms of monographs, *Widening participation in post-compulsory education* by Liz Thomas (2005) provides a good overview of the determinants of participation. The book has a rather strong focus on the UK, but also includes cases from Ireland and Sweden. Several monographs have resulted from the LLL2010 project too. Hefler (2013) published *Taking steps* in which he also explores participation issues from the perspective of formal training and from a background in workplace learning. Earlier, Holford et al. (2008) published *Patterns of lifelong learning: policy & practice in an expanding Europe* based on a review of participation statistics and supporting policies in a range of Western and Eastern European countries. Finally, Downes (2014) published *Access to education in Europe: a framework and agenda for system change* as part of the Springer Lifelong Learning Book Series.

Europe

Benchmarks and indicators in European education and training are measured regularly and since 2003/2004 the European Commission has started producing annual 'progress towards the Lisbon bench-marks and indicators' reports. The aim is to show countries how well they perform in comparison to other countries in the hope that this will put peer pressure on the weakest performing countries to engage in a policy learning process, as explained in the previous chapter. One way of doing this is by presenting the share of information and good practices between countries. In producing these statistics, the European Union claims to adopt an evidence-based policy process based on empirical data.

In the field of adult education participation, we have noticed significant differences in performance between the Member States. The benchmark of 15 percent – measured on a four week basis targeted at 25–64 year olds – has not yet been met by many countries, based on the latest participation rates published in 2014. In general, in exploring the data, a north-to-south and west-to-east pattern emerges: Scandinavian countries score higher on adult education participation and West-European countries score higher than East-European 'catching up' countries (Holford et al., 2008; Boateng, 2009). Research into these differences has made clear how the macro level context, such as levels of innovation, employment rates and the structure of compulsory education, relates to participation rates in adult education, which will be explored in Chapter 6 (Desmedt et al., 2006).

Based on available data, it is possible to see some patterns of participation, as summarised in Figure 2.1. These statistics have been sorted into five categories and reflect a participation reference period of four weeks. Detailed figures and tables, including distributions for a set of socio-economic and socio-demographic variables, can be extracted from the Eurostat website, which is an important tool for researchers, policy makers and practitioners interested in adult lifelong learning participation in the European context. Eurostat,

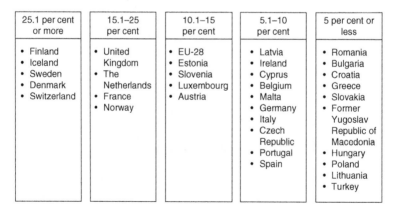

25.1 per cent or more	15.1–25 per cent	10.1–15 per cent	5.1–10 per cent	5 per cent or less
• Finland • Iceland • Sweden • Denmark • Switzerland	• United Kingdom • The Netherlands • France • Norway	• EU-28 • Estonia • Slovenia • Luxembourg • Austria	• Latvia • Ireland • Cyprus • Belgium • Malta • Germany • Italy • Czech Republic • Portugal • Spain	• Romania • Bulgaria • Croatia • Greece • Slovakia • Former Yugoslav Republic of Macedonia • Hungary • Poland • Lithuania • Turkey

Figure 2.1 Percentage of adults (25–64) participating in adult lifelong learning activities by country (2014)
Source: Own ranking based on available data.

the European Commission's statistical office, has its headquarters in Luxembourg. Founded in 1953, Eurostat strives toward the harmonisation of data in the Members States of the European Union, the candidate countries and the EFTA countries (Iceland, Norway and Switzerland) (Lawn & Grek, 2012).

The data collected about education is from the ESIS/EL: the European Union Statistical Information System on Education and Learning. The three strands of ESIS/EL are: (1) the collection of administrative data in cooperation with OECD and UNESCO; (2) the collection of data on vocational education and training based on the CVTS (Continuing Vocational Training Survey); and (3) the development and use of household surveys measuring lifelong learning participation, such as the Labour Force Survey, the Adult Education Survey and the EU-SILC (Survey on Income and Living Conditions). While micro data is only available upon detailed application, macro data can be accessed on the website for free and can be extracted in Excel files.

An alternative way of exploring participation rates in Europe is to analyse data from the recent Survey of Adult Skills, conducted as part of the PIAAC, which is managed by OECD, and thus includes a number of non-European countries as well (Desjardins, 2015). The reference period for participation is 12 months, not four weeks, as is the case for the Labour Force Survey. Based on the PIAAC survey data, we know that countries with participation rates of higher than 60 percent include the Scandinavian countries (Denmark, Finland, Sweden and Norway), while the Netherlands, Germany, Estonia, the UK and Ireland scored higher than 50 percent. Belgium, Czech Republic, Austria and Spain obtained participation rates in the upper 40 percentage. Poland, Cyprus, France and Slovakia scored higher than 30 percent, while Italy just managed to reach 20 percent participation in adult lifelong learning activities. While these numbers are, of course, different from those obtained through the Labour Force Survey because of the differences in reference periods, it is clear that participation rates in Europe tend to be highest in Scandinavian countries. While North-South and East-Western patterns exist, they are not completely accurate. A country like Estonia scores higher and is here in the same group with Western European countries, while France scores rather weakly in comparison with other Western continental countries.

North America

Both the United States and Canada achieved participation rates between 50 and 60 percent in the PIAAC's Survey of Adult Skills (Desjardins, 2015). They do not, therefore, belong to the group of highest achievers, like the Scandinavian countries, but they do better than a range of continental European countries. It is also important to provide more insight into the specific foci in both the United States of America and Canada.

United States of America

The political situation of the United States has been analysed by Milana and McBain (2014), who have identified the 1998 Workforce Investment Act as an important guide to education, a program that ran from 1998 till 2003. While the Act expired in 2003, it can be argued that annual funding streams have since been maintained. A new act, the Workforce Investment and Opportunity Act was signed in the summer of 2014. Milana and McBain (2014) argue that emphasis has been put on civic learning – e.g. through teaching English to those who lack proficiency – and the development of the workforce, particularly after the economic crisis. While these two strands are focus points of both Democratic and Republican parties, they tend to have different positions on a number of issues, such as the devolution of funding from the federal level to the states and the role of funding for learning activities that take place in for-profit organisations or in organisations with a religious ideology.

Participation statistics in the American context have also been produced, for example through the Adult Education Program and Learner Survey (AEPS) (Tamassia et al., 2007). Similar to the global context, Tamassia et al.'s report places a strong emphasis on the need for individuals to maintain human capital in the form of knowledge and skills, such as numeracy and literacy skills, in order to survive in society. While there is a strong focus on economic returns and participation in the labour market, there is a recognition of the relationship between human capital, citizenship, social cohesion, health and well-being.

The AEPS consists, in fact, of two separate surveys: the 'Program Survey' and the 'Learner Survey'. It is important to note that the focus regarding adult learners in this survey has been on those enrolled in basic skills education, those who enrolled in courses to improve their English, and those who sought to finish and obtain a qualification of secondary education. Comparing the adult learners' population with the general population based on representative household surveys, Tamassia et al. (2007) found that adult learners represent a younger and ethnically more diverse group with more people speaking a language other than English as their first language. They were hence more likely to be unemployed and scored lower on tests measuring their numeracy and literacy skills.

While these results may suggest that the system is able to attract learners from disadvantaged groups, the disappointing fact is that the proportion of these adult learners in the entire population is very small (1.3 percent of the US adult population) and adult learning activities in colleges and universities were not included in the definition of adult lifelong learning, which is the case in relation to the 15 percent participation benchmark in the European context. A report by Allan, Solomon, Storan and Thomas (nd) on widening participation in the higher education context underlines that degree attainment in the United States is clearly widening instead of narrowing. Students from stronger socio-economic family backgrounds have a higher chance of entering higher education. However, they also state that universities and colleges in the US have been quicker to adapt to the needs of lifelong learners compared to, for instance, England, through offering opportunities for part-time study modes.

In fact, Ginsberg and Wlodkowski (in Kasworm et al., 2010, p. 27) provide a to-the-point summary on the types of adult lifelong learners in the US context:

> Researchers have found that in the U.S. within the last decade those workers most likely to participate in nonformal and formal education are 45 to 54 years old, White or Asian American, have a professional or master's degree, earn more than $75,000 per year, and work in professional fields such as education and health care. (Hudson et al., 2005)

Participants in postsecondary education among adults 25 and older are predominantly white women married with children, with above average family incomes (60 percent) (Cook & King, 2004; Paulson & Boeke, 2006). Despite the existence of basic education and the recognised need to offer flexible education, it is still clear that those on higher salaries and those within white communities will have more chances of participating in workplace learning and higher education. The differences in participation rates between different socio-economic groups have also been demonstrated through analysis of the PIAAC Survey of Adult Skills (Desjardins, 2015). Among US respondents with less than secondary education qualifications, 31 percent take part, in contrast with 79 percent of those who do have qualifications higher than upper secondary education. While 27 percent of those with the lowest level of literacy take part, the participation rates amongst those with the highest levels of literacy is 84 percent, a strong statistical difference. There is also a statistically significant difference in participation rates between those with and without parents educated to at least upper secondary education. Those from lower socio-economic backgrounds have a participation rate of 39 percent while the participation rate among those from higher socio-economic status groups is 72 percent.

Canada

For a general overview of educational statistics, one can consult the 'Composite Learning Index', which is based on 'a combination of statistical indicators that reflect the many ways Canadians learn, whether in school, in the home, at work or within the community' (UNESCO, 2015 – http://www.unesco.org/new/en/education/themes/strengthening-education-systems/quality-framework/technical-notes/composite-learning-index/). The CLI is also based on a set of different indicators derived from UNESCO's division between 'learning to know', 'learning to do', 'learning to be' and 'learning to live together' and thus similar in format to the European Lifelong Learning Index, which has been developed drawing on Canadian expertise with the CLI (Canadian Council on Learning, 2010). Results from Canada can be tracked from 2006 to 2010 and can be found on the CLI website. The 'learning to do' component provides strong reflections on workplace learning and adult learning for job-related reasons. The 'learning to know' component measures the proportion of adults who obtained university level qualifications.

Participation rates in relation to adult lifelong learning in Canada have been analysed by Kjell Rubenson at the University of British Columbia. One of his extensive reports about the Canadian context was published in 2007, together with the research of Desjardins and Yoon (Rubenson et al., 2007). It provided an in-depth analysis of the results of the Adult Literacy and Life Skills Survey. As the results should be analysed per jurisdiction, the report provides separate statistics for adult learning in Alberta, British Columbia, Manitoba, New Brunswick, Newfoundland and Labrador, Northwest Territories, Nova Scotia, Nunavut, Ontario, Prince Edwards Island, Quebec, Saskatchewan and Yukon. While the general participation rate in organised learning for the entire country was around 50 percent, the lowest rates were found in Newfoundland and Labrador, and the highest in British Columbia.

Apart from the participation variation per province, the report also makes clear that participation rates were unequal in all the regions, based on socio-economic and socio-demographic indicators. Those with low literacy levels, low levels of education, older adults, the unemployed and those from low income backgrounds have fewer chances to be a participant. This trend has also been confirmed by more recent statistics from the PIAAC Survey of Adult Skills (Desjardins, 2015). Participation rates for those without upper secondary education and those with qualifications higher than secondary education are 31 versus 74 percent. There is also a significant difference between those with the lowest and highest literacy levels – 24 versus 79 percent – which is one of the highest differences across all the countries that took part in the Survey of Adult Skills. While those from lower SES backgrounds have a participation rate of 42 percent, for those from higher SES backgrounds the participation rate is 71 percent. In general, it is thus quite clear that there are persistent inequalities based on people's backgrounds.

South America

While lifelong learning debates have been mostly shaped in the Western world, it is also important to explore the situation in other contexts. The UNESCO website contains information on adult lifelong learning data in different regions of the world, including statistics on participation in Latin America and the Caribbean, and it is important to know that the Sixth CONFINTEA conference was organised in Belem, Brazil, in December 2009 (UNESCO, 2015). This conference concluded with the Belem 'Framework for Action', a strategic framework for enhancing lifelong learning and the development of stronger levels of adult literacy. Statistics provided by UNESCO show strong connections to this theme of adult literacy.

The data here shows that just over 10 million adults in this region participate in adult lifelong learning activities, around 25 percent at the primary educational level and 75 percent at the secondary educational level. Interestingly, the title appearing above the broad figures shows '(Adult education helps make up for lost opportunities)' (UNESCO Institute for Statistics). While primary and secondary education in Latin America and the Caribbean is targeted in the first place at young people, 4 percent of the primary level and 12 percent of the secondary level population are adult learners. Similar to the problems of access outlined above in relation to the North-American context, participation and return to primary education amongst those who did not complete (or even start) initial primary schooling is very small. In Colombia and Honduras, this represents around 4–5 percent of the population without primary education, but in a range of countries, it is less even than one percent (Ecuador, Venezuela, Chile, El Salvador, Uruguay and Bolivia). However, the return to secondary education is the highest in Bolivia and Ecuador, although around 9–12 percent of the entire population do not finish secondary schooling.

Amongst those who return to the education system across the Latin American and Caribbean countries, the majority is still younger than age 25, demonstrating that the system is mainly used for school drop-outs who go back into the system only a few years after they have left. On average, around 9 percent of the entire adult population is illiterate, a problem more common amongst women compared to men. Countries like Mexico, Peru and Guatemala have a strong overrepresentation of women in their literacy courses (around 75 percent and higher of participants are female) while women only represent around 20 percent of adult learners in literacy courses in Cuba. Bolivia has been very successful in getting illiterate adults into the course system, with more than 50 percent of all illiterate adults being enrolled in a literacy course. In some countries, like Puerto Rico, Jamaica, Brazil and Paraguay, this is less than 5 percent. Thus, in general, it is clear that this part of the world is still dealing with issues relating to basic education and basic skills like literacy and that, here, a lot of work will still have to be done.

Australia

Similar to other countries and regions in the world, the Australian Department of Education, Employment and Workplace Relations (2009) did preparatory work for the CONFINTEA conference that took place in 2009 in Belem, Brazil. The Australian system consists of a straightforward flow of primary, secondary and higher education, but also has a Vocational Education and Training (VET) as well as an Adult and Community Education (ACE) system in place. The main priorities for adult learning and education are to cope with the demands of the labour market and to supply training for the skills needed by employers in order to stimulate productivity and to widen access to educational activities as a means of generating higher levels of social inclusion. Similar to the European system, the Australian system thus focuses on the need for competitiveness, although notions of social themes are also addressed. A number of measurable targets have also been formulated, such as halving the proportion of low-qualified adults and doubling the number of higher education students obtaining their qualifications by 2020.

In relation to participation, a Survey of Adult Learners was organised in 2006 and 2007. Participation in adult lifelong learning activities was measured in a similar way as in Europe, through surveying adults between the age of 25 and 64 and asking for their participation in both formal and non-formal activities in the 12 months prior to the completion of the survey (Australian Bureau of Statistics, 2007). Results indicate that 38 percent of adults participated more in non-formal than formal activities, similar to the findings in Europe. Older, low-qualified adults tended to participate less, while gender differences in terms of general participation did not seem to be significant. Motivations for participation are mainly work-related, both for formal and non-formal education. Similar to general awareness and research evidence of barriers, time and costs were indicated as the two major barriers constraining participation in adult lifelong learning activities. Here, specific attention has been paid to mobilising adults from underrepresented groups, such as those with a low socio-economic status, those with disabilities, not native English speakers and those living in remote areas. Participation and unequal patterns of participation thus seem to be in line with what is happening in other developed countries.

Asia and the Pacific

Ahmed (2009) has produced the synthesis report for the Asian and Pacific region in preparation of CONFINTEA VI. The Asian continent has a high proportion of the world's population and hosts a diverse range of cultures. Literacy is one of the focal points for the region and, as in other parts of the world, is a problem that mainly effects women. However, literacy levels are higher than in Africa and Latin America. Equity is also one of the core strategies, with the aim of increasing participation amongst adults from disadvantaged groups. Low levels of basic education are found in particular in countries like Mongolia, Pakistan and Bangladesh, while they are much more advanced in the Philippines, Indonesia, Malaysia and Thailand. China is a very large country and therefore hosts a large proportion of the world's illiterate adults, resulting in a strong focus on the education of women and those living in rural areas.

In relation to participation in adult lifelong learning activities, it is generally accepted that both women and adults aged 45 and over are underrepresented. Those in rural areas are also underrepresented. In short, there is a clear correlation between low levels of literacy and low levels of participation. Disadvantages are also felt amongst those from ethnically underrepresented groups in specific areas. Findings in preparation for CONFINTEA VI showed that, in general, Asian countries are not spending high levels of public funding on education. A commitment to work towards a learning society is therefore needed with mechanisms in place to support learners' needs, both in formal and non-formal types of education. The region also requires stronger development of quality control mechanisms, further development of the use of technologies in learning and the installment of a strong managerial and governing structure.

As we have touched upon, Asia is a diverse continent. Japan and Korea are included within the OECD, which groups the most advanced countries. This means that they also participate in surveys such as PISA and PIAAC. Based on data from PISA, both Korea and Japan are countries in which 15-year-olds score above average on reading skills and countries that also score above average on adult literacy skills, as measured in the Survey of Adult Skills. This means that the most advanced Asian countries are, in fact, doing well in terms of literacy compared to other parts of the developed world, with the exception of the Scandinavian countries. These are also Asian countries in which skills inequality is rather low, while income inequality is around the average compared to other OECD countries (OECD, 2013c). In the general participation rates obtained through the PIAAC Survey of Adult Skills, Korea had a participation rate of 50 percent and Japan of 40 percent. This in fact puts them in the middle group, not in the strongest performing group in regard to this indicator, but also not in the weakest group.

In Asia, India is also a country with a very large population, but one putting itself on the map for its large economy and its fast development over the past 20 years (Chauhan in Jarvis 2009, p. 492). However, the country still has a significant proportion of illiterate adults, with the majority of them being women. An important focus of Indian education policy is on reducing inequalities in a number of areas, both economically and socially, including gender related inequalities, as identified in the 1986 National Policy on Education, modified in 1992 (Ministry of Human Resource Development, 1986). Owing to the literacy problem, a significant focus has been on literacy skills, for example through the implementation of the National Literacy Mission.

In 1996, Continuous Education Centres came into practice for illiterate adults to improve and maintain their literacy skills. While the year 2000 was important in Europe because of the signing of the Lisbon Treaty, putting lifelong learning in the picture, it was also the year in which the Indian government ran its own 'Education for All' campaign, with the aim of providing children in India with a solid educational basis and preventing the risk of illiteracy in adult life. Benchmarks and indicators in the Indian context mainly refer to the projected decrease of the proportion of illiterate adults.

Africa and the Middle East

Educational reports on the situation in the African continent are divided into two regions: (1) Sub-Saharan Africa and (2) North Africa together with the Middle East, called the MENA countries (Middle East and North Africa).

Aitchison and Alidou (2009) prepared the synthesis report *The state and development of adult learning and education in sub-Saharan Africa*, published by the UNESCO Institute for Lifelong Learning in the year that CONFITEA VI took place. The report inevitably focuses on the region's problems in relation to poverty, illiteracy and under-education. Statistics provided on the proportion of illiterate adults, as collected by the UNESCO Institute for Statistics, demonstrate that the need for adult basic education is very high, while well-developed curricula are not available in most countries. There also seems to be a lack of priority for adult education by policy makers. In the case of existing provisions, educators tend to be under-trained in the area of teaching adults and are mainly recruited from initial school settings. Unlike the developed world, monitoring and evaluation systems are weakly developed or lacking, while research evidence from this region is lacking in the international literature, making it more difficult for policy makers and practitioners to implement evidence-based strategies.

Owing to the typical problems of the region, it is recommended that a good basic education system be implemented with specific attention to creating opportunities for women and for illiterate people and helping adults to find their way out of poverty. Providing insight into trends of adult lifelong learning participation is difficult as most countries struggle to collect statistical data on the adult lifelong learning situation. On the other hand, it is known that different types of educational programmes exist, such as numeracy and literacy programmes, including programmes to maintain these skills, as well as basic education, second chance education, higher education, continuing education and professional development (mostly targeted towards those working in business environments). There are also vocationally-oriented programmes, ICT training, community development and education programmes available.

In the context of the region's initial schooling system, several countries provide opportunities for teachers to develop their teaching and training skills further. While some countries have already taken steps towards developing National Qualifications Frameworks, it is expected that other countries will focus on this in the next few years. Examples of quality assurance, monitoring and evaluation policies are weakly defined. While research into the field of adult lifelong learning is mainly lacking, Nigeria seems to be the exception.

The state of adult education in the Arab world has been synthesised by Yousif (2009) as part of the UNESCO's CONFINTEA regional reports. Similar to the sub-Saharan region, participation of women in learning activities is limited and there is a relation between the lack of human capital and knowledge and the state of income. Around 65 million adults in this region are thought to be illiterate and, as in sub-Saharan Africa, this problem effects women more than men. Although more girls receive primary education nowadays, a significant proportion of children still do not attend school. Connections between education policies and labour market policies are largely lacking, resulting in a mismatch between what employers need and what levels of skills and knowledge the education system is providing.

Given the situation, recommendations for adult education involve a focus on literacy programmes, the empowerment of women, 'return to education' programmes for school drop-outs, and a general focus on up-skilling disadvantaged groups in society. The region also needs more high quality research on adult education in order to provide evidence-based input for policy making. In the case of existing educational provision, there is a general perception that this tends to be low in terms of quality, while quality controls including learners' evaluation of courses seem to be absent from the debate. A final concern in this region is that access to the internet and other ICT related tools is amongst the lowest in the world, making it hard to catch up with other regions.

General trends

Having explored adult lifelong learning participation trends in various continents, it is clear that disadvantaged groups throughout society are likely to be underrepresented in the education system. In the developed world, the adult lifelong learning system focuses on skills and knowledge in order to survive in the competitive knowledge-based economy, while developing countries' core actions are mostly concerned with the combat of poverty and illiteracy. However, as will be explored later in this book, the way in which separate countries support the participation of adults in lifelong learning activities differs. It is important to know how this affects participation rates, although it has to be said that most of the scholarly evidence for my arguments has been assembled in the developed world.

Barriers preventing adult lifelong learning participation

Apart from understanding trends in adult lifelong learning participation, usually obtained through the analysis of participation statistics, another major interest for the field is understanding what prevents adults from participating, in order that actions be taken to help adults overcome these barriers, or even to remove them (Skilbeck, in Chapman et al., 2006, p. 47). While possible answers to this question will be provided in the next chapters, it is important to provide a general overview of the concepts and definitions of barriers as discussed in the international literature. Understanding barriers is also essential to understanding the differences between participants and non-participants (Scanlan & Darkenwald, 1984).

Traditionally, research into barriers in adult lifelong learning would start with reference to Cross (1981), who distinguished between 'situational', 'dispositional' and 'institutional' barriers. Situational barriers refer to barriers resulting from an adult's life situation, e.g. not being able to participate because of childcare duties. A range of situations, often related to lack of time and money, can prevent people from participating. Dispositional barriers relate to confidence issues and a lack of self-efficacy and will therefore be discussed in the following chapter explaining the psychological dimensions of participation.

Institutional barriers are then those barriers produced by the institutional structures themselves, e.g. when they ask for very high enrolment fees or offer courses at inconvenient and inaccessible places. Even adults without any situational and dispositional constraints will not participate in adult lifelong learning activities if the offer is not available. While these three types of barriers are widely used and confirmed in the international literature, it is important to mention that Darkenwald and Merriam (1982) included a fourth type which they name 'informational' barriers. Lack of communication in regard to available learning opportunities will prevent people from participating because they simply do not know that specific courses exist. As McDonald (2003) argues, informational barriers relate to institutional barriers as lack of information is often caused by a lack of communication at the institutional level. Institutional and informational barriers will therefore be discussed in Chapter 5.

While Cross (1981) has earned an international reputation in the field of adult lifelong learning participation through the publication of her Chain of Response model, which includes these barriers as part of her decision-making model, she was not the first person to explore barriers. Johnstone and Rivera (1965) were the first to conduct empirical research in the North-American context and distinguished between two major types of barriers: internal and external barriers. The meaning behind the notion of internal barriers is similar to what Cross (1981) label as 'dispositional' barriers, while external barriers represent the 'situational barriers'.

In the 1970s, Carp et al. (1973) surveyed adult learners and collected information regarding barriers to learning based on 24 response items, which were later used by Cross (1981) who classified the 24 statements as 'situational', 'dispositional' or 'institutional'. Carp et al.'s (1973) questionnaire has been used by other scholars in the field, such as Byrd (1990) and Green (1998).

After Cross' work was published, Valentine and Darkenwald (1990) further researched barriers and constructed the 'deterrents to participation scale', based on earlier research in which they had distinguished six 'factors of deterrence': 'lack of confidence, lack of course relevance, time constraints, low personal priority, cost, and personal problems' (Darkenwald & Valentine, 1985; Valentine & Darkenwald, 1990, p. 30). Their 1990 *Adult Education Quarterly* paper distinguishes between five types of non-participants based on their deterrents: (1) people deterred by personal problems, (2) people deterred by a lack of confidence, (3) people deterred by educational costs, (4) people not interested in organised education and (5) people not interested in available courses.

Another group of researchers who have explored barriers in relation to adults living in rural areas, are Chapman et al. (in Chapman et al., 2006, pp. 155–157). The five groups of barriers they recognised are (1) personal and societal barriers, (2) financial barriers, (3) geographic barriers, (4) management barriers and (5) vision, mission and identity barriers. In the context of adult lifelong learning participation, it makes absolute sense to include geographical barriers as a separate category of barriers, especially for those who live in rural areas in which educational institutions or training offers are often absent. While personal and societal barriers can include issues like lack of confidence, often reinforced by peers and family, Chapman et al.'s fourth and fifth barriers relate to the strong management, vision and mission ethos that needs to be developed at the level of the educational institutions in order to make lifelong learning activities attractive to the individual. In fact, the existence of barriers is one thing, but the structures and strategies put in place to overcome these barriers is vital to the generation of widened participation.

In general, it can be concluded that new empirical research on barriers mostly confirms Cross' classification. Overall, it can be said that the dominant barriers preventing adult lifelong learning participation are the lack of time and costs (Boeren, 2011). In relation to time, the reasons for non-participation include both family and job-related time constraints. In fact, barriers can be classified and explained from different perspectives. A cost barrier might be a situational barrier for someone who does not have a high income or lives on benefits, but it can equally be explained as an institutional barrier, in the case of the institution requiring adult learners to pay high enrolment fees.

One of the critical comments that needs to be introduced in relation to the typologies and categories of barriers is that these research projects were undertaken in the North-American context and that nowadays, in a globalised world, there is a need to include the level of countries and their system characteristics as countries differ from each other in terms of economic competitiveness, their education and labour market systems and general culture and values. It is thus important to understand the processes of interplay between these barriers and it is the aim of this book to generate higher levels of insight into the interdisciplinary nature of adult lifelong learning participation theory. Reflections on institutional barriers will therefore include reference to research on how educational institutions are constraining adults, but also on how the broader institutional features of countries correlate with the odds of being a participant or non-participant in adult lifelong learning activities.

Conclusions

The first part of this book has explored trends in relation to adult lifelong learning participation, but also how policy discourse has changed since the second half of the last century. The shift towards individual responsibilities and economic focus has been underlined. There are multiple explanations as to why certain groups of adults do or do not participate in adult lifelong learning activities. It is the aim of the following chapters to provide explanations from different viewpoints and then to discuss combined and integrated perspectives.

Part II
The Contribution of Disciplines to an Interdisciplinary Theory

3

Lifelong Learning Participation: The Behavioural Perspective

Having outlined the context regarding the current state of adult lifelong learning participation, I will now turn to exploring the mechanisms behind why certain adults do and other adults do not participate in adult lifelong learning. I will thus explore why, from the policy point of view, these mechanisms do or do not contribute to the benchmarks and indicators relating to adult lifelong learning participation.

This third chapter, the first within Part II, therefore explores participation from a behavioural perspective. Here the psychological literature principally focuses on a range of explanations, including the role of decision-making processes as a means to fulfil needs, the role of motivation and the role of development in adulthood. As will be demonstrated, all theories bring important aspects to understanding the puzzle of participation, but have their limitations too.

Participation as the result of an underlying decision-making process

While surveys have the tendency to measure participation through a simple yes-no question, participation can be regarded as the result of a rather complex underlying decision-making process, one that captures a wide range of elements, including motivation and expectations (Baert et al., 2006). Many of these decision-making models were developed in the 1970s and 1980s, and are discussed in Courtney's *Why adults learn: towards a theory of participation in adult education*, e.g. not only Cross's well-known Chain-of-Response model, but also contributions by Miller (1967), Rubenson (1977), Grotelueschen and Cauley (1977), Darkenwald and Merriam (1982) and Cookson (1983, 1986) (Courtney, 1992).

What the models all have in common is that they start from decision making being internalised within the individual, while some theories also focus on the surrounding social environment (Boeren et al., 2010). It can therefore be said that these participation models originate from a social psychological tradition. While such models have been around for a long time, and have been discussed before, it is important to analyse how the idea of decision-making processes in the lifelong learning literature has been developed following the publication of Courtney's work in 1992.

The role of needs, intentions and planning

It may be noted that work built on previous participation modelling has expanded into other disciplines, such as sociology, economics and politics, thus creating an interdisciplinary theory. In relation to the psychological component, some significant and influential work in the field of adult lifelong learning participation has been undertaken based on Fishbein and Ajzen's work on 'planned and intended behaviour' and 'reasoned actions', research further developed by Flemish scholars Baert et al. (2006) (Fishbein & Ajzen, 1980). The notion of 'intention' is – as in Fishbein and Ajzen's work – central to their theory. Reflections and empirical studies on the importance of 'intentions' in participation research, grounded in work by Fishbein and Ajzen, can also be found in the work of Maurer et al. (2003), Hurtz and Williams (2009) and Kyndt et al. (2013). Although not based on Fishbein and Ajzen's research, it is also worthwhile to mention the work undertaken by Grotluschen, in what she labels – in German – as 'Interessetheorie'. Similar to the work of Baert et al. (2006), she argues that non-participation can also be the result of a lack of interest. In accordance with my understanding of participation, she refers to psychological concepts like motivation, as well as to concepts of 'habitus' as developed by Bourdieu, one of the elements discussed in the following chapter.

Going back to Fishbein and Ajzen, three key factors have been determined by them as central predictors as to whether people will intend and plan to follow certain behaviour patterns. Firstly, the attitude towards specific behaviour; secondly, the subjective norms attached to the behaviour; and thirdly, the perceived behavioural control, e.g. feeling the need to participate due to pressure to do so. The development and formulation of an intention to participate, usually generated through a combination of these predictors, is therefore an essential step in the decision-making process.

Baert et al. (2006) include 'intention' as a central focus point in their participation theory. They argue that becoming an adult learner starts from developing a specific need, which needs to be transformed into an educational need. Once this educational need has been recognised, the intention to participate in an adult learning course can be formed. During the next phase, the intention will flow over into an educational demand, and only after demand and offer have matched – when the learning activity fulfilling the initial need is available to the potential adult learner – can participation then take place.

Baert et al. (2006) do not isolate needs, educational needs, intentions and the educational demands cycle, but demonstrate that the decision-making process is heavily influenced by other factors. They distinguish between the individual characteristics of the adults, including psychological and socio-economic characteristics, and the characteristics of existing adult learning programmes as influential factors. However, they also connect the two through the notion of intention, borrowed from psychological theory. Participation is thus the result of an underlying decision-making process in which individual needs have been converted into educational needs, intentions and demands, and for which a matching educational offer has been found. There will be further exploration of the role of socio-economic factors and institutional offers in the following chapters.

It is interesting that Baert et al. (2006) reflect on 'needs'. Furthermore, it would be interesting to explore in more depth when exactly needs are to be translated into educational needs. It might also be the case that needs are being fulfilled in other ways than through participation in lifelong learning activities, discussed by Courtney (1992) as the necessity to compare educational offers with the spectrum of alternative activities. One recognised way of understanding needs was constructed by Maslow (1943) in his 'Theory of Human Motivation'. In this work, needs are represented in a pyramid, representing the hierarchical nature of needs. Maslow argues that it is important to fulfil the needs at the bottom first, before one starts focussing on needs concentrated at a higher level. Needs such as 'physiological needs' and 'safety needs' are perceived as basic needs which are necessary for survival, such as food, drink and shelter. Belongingness, love and esteem are important psychological needs, which are above the basic needs. Moreover, individuals need connections with friends and family alongside the need to feel respected by others, yet they also need to develop a sense of self-respect. Finally, at the top of the pyramid, Maslow distinguishes the need for 'self-actualisation', which mainly refers to the need of humans to reach their full potential. While Maslow's work has been widely influential, it has also been criticised, e.g. by Dutch social psychologist Hofstede (1984), who argues that Maslow's needs hierarchy does not succeed in distinguishing between the different structures according to which societies are organised. I tend to agree with this criticism about the isolated nature of Maslow's work, but perceive it as an interesting puzzle that contributes to an overarching integrated lifelong learning participation theory. Similar critique of lack of cultural contexts in relation to adult lifelong learning participation modelling has been published by myself based on doctoral research supervised by Baert (and Nicaise). It can be argued that the planning and the formulation of intention still lies at the core of persuading people to participate. Psychological insights cannot therefore be ignored, and it is recommended that policy makers generate strategies for encouraging adults to develop positive feelings towards adult lifelong learning, entailing that adults are aware of the educational opportunities available to fulfil their needs.

Rational Choice Theory

Another theory often used to explain human decision making, and thus the decision to participate in lifelong learning activities, is based on Rational Choice Theory, which is also referred to as 'Choice Theory' or 'Rational Action Theory' (Allingham, 2002). This theory is often used by behavioural economists to *'understand and predict individual action ...'* (Wang, 2008, p. 52). Explained in a simple way, Rational Choice Theory argues that when people have the choice between different options, they will choose the one that will provide them with the highest level of utility (Bohman, 1992; Abell, 2000). The core elements that will influence whether the individual is going to undertake a specific action will be based on the desires and beliefs of the individual, and the preferences they have. However, they will also be based on the information that he or she is able to consult about the available options from which he or she can choose.

In fact, to start from the assumption that adults will choose to participate in order to maximise their profits or utilities is to focus significantly on the human capital approach of lifelong learning in which economic competitiveness is perceived as vital. It is therefore not surprising that Rational Choice Theory has been criticised as being a form of *'economic reductionism'* (Wang, 2008, p. 66). Weighing up the costs versus the benefits before deciding to participate does sound reasonable, but it is important to point out that this process will not be the same for everyone. An engagement with different levels of costs and benefits for different socio-economic and sociodemographic groups in order to increase our understanding of these relationships will thus be pursued in the following chapter.

The role of motivation

Motivation is an important construct in the study of psychology, and exploring the motivations behind adults' participation in lifelong learning activities is strongly present in the scholarly literature in the field. It is important to know that 'motivation' is derived from the Latin word 'movere', 'to move', which reflects the effort one is willing to make to 'move' in the desired direction (Rathus, 2012). Motivation is thus likely to be a construct that can help people in their decision-making process of whether to participate or not.

This section on motivation refers to a range of motivational theories but, in the first instance, to the pioneering work of Cyril O. Houle. Later, I will also concentrate on the use of other motivational theories in adult lifelong learning research, such as the self-determination theory, and provide details on recent motivational research in the field of adult lifelong learning participation.

The Inquiring Mind

Cyril Orvin Houle was born more than 100 years ago on the 26th of March 1913 and is recognised as one of the major influential thinkers in the history of adult education research (Griffith, 1991). Houle attended the University of Florida at Gainesville and received his PhD degree from the University of Chicago under the supervision of

Floyd W Reeves. His PhD, awarded in 1940, was entitled *'The coordination of adult education at the state level'*. Together with Reeves, Houle has been involved in projects on national and state level education, such as the *'Regents' Inquiry into the character and cost of public education in the State of New York'* (1938), which was published even before he obtained his PhD degree. Houle remained active at the University of Chicago until 1978, taking up a position as an assistant professor in 1942 and becoming a full professor in 1952, before retiring in the late '70s. Houle died in 1998 at the age of 85. Even before his death, Houle was described as one of the most influential thinkers in adult education in the twentieth century (Jarvis, 1991).

Houle indeed compiled an impressive curriculum vitae. He won numerous awards, received more than 10 Honorary Doctorates and served on the Advisory Committee on Education under president Roosevelt. Houle had a special interest in the design and planning of education and was known to have an extraordinary level of productivity and self-discipline, as well as a highly developed competence for dealing with administration (Griffith, 1991). His work on institutional providers of adult education investigates a variety of sectors, such as the library sector and the armed services. Houle was active at the Universities of Leeds and Oxford in the UK for which he received a Fullbright scholarship, while he also held the Knapp visiting professorship at the University of Wisconsin-Milwaukee. In addition, he worked at California-Berkeley and Washington. Outside the Anglophone academic world, Houle undertook activities in Africa and the Caribbean. He also acted on various education boards, including UNESCO's committee for the Advancement of Education.

Although Houle published many books, reports and articles, including *The effective board* (1960), *Continuing your education* (1964), *The design of education* (1972), *The external degree* (1973), *Continuing learning in the professions* (1980), *Patterns of learning: new perspectives on life-span education* (1984), he is, specifically in relation to adult lifelong learning participation, mostly known for his 1961 work, *The inquiring mind: a study of the adult who continues to learn*. This publication emerged as the result of a lecture series he gave while active as a Knapp visiting professor at the University of Wisconsin, Milwaukee, and is regarded as a core reference study in the field of adult motivation.

His research here was based on qualitative interviews with 22 adult learners. Houle grouped them into 'goal-oriented', 'activity-oriented' and 'learning-oriented' participants. Goal-oriented learners participate because they want to achieve clear-cut objectives, activity-oriented learners are mainly interested in the act of taking part as opposed to the content of the course, while learning-oriented participants take part for the sake of content-related knowledge. Houle followed a qualitative paradigm, in which he inductively explored the orientations towards learning adopted by adult learners (Robson, 2011).

Later, researchers have engaged in a quantitative paradigm, testing Houle's typology in a deductive way by employing factor analysis of items that have been developed to confirm or reject the three dimensions theorised by Houle. Boshier developed the Education Participation Scale in 1971 in order to test Houle's typology (Boshier & Collins, 1985). Boshier concluded that, based on factor analysis, while the learning- and goal-oriented learners were a clearly distinguished group, the activity-oriented group is diversified. He further distinguished four dimensions of the activity-oriented learner: those who participate because of the social stimulation; those who are in search of social contact; those who participate to fulfil external expectations; and those who want to contribute to community service (Boshier, 1971).

The Education Participation Scale is a well-known instrument in motivational research in the adult education field and various research projects have used the scale, including the European LLL2010 project 'Towards a Lifelong Learning Society in Europe, the Contribution of the Education System'. A survey of 13,000 adult learners across Europe in formal education and training has contributed a shortened version of Boshier's scale, including two statements on each of the six dimensions (Boeren et al., in Riddell et al., 2012, p. 63). Here, factor analysis has demonstrated two major dimensions: one referring to specific qualification and vocationally oriented goals and the other referring to social motivation and intrinsic interest in the subject of the course. While new empirical research has been undertaken based on the Education Participation scale, Houle's initial typology appears to remain valid. Indeed, more than twenty years ago, and yet thirty years after publication of Houle's *Inquiring Mind*, Griffith (1991, p. 155) stated that additional research activities in the field of adult learning motivation have *'not cast doubt on the soundness of the original conception'* as constructed in Houle's typology.

Going back to the original question to be answered in this book – Why do certain adults participate in lifelong learning activities while others do not? – Houle (1961) offers an answer in terms of those who do. This group has specific reasons or interests for why participating in adult learning is important or relevant for them. However, merely making a simple reflection on the distinction between these three types will not give a satisfactory answer to the question of why certain people did not participate. What do alternative motivational models have to offer?

Expectancy-value theory

The question of whether adults will decide to participate in lifelong learning activities or not might be approached through exploring the values they attach to lifelong learning, and the specific expectations they have about their participation which drive their motivational forces. Expectancy and value were also used by Rubenson in his earlier work in the 1970s, and this is one of the participation models discussed by Courtney (1992) (Rubenson, 1977). The foundations of expectancy-value theory are often linked to the work of Vroom (1964). Several scholars in the field have either critiqued or tried to advance his work.

Keller (1987) has also focused his work in the education context on distinguishing aspects of expectancy and value, coming to the conclusion that once someone has become 'Attracted' to a specific activity or behaviour, then he or she will have to recognise the 'Relevance' of this participation for his or her own life. A good level of 'Confidence' in one's own abilities will be needed, being that the potential participant needs to be sure that s/he will be able to finish the course successfully. Finally, argues Keller, 'Satisfaction' is required in order to sustain the motivation. In short, the adult must believe that they will benefit from participation, either directly or indirectly, but they also need to believe that they have the abilities to succeed.

Several aspects of this theory are important to consider here. In relation to value, I would argue that this theory is right to focus upon the attitudes attached to the activity, as expressed earlier in this chapter as an important predictor of intentions in the work of Fishbein and Azjen (1980). Recognition of the 'value of education' is also made explicit in Rubenson's Expectancy-Valence Model (Rubenson, 1977). Work in relation to attitude and lifelong learning has been undertaken by Blunt and Yang (2002), scholars who have developed the Adult Attitudes towards Continuing Education Scale draw upon earlier attitude research by Rokeach (1968).

Blunt and Yang revised their research instrument following pilot studies and tested the final version of their scale with 275 adult learners who participated in a learning activity taking place 12 months before the survey. Based on the data, Blunt and Yang extracted three dimensions of attitudes, leading to a revised scale with nine items: (1) enjoyment of learning, represented in the statements 'I dislike studying', 'I'm fed up with teachers and classes' and 'I enjoy education activities that allow me to learn with others'; (2) the importance of adult education, correlating with the statements 'successful people do not need adult education', 'adult education is mostly for people with little else to do' and 'money employers spend on education/training is well spent'; (3) intrinsic value, measured through the statements 'adult education helps people make better use of their lives', 'continuing my education would make me feel better about myself' and 'adult education is an important way to help people cope with changes in their lives'. Hence, all of the above statements formulated in a negative way were reversed in a positive way for analysis.

Nowadays, the Eurostat Adult Education Survey also includes items on attitude. The analysis that I have earlier undertaken, reported in Boeren (2011), is based on the Flemish Adult Education Survey. It demonstrates that attitude is a significant predictor for participation in adult lifelong learning activities, and also for the development of an intention to participate among non-participants. However, the attitudinal predictor was not significant in exploring the differences between participants and non-participants with an intention. This finding is thus a confirmation of Fishbein and Ajzen's hypothesis that intention is a predictor of attitudes. However, the results demonstrated that intentions do not automatically translate into participation, because of the barriers in the 'intention-behaviour gap', a term frequently used by Sniehotta and colleagues, although their work does not relate to lifelong learning (Sniehotta et al., 2005). In general, it can thus be argued that it is important for policy makers and educators to focus on the development of positive attitudes; if they do not, it is unlikely that participation rates will increase. Similar critical analyses were carried out by Rubenson (2011b). While a lack of time and money are often mentioned as the major barriers preventing adults from participation in learning activities, it may be argued that the major reason for non-participation is, in fact, a lack of interest and, as mentioned above, a non-engagement in formulating an intention or planning to participate.

We can therefore expect that a lack of positive attitudes and values towards lifelong learning is a strong explanation of why a significant proportion of the adult population does not participate in adult learning activities. The large proportion of adults who lack any interest in participation in adult lifelong learning has also been demonstrated by PIAAC's Survey of Adult Skills (Desjardins, 2015). Amongst those who do not obtain a qualification of upper secondary education, in all the countries surveyed, more than 20 percent have no demand for participation. This is even the case in Scandinavian countries, traditionally the countries with the highest participation rates (Norway, Sweden, Finland and Denmark). In the Slovak Republic and Italy, the proportion of this subpopulation with a lack of interest in participation is even higher than 60 percent.

Apart from 'values', the 'expectations' of potential adult learners are important because a failure to fulfil expectations will lead to disappointment, or a decision not to participate, or the decision to drop out during participation. Expectations are not only projected towards what potential learners expect to happen in the institutional context, and the expected benefits or rewards of participation – e.g. obtaining a better job or salary, making new friends etc. – but they are also projected towards the individual him or herself. Confidence in one's own abilities and the belief that one will be able to participate successfully are important and, in being related to the concept of self-efficacy developed by Bandura (1977), widely used in educational research.

The concept of self-efficacy is important because it has the potential to affect people's behaviour, the goals they want to reach and the tasks and challenges they are willing to undertake. In relation to lifelong learning, those with higher levels of self-efficacy are usually strongly motivated to participate, while for those with low levels of self-efficacy, participation can be perceived as more difficult than it actually is (Maurer et al., 2003; Sahu & Sageeta, 2004). Being that it is linked with previous success and failure, self-efficacy is thus likely to be part of the puzzle of explaining the patterns of unequal participation between high versus low educated adults. Adults who have gone through successful educational experiences are expected to have higher levels of self-efficacy, and it will therefore be more likely that they undertake additional learning challenges in the future because they have confidence that they can do it.

Self-determination

A motivational theory widely used nowadays is the self-determination theory (SDT). SDT starts from the assumption that, in psychological terms, human beings have three basic needs: the 'need for competence', 'need for relatedness' and 'need for autonomy' (Deci & Ryan, 2013). People want to have their lives under control and want to be able to behave in an effective way, in relationships with others which are close and meaningful to them. Humans also want to experience agency in controlling their own lives. While Houle's typology is based on the motivation to distinguish between types of adult learners, the SDT views motivation as a continuum with regard to which people can move between very 'self-determined' or 'not being self-determined' at all. This makes sense as motivation can change over a period of time.

In SDT, a distinction is made between 'autonomous' and 'controlled' motivation, which nowadays is more frequently used than 'intrinsic' versus 'extrinsic' motivation. In exploring adult lifelong learning participation, it is expected that adults who have developed a specific interest in a specific learning activity, who enjoy learning and who experience satisfaction in undertaking these activities are most likely to become adult learners in the future (again) (Deci & Ryan, 2013).

On the other hand, those who experience 'amotivation' are the least self-determined adults, those who have no intention of participating. As we have explored above, this is a significant group backed up by evidence from PIAAC's Survey of Adult Skills (Desjardins, 2015). This group might have developed an alienation from learning because of negative learning experiences in the past and therefore have developed feelings of incompetence. However, amongst those who do participate, we would expect there to be learners who also develop these feelings because of 'external regulations', such as compliance with rules and regulations to keep a job-seekers allowance, as a compulsory part of the job and so on, which refers to what Fishbein and Ajzen (1980) called 'perceived behavioural control'.

For other groups of adults, participation will be driven by the notion of proving to others – usually peers, colleagues, family members – that one is capable of achieving positive outcomes, or to boost one's ego (introjected regulation). Aspirations differ amongst adults, being that some have more 'intrinsic' aspirations which are largely centred on their personal development and relationships with others, while those with 'extrinsic' aspirations are more likely to fulfil needs of becoming rich, famous and being perceived as successful by others. In general, research has demonstrated that people with higher levels of intrinsic aspirations score higher on measures in relation to health and well-being. It is therefore important to stimulate people to recognise the value and joy of learning on top of the external benefits it can generate (Vansteenkiste et al., 2010).

As we have explained, for those who had positive learning experiences in the past, it is more likely that they will have developed higher levels of self-determination, intrinsic aspirations and that the choice to become a lifelong learning participant will be an 'internal' choice, coming from within. While adult educators will be able to stimulate higher levels of self-determination amongst adult learners through facilitating specific teaching and learning approaches such as self-directed learning, it is important that high levels of positive attitudes and autonomous motivation are developed early in the life span, in order to maximise chances in later life, including becoming a participant in adult lifelong learning activities. Interestingly, in relation to self-determination and lifelong learning, the term 'heutagogy' has been used by a range of authors to discuss the need for autonomy and self-determination amongst adults in enabling them to deal with the complexities of functioning efficiently in the current knowledge based economy (Hase & Kenyon, 2000; Blaschke, 2012). Self-determination is distinguished from the traditional concept of self-directed learning as central in andragogy, being that it places a stronger focus on the development of capacities and capabilities to survive in the complex world, instead of focusing on the development of competencies. Blaschke (2012) also argues that, within self-determined learning, there is a stronger focus on learning how to learn, instead of a self-directed approach to learning new content.

In short, both Expectancy-Value Theory and Self-Determination Theory are useful for understanding why adults do or do not participate in adult lifelong learning activities. Aside from referring to theories capable of assisting in the prediction of participation behaviour, it is also important to understand the different motivations of adults who do participate, as it might generate insights for those responsible for attracting new adult learners. Understanding adult learners' motivations might help in understanding what potential learners want.

Motivational patterns of adult learners

Owing to Houle's influential work in the area of adult motivation, I have first mentioned his work in this related section. However, while Houle's typology and the research undertaken by Boshier dates from the 1960s and 1970s, more recent research is based on new empirical data in order to understand the different types of adult learners and the different reasons why they have chosen to participate.

Hefler and Markowitsch (2010) have created a typology of adult learners in formal educational activities based on evidence gathered in case studies of 89 small and medium enterprises across Europe. The first type of learners who have been distinguished represents those in the process of *'completing'* their formal education while having already started to work for a company. These adult learners tend to be young adults in regard to which the responsibility is to provide the resources to complete their education and to make sure they finish their studies instead of dropping out.

The second type was labelled as those *'returning'* to education. These adults have usually left their previous studies unqualified or have taken a break to focus on other developments in their lives, such as having children or doing some temporary work which is difficult to combine with participation in learning. The third type is centred on the notion of *'transforming'*. Adult learning is focused on transition between different types of professions or between different stages in life. While those 'completing' and 'returning' to formal education are more likely to be young, those 'transforming' their lives tend to be older. Those who seek to develop themselves further in their chosen life and career pathways can participate in learning activities because of *'reinforcing'*. This type of adult learner is usually already in a rather good societal position, which he or she wants to maintain through progression to the next step on the hierarchical ladder, either specialising in a particular area or adopting a new field parallel to their existing work. Finally, Hefler and Markowitsch

(2010) refer to the dimension of *'compensating'*. In order to belong to this group, adults will have to experience a sense of disappointment in a part or parts of their lives, which they then desire to change with the aim of generating a more beneficial position.

Further work on motivations of adult learners has been published in the leading lifelong learning journals, but it is hard to say that many of these articles have engaged in providing new theories in relation to motivation. However, many of them increase the knowledge base in relation to specific groups of workers, or specific groups of adult learners attending higher education institutions. To name a range of papers published in recent years: Williams and LeMire (2011) conducted research with Air Force Commanders, Liang and Wu (2010) explored the motivation of clinical nurses, Smith et al. (2006) dealt with social workers, Landers et al. (2005) looked at physical therapists, Livneh and Livneh (1999) studied participation in professional development among educators and Becker and Gibson (1998) were interested in care practitioners. Basham and Buchanan (2009) explored the motivations of working students undertaking a Master's course in social work and business. Jauhiainen et al. (2007) explored the context of the Finnish Open University. Oplatka and Tevel (2006) looked at perceptions of female students in mid-life at a HEI in Israel while Bennett explored the motivations of students who plagiarise in the British context, studying undergraduate business students. Walters (2000) investigated experiences of mature students in higher education in the UK context. Scott et al. (1998) looked at female mature students within an Australian higher education context; Simpson (1997) studied Australians undertaking a Bachelor of Education programme. Fujita-Starck (1996) dealt with American students in a state university and West (1996) investigated the motivations of different generation students at the University of Kent in England. Unsurprisingly, many of these papers refer to Houle's typology in the theoretical section of their papers.

Participation persistence among current adult learners

Apart from motivational discourses that help us to understand why certain adults do and others do not participate in adult learning activities, it is also important to note that influential research has been undertaken to understand how to motivate adult learners once they have decided to participate, e.g. to prevent them from dropping out, as they will disappear from the participation statistics. In the context of higher education in the UK, Milburn (2012) distinguishes between four stages of participation: 'getting ready', 'getting in', 'staying in' and 'getting on'. 'Getting ready' starts before entering higher education where learners prepare for their participation. 'Getting in' is linked with the admission procedures of educational institutions, while 'staying in' refers to the retention of learners in preventing them from dropping out. 'Getting on' refers to the outcomes that learners will achieve and the next steps they will take as a result of their successful participation. The focus on 'staying in' is important, being that those who do participate in learning activities are not automatically successful learners. However, it is important to explore what action can be taken by educational institutions to support and stimulate learners' progress. While structural support can be provided, it is also important to focus on the role of the adult educator as an agent facilitating the participation process.

The role of the educator as facilitator of participation satisfaction

An example is Wlodkowski's *Motivational Framework for Culturally Responsive Teaching* (Wlodkowski & Ginsberg, 1995). This model focuses on four aspects: (1) establish inclusion, (2) develop positive attitude, (3) enhance meaning and (4) engender competence (Ginsberg, 2004; Rhodes, 2013). It is built around the idea that good teaching practices occur through sensitivity and acknowledgement of the diverse backgrounds from which learners come. Wlodkowski argues that inclusion relates to developing respect and connectedness amongst learners with the aim to develop a learning community in which learners feel happy. This was also found to be one of the major determinants of adult learners' satisfaction based on a survey of 13,000 adult learners in Europe, so reflecting a consistent pattern across all countries (Boeren, 2011).

Darkenwald and Valentine's (1986) Adult Classroom Environment scale had been included in the LLL2010 Adult Learners' Survey. It measured the elements of support, sense of organisation and adult learners' sense of receiving autonomy in their learning process. In order to motivate adult learners, it is thus important for adult educators to know how to treat learners with respect and how to engage with learners so that they feel included and represented. In relation to attitude, similar to the work of Blunt and Yang (2002), it is important that adult learners experience the learning activities as meaningful and that they have the opportunity to make their own choices which are valuable to them. Adult educators thus need to be stimulated to enable students to communicate their learning preferences and to link learning content to the needs, interests and experiences of the adult learners.

Participation in adult lifelong learning activities also needs to be challenging and engaging. Learning needs to go beyond the level of memorising facts and figures to include, ideally, debates and discussions during which learners are challenged to develop different viewpoints and strong arguments. Finally, adult learners engage in learning to increase their competences in order to become effective learners and strive towards being perceived by others as being authentic. It is thus important that standards in the field of study are communicated towards and discussed with the students in a clear way. Hence, learning content should always be connected to processes going on in the real world in order that learners come to know how to be effective and authentic.

Changes across the life span

In acquiring knowledge of why adults do or do not participate in lifelong learning activities, the psychology of adult learning offers explanations relating to adult development and the manner in which adults are changing across the life span. Put simply, there is a clear overall pattern indicating that older adults participate less in adult learning activities, and this decline starts in mid-life, around the age of 45. While the following chapters will focus on social and economic explanations, the focus here will be upon the psychological aspects of ageing, and how these elements affect participation in adult learning activities.

The cognitive reserve

Explanations on the cognitive aspects of learning during the life span have been offered by Stine-Morrow and Parisi (in Rubenson, 2011). In short, they focus on the interplay of two aspects. On the one hand, the older one becomes, the more knowledge and skills one will have accumulated as a result of building expertise in different life domains. On the other hand, the realities of declining age stand in contrast to knowledge accumulation, perhaps involving a reduced speed of control processes and a weakened working memory. The reason older adults participate less in adult learning activities, from a psychological perspective, might thus be that learning something new becoming more difficult for them.

Owing to the effect outlined above, Stine-Morrow and Parisi (2011) expand upon the importance of the 'cognitive reserve' (see e.g. Stern, 2006, 2009). The mind's decline might be slowed down due to the fact that participation in early education can have lifelong effects on people's learning capacities. Nowadays, it is clear that positive learning experiences at a younger age are related to stronger cognitive development in adulthood through education or performing tasks that stimulate the brain (see e.g. Richards & Sacker, 2003). Moreover, this may be one of the explanations of why highly educated adults are overrepresented in the lifelong learning system. Children growing up in intellectually stimulating environments will develop a wider set of self-regulatory skills and develop a higher level of innate vitality. While this explanation is driven by a psychological viewpoint, it suggests that an association between cognitive development and socio-economic status and culture exists, which will be discussed in more depth in the following chapter.

Life cycle theories

Core work on the psychology of adult learning has been undertaken by Tennant (1997). In his book *Psychology and Adult Learning* he places a strong emphasis on the development of 'identity' during adulthood, drawing upon work of various developmental psychologists like Loevinger (1976), Lowenthal et al. (1977), Vaillant (1977), Levinson (1986), Gilligan (1986) and Gould (1990). Within Tennant's book, work by Chickering and Havighurst (1981) is employed to demonstrate how developmental tasks change during adulthood, here distinguishing between 'late adolescence and youth' (16–23), 'early adulthood' (23–35), 'mid-life transition' (35–45), 'middle adulthood' (57–65) and 'late adulthood (65 plus). The work undertaken by these developmental psychologists is built upon the argument that development does not end at the beginning of adulthood, but is rather something that takes place from cradle to grave, similar to current lifelong learning discourses. The changing tasks undertaken by adults, such as 'choosing and preparing for a career' during late adolescence and youth versus 'preparing for retirement' during late adult transition are likely to result in different adult lifelong learning participation patterns.

It is important to underline that the continuous development resulting in change demands measures to help cope with and adapt to the changes. Lifelong learning participation can play a supporting role here. Qualifications may be needed to carry out certain professions, but a specific educational certificate is not needed to go into retirement. It is not only the manner in which we learn that will be affected by age, development – both the psyche and the body – and stage of life, but also whether we will decide to participate in learning activities, and what exactly we would like to learn. Similarly, Levinson developed a 'seasons of life' theory in which he distinguishes between 'early adult transition' (17–22), 'entering the adult world' (22–28), 'age 30 transitions' (28–33), 'settling down' (33–40), 'mid-life transition' (40–45), 'entering middle adulthood' (45–50), 'age 50 transition' (50–55), 'ending middle adulthood' (55–60), 'late adult transition' (60–65).

The underlying concepts behind these scholars' work are meant to express the fact that human beings change and develop during the life span. Moreover, they also put an emphasis on the importance of individual agency within his/her own self-development. For those involved in adult lifelong learning, it is thus important to understand these changes. A critical note to include in relation to life cycle models is the changing nature of society as a whole. Examples provided in many of these theories refer to the need to be married by the age of 30, to have children and to move into retirement at a younger age than people do nowadays. In a postmodern society, the grand structures have weakened and it is now more accepted that people's lives will vary. In relation to lifelong learning, Evans et al. (2013) refer to the 'de-standardisation of the life course'. The idea of changing perceptions and meanings of life amongst adults has also been explored by Merizow (1991) as part of his Transformative Learning Theory, in which he states that people might feel disoriented at certain life stages, and that they will need to find coping mechanisms to adapt to new meanings of life (Cranton, 2006). One of the actions required to achieve this goal might be to participate in adult lifelong learning activities.

Specifically applying his research to adult learning, Illeris (2009, in Jarvis, 2010) has critically explored lifelong learning from a psychological point of view. Similar to other psychological insights, Illeris describes adult learning as something that takes place in interaction with the environment, which can only take place if the individual is undergoing a process of acquisition, in the sense of acquiring a new set of skills and knowledge. In proximity to the work of developmental psychologists, Illeris defines a set of different life stages, arguing that the reasons for lifelong learning participation differ. Childhood is characterised by confident learning in an uncensored way, while learning in youth focuses around the notion of building an identity, much of the learning processes then taking place in formalised, compulsory settings. During adulthood, the reasons for engaging with learning change, as adults become much more selective and will only choose to participate intentionally in adult lifelong learning activities if they feel confident about the goals they will be achieving through participation.

However, Illeris is aware of the compulsory nature of specific forms of adult lifelong learning activities, such as those which are compulsory before one is allowed to claim welfare benefits, or those which are compulsory training to be undertaken in order to maintain a specific job. This compulsory element of lifelong learning conflicts with the initial ideas of lifelong learning as something which is characterised by the self-directness of the adult learner (see e.g. Knowles, 1975; Brockett & Hiemstra, 1991), so fitting into a discourse of lifelong learning that has been dominated by an economic perspective since the mid-1990s. Another shift on which Illeris reflects is the end of the big choices made for life at the end of youth, and the diverse patterns that adults will experience throughout life. In terms of adult lifelong learning participation, this changes the notion of learning as something that ends after initial education towards a notion of learning as something which is needed to adapt to new life circumstances.

The idea of changes across the life span has also been discussed in the British context by Schuller and Watson (2009). In *Learning Through Life: Inquiry into the Future for Lifelong Learning,* and in an inquiry investigated by NIACE (National Institute for Adult Continuing Education), they have specifically focused on a four stage model, distinguishing between childhood and adolescence up to the age of 25, the first half of the active life stage from 25 to 50, and the second active life stage from 50 to 75. The fourth stage is then defined as those who are older than 75, which should be seen as the new transition age for inactivity. The authors argue that people in these specific age groups have different needs and that it would therefore be fair to rebalance resources across these four groups. Such measures are particularly required in an ageing society; hence, they refer to the 'Fourth Age' of life, focusing on the needs of the oldest group in society. While the current spending ratio is now 86:11:2.5:0.5, Schuller and Watson propose to have this changed to 80:15:4:1.

Life events

As explained in the previous chapter, barriers preventing participation can be dispositional, but also situational (Cross, 1981). Tennant and Pogson (2002) have written about 'learning and change in the adult years', but apart from the different life 'stages' as developed by e.g. Levinson, life 'events' can also have an impact on people's engagement with learning processes. Development or the occurrence of life stages does not automatically present a linear or continuous process and can be interrupted by a range of factors (Smith, 1999, infed.org). Life-changing events have an impact on adults' health and well-being and adult lifelong learning participation might be used by people affected by these events. Examples of these events that have a strong impact, as developed by Holmes and Rahe (1967), include events such as the death of a spouse or another close family member, divorce and separation, imprisonment, becoming unemployed or going on a retirement, but other events like changing job, taking up a new hobby or going on a holiday can also affect participants.

Biographical research

From a research perspective, it is interesting to know how people's lives are changing over time and how this affects their decisions in relation to lifelong learning participation. Quantitative research would explore this matter through the analysis of longitudinal datasets. However, not many of these are widely available for this type of research, upon which I will critically reflect later in this book.

One qualitative approach is 'biographical research', also referred to as 'life history research' (Field et al., 2012). Finger (1989) wrote about the 'biographical method in adult education research' more than 25 years ago and distinguishes between 'life history' approaches and 'biographical' approaches, arguing that both rely upon different epistemologies. Life histories puts a stronger focus on 'objective' descriptions of people's lives, while the biographical method is more concerned with answers to underlying questions of 'why', 'how' and 'what for', and is thus more subjective in nature. Merrill and West (2009) have also written about the use of biographical methods in social sciences, including critical discussions on the differences between 'life history' research and 'biographical' research. However, both researchers have co-authored a paper on the results of the RANLHE project (Access and Retention: Experiences of Non-traditional Learners in Higher Education – see Finnegan et al., 2014) in which they use both the above terms interchangeably (Field et al., 2012, p. 79): *'Life history or biographical research (and for present purposes we are using these terms interchangeably, which can be a point of contention for some (Merrill & West, 2009)) is by no means a single, unified field, with its own clearly defined and universally accepted methods.'*

Both Finger (1989) and Field et al. (2012) refer back to the work undertaken by the Chicago School of Sociology, as one of the pioneers in life history research. At the same time, they recognise a stronger shift towards research methods influenced by discourses on reflexivity and understanding of the self. The core characteristics of biographical research involve a focus on transformations and changes in people's lives, and the opportunity for the researcher to understand these processes. As Field et al. (2012, p. 80) argue:

> Biographical approaches thus allows researchers to explore the meanings and importance that people attach to particular changes in their lives, including those that have to do with transitions between different life stages, which we probably expect to go through at some time as we grow older, and those that involve significant and often unexpected challenges to someone's status and roles. (Field et al., 2012, p. 80)

Furthermore, Finger (1989) underlines that biographical research deals with the retrospective subjectivities of people's lives. Only after a critical examination of the past will the adult then be able to reflect on more objective aspects of his own history. In this regard,

Merrill and West (2009) refer to the 'turn' from strong positivist research methods in the social sciences, often based on quantitative research pretending to be 'objective', towards a recognised need to understand subjective perspectives as well. Life events, changes and transitions are strongly linked with learning, part of everyone's life. While biographical research is often criticised as too narrowly focussing on the role of the individual, Merrill (2014) demonstrates that biographical research does take the individual's social environment into account, an approach I will further approve in the following chapters of this book.

Conclusions

This chapter has demonstrated that from a behavioural perspective, participation in adult lifelong learning activities can be explained in terms of the results of an underlying decision-making process. The decision whether or not to participate will be influenced by the predicted fulfilment of needs, intentions, motivational orientations including expected benefits, attitudes and self-confidence, as explored in different motivational theories. However, it is important to understand that decisions to participate can be formulated at different points of life and it is therefore important to understand the changing nature of adults' lives as they develop and grow older, including their biological development. It is hence important for time to be taken into account. These aspects will be included in the proposed integrated theory of adult lifelong learning participation.

4

Lifelong Learning Participation: The Micro Sociological Perspective

Similar to the previous chapter, this chapter discusses the determinants of participation, but from the sociologist's perspective. A central theme in this chapter will be the notion of social class, and the way in which adult education is often discussed in relation to climbing the social ladder. Notions of inequality and class differences are pertinent to this discourse. Understanding these social mechanisms to strive towards a fairer uptake of education and training is extremely important, as Torres states (2013, p. 26), whose work makes regular references to Freire (1970) who argued against oppression and domination, and how social structures and relations in fact lead to maintained levels of inequality and injustice:

> in the end, key dimensions in policy formation, such as social class differences, gender, ethnic or racial discrimination, or discrimination based on region of origin, immigration status, or religion remains understated in the narratives of policymakers. (Butterwick & Egan, in Kasworm et al., 2010, p. 114)

This entire discourse is thus closely linked to the aim of achieving higher levels of social justice.

Social class

Social class has been the focus of much educational research in the capitalist world, often informed by the work of theorists such as Marx, Weber and Bourdieu. In short, as mentioned in the background section of this book, participation patterns in adult lifelong learning across the globe have shown that those in the weakest societal groups are strongly underrepresented, such as those in unemployment, or with low incomes and with low levels of previous educational attainment. From a sociological viewpoint, this pattern is to be explained through the lens of class distributions in society; the levels of power possessed by the leading classes in society, and the easier access that the middle- and upper-class adult have to power compared to those from lower classes (see e.g. Nesbit, 2005a, 2005b).

While lifelong learning participation could be a means of reducing inequality and the levels of social stratification, it is often argued that the education system in fact represents only middle-class values. Reay (in Apple et al., 2010, p. 399) writes about 'winners' and 'losers' in relation to schooling, in regard to which middle-class children are well informed about the fact that 'failure' is not a characteristic of the groups they belong to. They also differ from working-class families as they develop a stronger cosmopolitan worldview compared to the geographical borders set by those who belong to working-class groups who are less likely to be willing to move for educational or occupational reasons because they do not feel comfortable about the idea of leaving the local community. This inevitably leads to widening of gaps in society, instead of narrowing them. Moreover, Brookfield (in Kasworm et al., 2010, p. 75), reflecting on the contribution of critical theory to adult learning, argues *'that a state of permanent inequality has become accepted as normal'*. It is thus important to understand the notion of class if one wants to increase participation chances among the most disadvantaged groups, who are nowadays widely absent from participation statistics.

Going back in time then, we can see that class has been explained in various ways, focusing on a range of different aspects. While Marx mostly focused on the materialistic differences originating in the Industrial Revolution, Weber and Bourdieu have widened this notion to include people's social and cultural backgrounds. Educational research often refers to Bourdieu's different forms of capitals, including economic, cultural, social and symbolic capital (Bourdieu, 1984; Sullivan, 2002; Butterwick & Egan, in Kasworm et al., 2010). Starting from this viewpoint, participation in adult learning activities is thus determined not only by one's ability to pay, but also by one's taste and the social circles with which one familiarises him or herself.

In other words, the importance of knowing how to behave in specific educational circles and knowing the implicit rules of how to be successful. Adults who have a high level of social capital, and whose peers are actively participating in learning activities, will be thus be more likely to participate themselves.

London et al. (1963) found that social capital is not only relevant to the field of adult education but also to other 'participation' activities in society, such as participation in specific professions, or participation in specific types of leisure activities. Social capital, widely discussed by specialist Putnam (e.g. 2000; 2004), has been extensively researched in relation to lifelong learning by Field (2005). In short, the entire notion of social capital resolves around the idea of relationships and how strong connections can help people to acquire better resources. Social capital is therefore thought to have a strong correlation with human capital as well, perceived as one of the dominant values within a lifelong learning policy that focuses primarily on knowledge, economic innovation and competitiveness. High levels of social capital are also relevant to accessing work and education or training, being that those with strong social capital are expected to be more knowledgeable about existing opportunities and might already have a range of connections in place that can offer help in navigating the system.

Apart from human and social capital, Bourdieu also focuses on the notion of 'cultural' capital, which is strongly linked to the concept of 'habitus' (Wacquant, 2004). Lifestyles, attitudes, values and the development of taste are indicators of people's position in society. Savage and Bennett (2005) have undertaken a wide range of research projects in the field of cultural capital and have written about its relation to social inequality. In the education field, Hodkinson et al. (1996) has worked further on the concept of cultural capital and habitus to develop the 'Horizons for actions' theory, referring to the way in which people make decisions about their futures based on their self-beliefs and knowledge about opportunities to increase their levels of skills and knowledge (Bassot et al., 2014). In relation to answering the question of who does and who does not participate in adult lifelong learning activities, it is generally accepted that adults with a middle-class level of cultural capital and habitus, as well as strong levels of social capital, will be more likely to participate compared to adults from a working-class background. Apart from the mechanisms at the level of the individual and the family, it is also important to recognise that educational institutions themselves are often developed based on middle-class values and tastes, so reproducing middle-class values. It is not hard to imagine how this situation becomes a vicious circle.

Social mobility

Social class is an important focus of lifelong learning research. Through participation in learning activities and through participation in knowledge intensive jobs, an individual should be able to climb the social ladder. In fact, there are two ways through which adults can achieve class mobility. Firstly, inter-generational mobility refers to children passing successfully through the education system at a higher level than their parents; this may mean successfully finishing higher education and being employed in a graduate job (Erikson & Goldthorpe, 1992, 2010; Heath & Payne, 1999; Iannelli & Paterson, 2005; Goldthorpe & Jackson, 2007; Paterson & Iannelli, 2007; Milburn, 2012; Brown, 2013).

Secondly, and less frequently researched in the field of adult lifelong learning, intra-generational mobility can occur during adult life; that is, when adults work themselves up towards a higher stratum, e.g. through participation in (part-time) higher education as a mature student (Callender, in Jackson, 2013). Adults' positions are thus compared over time instead of comparing their position in society with that of their parents. Participation in lifelong learning might provide adults with the opportunity to become socially mobile. However, previous research has not presented a clear and consistent conclusion as to whether economic benefits of lifelong learning in relation to social mobility really exist, to return to the discussion on the benefits of lifelong learning discussed in Part I.

Exploring change of income over time using data from the longitudinal British Household Panel Survey, Blanden et al. (2010) argue that monetary returns on investment in lifelong learning participation are low, and that it is therefore acceptable for public funding of lifelong learning activities not to be so high. Evans et al. (2013) contest this idea by focusing on the cumulative effect of lifelong learning participation over time, also based on data from the British Household Panel Survey. Here, the skills and knowledge acquired during participation can become more visible at a later stage, rather than immediately after participation. Research on social mobility thus often explores increased levels of educational attainment or income, but can also reflect on occupational classes to which adults belong, as developed by Erikson and Goldthorpe (1992).

The EGP class schema (Erikson – Goldthorpe – Portocarero) consists of eight different categories: (I) Professional, administrative and managerial employees, higher grade, (II) Professional, administrative and managerial employees, lower grade; technicians, higher grade, (IIIa) Routine non-manual employees, higher grade, (IV) Small employers and self-employed workers, (V) Supervisors of manual workers; technicians, lower grade, (VI) Skilled manual workers, (IIIb) Routine non-manual workers, lower grade and (VII) Semi- and unskilled manual workers. The higher one's positioning in this list (I) the higher one is positioned on the social ladder. The question remains as to whether or not participation in lifelong learning activities will help people to climb this ladder. However, it is generally accepted that those who are already higher in the hierarchy receive more training opportunities compared to those in the lower strata. Indeed, the latter are often stuck carrying out repetitive and low-skilled work for which continuous training is not needed.

Cost–benefit analysis

As stated in the previous 'behavioural' chapter, participation can be perceived as the result of an underlying decision-making process. While the psychological literature tends to focus on the importance of attitudes, confidence, intentions and motivation driven by expectations, the economic and sociological literature tends to focus on cost–benefit investment and returns on investment. From a sociological point of view, it is important to mention that the outcomes of the underlying decision-making process and the cost–benefit analysis will vary for different groups in society. In a risk society, as explored by Beck (1992), people are expected to plan their own lives, which introduces a range of uncertainties and insecurities – the world as a dangerous place – which might lead to a range of disadvantages (Bialostok & Withman, in Bialostok et al., 2012).

Based on previous research (Rubenson et al., 2006; Boeren, 2011; Robert, 2012), it is clear that participation rates in adult lifelong learning show significant differences in relation to a set of core sociological variables. It is in the following section that I attempt to explain why these differences exist. While Chapter 2 provides an overview of lifelong learning participation trends across the globe, it must be acknowledged that most of the research explaining the sociological determinants of adult lifelong learning participation has been developed in the Western world. Most of the insights generated in this chapter to understand why certain adults do and others do not participate in adult lifelong learning activities are thus based on Western scholarly literature.

Educational attainment and skill level

In Gorard's analysis of 'the potential lifelong learning impact of schooling', he reflects on the notion of lifelong learning participation as something which is deeply rooted in people's histories. However, the determinants of participation do not reflect a person's situation at the moment of enrolling in a course, instead being based on a range of longer-term aspects, such as one's experiences with the initial school system (Gorard, in Jarvis, 2009, p. 92). As argued in the previous chapter, the above analysis reinforces the importance of studying lifelong learning participation beyond a single point in time. Tuijnman (1991) has already argued that the best predictor for participation in adult lifelong learning activities is earlier participation in education; this is confirmed, for instance, by the review undertaken by Desjardins, Rubenson and Milana in 2006, and the analysis of the PIAAC Survey of Adult Skills by Desjardins in 2015.

From a sociological perspective, adult lifelong learning is therefore perceived as a mechanism that provides people with opportunities to 'accumulate' knowledge and skills, instead of a mechanism that is used to 'compensate' for a lack of knowledge and skills that an individual needs for full participation in society. Not only educational attainment, but also parental educational attainment is important within the exploration of this determinant, while recent research suggests that in relation to adult lifelong learning participation it has more of an indirect effect, mediated through the educational attainment of the adult itself. For example, Boeren (2011) found that the educational attainment of parents did not have any statistical power in predicting participation, based on data from the Eurostat Adult Education Survey; instead, parental education is a strong predictor for adults' educational attainment in itself. Put differently, those with highly educated parents are more likely to become highly educated themselves, and therefore have more chances to participate in adult lifelong learning activities. However, those who grew up in families with low-educated parents, but who managed to climb the educational ladder earlier, will be more likely to participate compared to those who did not increase their educational status (Boeren, 2011).

Doing well in the initial education system is thus a strong predictor of participation in adult lifelong learning activities. While 'educational attainment' could be classified as a sociological construct, it is important to make the link with psychological constructs such as motivation, confidence and attitude. Those who have been successful in the past are more likely to have developed positive feeling towards participation in educational activities, because they have done it before. It is also likely that these values are being transferred as part of the habitus or environment in which an adult grew up. The relationship between educational attainment, influenced by social background, and participation in adult lifelong learning activities has been labelled by Rubenson (1998, p. 261) as 'the long arm of the family', inspired by Meissner's use of 'the long arm' to refer to people's advantages in society based on their environment (Meissner, 1971). However, in explaining participation, it is also necessary to refer to adults' levels of skills, such as literacy and numeracy, but nowadays also ICT skills. Barros (2012) discussed the emphasis on competencies and the recent Survey of Adult Skills (PIAAC) has put the focus on skills in the spotlight (Desjardins, 2015). Especially in the developing world, but also in the developed world, a significant group of the adult population lack skills to function in society. Boudard and Rubenson (2003), based on analysis of the OECD's International Adult Literacy Survey (IALS) found that literacy level did not have the same predictive weight as educational attainment. However, Desjardins (2015) demonstrated, based on PIAAC data, that those with the highest levels of literacy are much more likely to participate than those with the lowest skill levels. The difference is significant in most countries. It is of course true that skill levels and educational attainment are correlated, hence the decision to discuss these variables together.

Gender

The sociology of lifelong learning and the notion of participation can be explained in terms of previous educational attainment and the specific relation to income and/or occupation. Through this entire discourse, we should not forget that adult lifelong learning participation is also a gendered subject, and that men and women differ in the way they engage with lifelong learning activities (Boeren, 2011). Lifelong learning participation theories are thus also influenced by feminist theory (Brookfield, in Kasworm et al., 2010, p. 75). Gender refers to differences between men and women based on social and cultural norms and beliefs, and is therefore different from the concept of 'sex', which refers to the biological differences between men and women (Appelbaum and Chambliss, 1997). Gender stratification exists when power and wealth are unequally distributed between men and women in society, as is generally the case (Macionis, 2013).

From a structural-functional perspective, Parsons (1942) reflected on the notion of men and women being assigned different roles in the family. Feminist voices have since reacted against this notion because limiting women to their role as mother and housewife leads to a waste of talent in other levels of society. Nowadays, women are thus more present in the capitalist market than they used to be. However, it is still clear that women participate less in STEM (Science, Technology, Engineering, Mathematics) related subjects, and if they do, they earn less than their male colleagues (Koch et al., 2013; Xu, 2015). In the workplace, women may be highly represented in fields like education, nursing and childcare. While more women enter and successfully finish higher education these days, a gender-based division of labour is still very much present. In relation to participation in the labour market there is a recognised pattern of unequal access as women are more likely to be employed in lower paid jobs and are known to receive lower compensations for overtime work, which might be explained by their overrepresented employment in the soft sector which is less dominated by 'old boy' networks (Shauman, 2006; Bobbitt-Zeher, 2007).

Additionally, it is more difficult for women to break through the 'glass ceiling', which might lead to them receiving fewer opportunities to participate in learning activities at the workplace or sponsored by the employer. As Dobele et al. (2014) argue, while the nature of work packages might have become more equal between men and women, status and pay definitely have not. Going back to the notion of social class as explored earlier in this chapter, Macionis (2013) concludes that within each stratum of social class, men usually have more power and resources compared to women with a similar social class status. More women work part-time or take parental leave in order to care for their children and their periodic absence from the labour market is therefore higher compared to the periodical absence of men. While it is positive that people receive opportunities to combine work and family, Puhani and Sonderhof (2011) point to evidence relating to the difficulties people face in these situations. It is mostly women who make use of these opportunities which can lead to negative effects in the workplace, e.g. fewer chances to participate in training or constraints on advancement into senior or managerial roles.

In general, it is also clear that women undertake most duties in the household such as cleaning and preparing meals. Although popular media likes us to believe the new man has arrived, research shows that this is very relative (Birch et al., 2009; Harkness, in Scott et al., 2009). It will be interesting to see whether and how quickly a better gender balance in society will appear, being that girls are now overtaking boys in the school system and more girls than boys enter higher education.

However, owing to the differences in subject choices, it might be that we still have to wait for some years before we will observe a more equal picture. Feminists still therefore have to undertake further work, while there remains some opposition to feminism by those who believe men and women are fundamentally different (Macionis, 2013). Liberal feminists will strive to stimulate women to develop their own skills and interests, while socialist feminists will put a stronger focus on the collective opportunities available for women to liberate themselves. Radical feminists are mostly interested in eliminating the idea of gender and creating an equal society in which gender no longer plays a role (Willis, 1984).

Age

Similar explanations can be given in relation to participation in adult lifelong learning activities and age, and an entire book entitled *Lifelong Learning in Later Life* has been published by Findsen and Formosa (2011). It is generally known that older adults participate less, and explanations from a psychological point of view have been provided in the previous chapter. From a sociological and economic viewpoint, older adults' contribution to society will be shorter, explaining their lowered participation, especially in formal learning activities (Descy, 2006). From an economic point of view in particular, employers prefer to invest in their younger employees because they will stay in the labour market for a longer period and will thus generate higher benefits compared to the initial investment made, although this might be rather stereotypical (Gaillard & Desmette, 2010). Whenever older adults do participate in learning activities, they are more likely to be in leisure related fields and their motivations will be more intrinsic or socially-oriented than goal-oriented; older adults tend to focus more on human growth and feeling fully mature than on achieving external rewards (Erikson, 1982). As Greller and Stroh (2004) argue, it is still important for older adults to have a fulfilling work life. This assertion can also be found in the work of Robson et al. (2006) who focus on the need for employees to 'successfully age' in the workplace.

However, it is clear that 'age' generates inequalities in society. Age stratification has been studied by sociology scholars for several decades, e.g. the leading work by Riley et al. (1972). Based on age, society tends to divide people into specific 'cohorts' or 'generations' – such as the Baby Boom generation referring to those born in the period after the Second World War. For each generation, society will expect them to undertake specific activities, such as attending school during childhood and teenage years, and being active in the labour market thereafter. From a Marxist perspective, we can explain this level of age segregation in relation to capitalism and the competitive labour market in which we function today. Younger workers will be put under pressure to generate profits while attention to older ones decreases because of their reduced input towards realisation of capitalist goals, which results in limited investment in their lifelong learning participation.

When referring to older adults, it very much sounds like exploring the learning patterns of those in retirement. However, statistics are very clear that the decline in adult lifelong learning participation starts as early as age 40–45 (Desjardins et al., 2006). It will be interesting to monitor the participation of these adults in the second half of their active lives over the next few years, during which many of the economic and social debates will be focused on the notion of an ageing society and the increase of retirement age; in many countries these have already been extended to above the age of 65. At present, several publications have given attention to the need of learning in later life; not only in the second half of the career, but also as a way to adapt to old age and a new life in retirement (Findsen & Formosa, 2011; Schmidt-Hertha et al., 2014). With an ever-increasing proportion of older adults due to changing demographics, it will be essential for policy makers and practitioners to develop sound lifelong learning strategies, in the sense of a real 'cradle to grave' approach.

Un/employment and work characteristics

It is often thought that unemployed adults are highly likely to profit from participation in adult learning activities, being that newly acquired knowledge and skills will help them in finding a job. However, the opposite is true. For those who already have a job, their employer might want to contribute to the cost of training – both financially and in terms of time – while the unemployed adult will not have this opportunity and is thus more reliant on personal investment, or initiatives set up by public funding, such as 'training-to-work' schemes (Wainwright et al., 2011). The adult who already has a job will be immediately able to translate new skills into practice, while the unemployed adult may be unclear about the benefits as he or she does not have a job and the initial cost of investment is likely to be higher, especially in case of lack of support. Income is thus also likely to play a role in deciding to participate. If private investment is required, it might not feasible for those with limited financial capacity to take part. However, there are also disadvantages for those who are in employment. One of the major reasons adults do not participate in adult lifelong learning activities is lack of time (Cross, 1981; Boeren, 2011). Women who work full-time and aim to combine work with family might decide that further participation in learning activities is not on their priority list for a number of years.

At first sight, the higher participation rates among and clear benefits for the employed appear slightly contradictory, as those in unemployment might appear in greater need for participation to increase their job chances. However, the unequal situation will not be resolved the moment all adults are in employment as adults' participation also differs based on occupation. Those in high-skilled, professional and managerial roles will receive more opportunities to train compared to those in monotone jobs for which a lower level of skills is required to carry out routine tasks. This situation confirms (again) the accumulation theory of adult lifelong learning participation. Kaufmann (2015) has investigated which groups received support from the employer to participate in training, drawing on a wide range of previous research conducted by Brunello et al. (2007), Desjardins and Rubenson (2011) and Kaufmann and Widany (2013). Unsurprisingly, men, younger employees, the high-skilled and those working in larger companies are more likely to receive employer support. Women, those on part-time and/or fixed-term contracts are more likely to receive no support, while those in medium-sized companies are more likely to be on co-financed training schemes. Similar predictors were found in a review undertaken by Kyndt and Baert (2013), who reviewed the antecedents of participation in work-related education and training for employees, based on consultation of relevant literature. They have distinguished a category of 'job characteristics', arguing that a range of factors at the job level are related to the opportunity to participate and thus thought to correlate with participation in lifelong learning: type of contract, level of income, level of control, demands and challenges the employee has to deal with in his or her job. The type and level of occupation determines level of autonomy, the variety of tasks the employee can undertake and whether he or she is involved in decision-making processes at the workplace. The stronger the overall job profile, the more likely the employee will receive training. Those carrying out low-skilled monotonous tasks are more likely to be ignored in relation to lifelong learning.

Race and ethnicity

The outcome of decision-making processes regarding participation in adult lifelong learning opportunities is also likely to be different for people of a different race or ethnicity than the dominant racial or ethnic group in the country, region or community in which they are living. I agree with White (2012) who argues that ethnicity is often ignored in lifelong learning participation research, or measured in a vague way: e.g. comparing 'White' adults with adults who do not belong to the dominant White group. One of the aspects that plays an important role here is the well-known racial discrimination that happens not only in the workplace but also in accessing post-compulsory educational institutions. Critical Race Theory is therefore to be acknowledged as one of the important theoretical frameworks in lifelong learning research (Brookfield, in Kasworm et al., 2010, p. 75). Its importance for adult lifelong learning participation has been underlined by Sheared et al.'s (2010) publication of *The Handbook of Race and Adult Education*, in which the authors provide strong evidence of ongoing examples of discrimination based on race and ethnicity.

As will be explored in a later chapter, different institutional cultures lead to different levels of engagement in prioritising access strategies for non-traditional groups. Elite universities are generally understood to enrol fewer students from certain ethnic groups, which might lead to less chance of an individual becoming a lifelong learning participant after initial education, as participation in lifelong learning activities are highly correlated with educational attainment and previous positive learning experiences. Racial discrimination in the workforce happens when equally skilled and qualified candidates do not succeed in finding employment because of their race, skin colour, nationality or ethnic origin (Cohn, 1999; Nilsson & Wrench, in Kraal et al., 2009). Experiments have shown that sending similar applications to employers which feature a different name – e.g. a typical name within the specific country or region and a more exotic name – lead to differences in the chances of being invited for a job interview. Not only is accessing the labour market a problem, but the chances of participation are also less for those not in employment, as we have explained in the previous section.

Conclusions

Based on micro sociological determinants, I can be quite short in my conclusions. Those with the strongest socio-economic profiles are overrepresented in adult lifelong learning activities. This finding contradicts the social justice perspective of lifelong learning and indicates a situation that runs the risk of widening rather than narrowing gaps in society.

Significant elements to be taken forward to the integrative approach include the role of educational attainment and skill level, age, gender, employment status, occupational status, income, work-life balance, social and cultural capital and place of living. As reviewed in this chapter, these factors relate to participation in adult lifelong learning activities, but are also correlated to each other.

5
Lifelong Learning Participation: Institutional Barriers

The previous chapters have generated insight into the psychological and sociological determinants of adult lifelong learning participation. They have very much focused on the level of the individual adult, the choices he or she is making and how his or her socio-economic and socio-demographic background influences the chances that he or she will participate. However, participation is much more than an individual responsibility and despite its strong focus in a changing policy context, there remain a number of institutional barriers.

Referring to both formal and non-formal education and training, an adult's decision whether or not to participate in lifelong learning activities is very dependent on the choice of learning activities being offered. Learning activities need to be offered in an accessible way so that the adult learner will be able to manage the workload and complete the course or training event successfully. In this regard, it is important for policy makers and practitioners to pay attention to individual differences between potential learners, as individualised measures may need to be taken in order to attract them, as recognised by Butterwick and Egan (in Kasworm et al., 2010, p. 120):

> Equal access is an important right, but it requires nuanced analysis and recognition of group differences, rather than policy and practices that assume all adult learners need and want the same opportunities. Equality of access and outcomes also means recognizing and challenging assumptions about difference and the dangers of stereotyping.

This situation reflects the level of institutional barriers identified by Cross (1981), who argues that overcoming situational and dispositional barriers will not be enough to enable an individual to succeed in entering a learning activity as long as these institutional barriers exist. This problem reflects the fact that some educational institutions' practices are deterring adults instead of stimulating them. This chapter will also critically explore the role of information, which has been identified by Darkenwald and Merriam (1982) as an additional barrier to participation. In addition, I will reflect on the importance of outreach strategies.

Exploration of the institutional side has often been ignored in previous theorisations of adult lifelong learning participation, and a critique of this lacking perspective has been published in the *International Journal of Lifelong Education* (Boeren et al., 2010). This statement on the lack of inclusion in theory is backed up by Hefler (2013, p. 109):

> theories on participation hardly explore specifics of the 'taught course': their length, workload, selectivity, prestige and so forth are taken as having no impact on a theory's explicative value.

Lifelong learning offers

The availability of offers – learning activities – is essential. Participation cannot take place without them. However, lifelong learning activities are not necessarily available to everyone. In the formal system in particular, entrance conditions will determine whether someone is allowed to participate or not. The formal system represents a 'ladder' structure (Vermeersch et al., 2009). Therefore, not having obtained a qualification at the bottom of this ladder is likely to result in being constrained from participation at a higher level. At the bottom of the educational ladder we find primary and secondary education; in the developed world, it is compulsory for children and teenagers to participate in these forms of initial schooling. However, it is also vital that 'adult versions' of these programmes exist in order to strive towards 'equity and equality of opportunity' (OECD, 2010, p. 67). Adults with low levels of literacy and no or low levels of qualifications will not be allowed into higher education courses unless they have increased their levels of knowledge and skills to the desired standards. Basic Skills Education and Second Chance Education is therefore needed for this group of people. The content of lifelong learning activities should match the needs of the potential adult learner, but it is also vital that the activities are being offered at convenient times and locations. Especially for the most disadvantaged groups, it does not make sense to travel for educational purposes.

When in employment, low-skilled adults are more likely to be found in routine manual jobs, and will therefore receive fewer opportunities at the workplace; it might thus be important for the public sector to guarantee that appropriate courses are available. Similar mechanisms apply to the needs of unemployed people who may need to retrain or update their skills and knowledge to perform a new profession for which employment opportunities are available. As will be demonstrated later in this chapter, the availability of lifelong learning opportunities in the workplace might vary and depend on a number of factors. Especially in relation to low-skilled and/or unemployed adults, partnerships or public initiatives are recommended.

Lifelong learning course modes

Adult learners often combine their learning activities with other life domains, such as work and/or family responsibilities. It is therefore extremely important that learning activities are designed flexibly. Research evidence in this area has mainly been established in the context of higher education. Schuetze and Slowey (2002) have researched the participation of lifelong learners in the higher education context and distinguished between the 'traditional mode' and the 'lifelong learning mode' of education. Traditional modes of education are harder to access for adult learners as they often consist of campus-based programmes for which the potential learner will need to have obtained a core set of entrance qualifications. Programmes will often be offered only in full-time mode. The lifelong learning mode represents a much more flexible model, in which learners can access courses based on the accreditation of prior learning, often organised in a modular way so that learners have more autonomy in selecting their own pace of study. Nowadays, the widespread supply of online courses is likely to lower some of the institutional barriers because learning can take place in the students' own living environment. It is thus important to understand that the modes in which courses are offered can play a vital role in adults' decisions to participate in lifelong learning activities. If courses are offered at inconvenient times, offering little flexibility, then the outcome of the decision-making process is likely to be negative. These arguments are reiterated by Pont (2004) who mentions the need for flexible programmes in order to stimulate participation.

Similar insights are offered by Thomas (2005) who has researched the context of widening participation in post-compulsory education, mainly from the British perspective. A number of institutional barriers constraining the entrance of non-traditional students are highlighted, such as the high level of fees, additional costs like transport, or even living costs if the adult learner wants to participate in higher education at an institution further away from home. In addition, indirect costs have to be taken into account, as the time spent in education cannot be spent in paid employment. This creates the need for flexible learning opportunities that enable mature students to learn at their own pace and combine participation with responsibilities in other life domains. In line with Schuetze and Slowey (2002), Thomas (2001) refers to barriers introduced by educational institutions because of strict entrance qualifications. In particular, non-traditional students will often lack qualifications, and it is therefore recommended that institutions offer a range of alternative access routes. But what is the willingness of educational institutions to adapt towards more flexible learning routes and to engage in widening access strategies? Furthermore, Thomas (2001) points to the barriers created by the initial compulsory school system, as those with negative learning experiences earlier in their lives will be put off returning to educational settings and might even feel stigmatised by the label of 'bad learner'. The notions of attitudes and confidence have been explored in an earlier chapter.

In relation to the higher education sector, Thomas (2001) distinguishes between four types of institutions that are known to have different 'institutional cultures'. These cultures provide a prediction as to the willingness to engage with alternatives in relation to non-traditional students. The first type as mentioned by Thomas (2001) is the 'traditional elite' type, referring to higher education institutions that are found at the top of the rankings, those that employ staff members with strong research profiles and that only weakly engage with widening participation initiatives. The second 'quasi-old' type consists of those institutions who understand the need for change, but are rather reluctant to widen their traditional pool of learners, who are mainly school leavers. While they are also older institutions, they have a less clear cut high profile identity compared to the elitist institutions. The third type, the 'quasi-new' type focuses on attracting both traditional school leavers and non-traditional learners such as adult learners. While their widening access strategies are important to them, they feel the need to catch up with the more research-intensive institutions, in the case of the UK, stimulated by the need to achieve excellent scores in the Research Excellence Framework exercises. The fourth and last type, the 'real new' type, refers to mainly teaching-focused institutions for whom widening access and offering learning opportunities to non-traditional learners is a top priority. The need for the higher education sector to be more inclusive is also an important feature of European higher education policy, through the notion of the 'social dimension' of higher education (Weedon & Riddell, 2012; Riddell et al., 2013). It is important that higher education participation is widened so that it represents class distribution in society. Whether this is a realistic goal is doubtful, but countries are encouraged to attract more learners from non-traditional and under-represented groups. Not only the higher education context, but also the context of other adult learning institutions is extremely important in this debate, being that educational provisions at lower levels will have a role to fulfil to prepare non-traditional learners to make the transition to participation in higher education. As discussed in an earlier chapter, social inequalities are also present in the American higher education system.

Three levels of access indicators

The ways in which educational institutions can work towards higher levels of access and higher levels of adults participating in lifelong learning activities can be explored in different ways. Downes (2014, p. 52) distinguishes between 'structural', 'process' and 'outcome' indicators in relation to access to education, which is indeed a more in-depth approach to dealing with benchmarks and indicators than is currently the case in education policy making. *Structural indicators* focus on the availability of services to help learners to access, and persist, such as schemes to include people from disadvantaged backgrounds, to have counselling services in place, and to offer access courses to make learners ready to enter a new course and finish it successfully. *Process indicators* are used to encourage a positive learning environment within the educational institution, such as building good relations between educators and learners, employing a diverse group of staff members representing different groups in society, and using student-centred approaches in which students have opportunities to contribute to the environment of the institution. *Outcome indicators* represent the statistics institutions want to achieve, such as the proportion of learners from underrepresented groups. Downes (2014), supported by others criticising the current lifelong learning policy climate such as Holford and Mohorcic-Spolar (2014), argues that too much emphasis is placed on the importance of 'outcome' indicators without paying enough attention to the processes that can be used to achieve these targets. This finding corresponds with the overview on benchmarks and indicators discussed in an earlier chapter, in which the 'governing by numbers' approach was explored. In the European context, a participation rate in adult lifelong learning of 15 percent is only useful if adequate attention is paid to the inclusion of disadvantaged and underrepresented groups; evaluation should thus go beyond a static numerical level.

Workplaces as institutional learning environments

Formalised or non-formalised lifelong learning activities do not necessarily have to take place in specific educational institutions; workplaces can also offer opportunities for participation. Eraut et al. (1998) argue that one of the most important aspects of determining the chances of employees receiving learning opportunities at work is the appointment of managers who are willing to promote learning. In their research, learning opportunities are defined in a broad sense including opportunities for coaching and mentoring, team learning and participation in secondments. While employees' motivation and self-efficacy are important as well, as discussed in an earlier chapter, the organisational context can also increase or decrease learning chances.

In relation to *'workplaces as learning environments'*, Fuller and Unwin (in Malloch et al. 2011) distinguished between 'expansive' and 'restrictive' learning environments. In 'expansive' environments, there is a strong tendency to think long-term and to provide learning opportunities which go beyond the level of the current job tasks, and there is also a stronger sense of community. In 'restrictive' environments, participation in learning activities will only be allowed if they are directly related to specific job tasks to be completed and work is strongly focused on reaching a set of targets, managed and controlled from the top.

Houman Sorensen (2008, in Markowitsch and Hefler, p. 218) has explored the relationship between innovation and enterprise training, focusing on the role of 'organisational flexibility', based on the work of Nielsen (2004), in which he explores three levels of flexibility in relation to structure, processes and culture. Firstly, the way in which enterprises are structured will inevitably have an impact on learning opportunities as some will offer their employees more interdisciplinary roles in which they have to combine functions while others might structure their employees' work in a more monotonous way. Hefler and Markowitsch (in Markowitsch & Hefler, 2008, p. 33) argue that there are various explanations at the structural level as to why enterprises are not offering learning opportunities to their employees. This might be because they do not have the funding or economic capacity to make the initial investment in training, being that the workplace environment is structured in such an inflexible way that it will be difficult to change anyway and employees participating in learning activities will unlikely affect the organisation. It might also be the case that employers do not have the know-how to develop or offer training due to lack of experience. Secondly, organisational processes can differ in the ways in which the planning of learning activities is incorporated into the work packages of the employees. Finally, enterprises have different cultures in the sense that in some workplaces employees will receive more opportunities and flexibility to plan their work while a more controlling culture can exist in other workplaces.

Hefler and Markowitsch (2008, in Markowitsch and Hefler, p. 39) conclude that quantitative research in the field, such as that based on the Continuing Vocational Training Survey (CVTS), demonstrates that workplaces offering more opportunities for lifelong learning participation tend to be larger, undertake innovative work, employ mostly highly-qualified employees and are active in knowledge-intensive sectors of the economy. Kyndt et al. (2009) have also found that the size and type of organisation is related to conditions being available to learn, although their research is only focused on non-formal and informal learning. Kyndt and Baert (2013) also reviewed the impact of job characteristics on participation in work-related learning and summarised factors at the organisational level. Apart from elements already discussed above, they mention 'internal mobility' as a stimulant to engage workers in learning activities as well as 'career encouragement'.

Hefler (2010) has focused on support for lifelong learning participation with specific regard to Small and Medium Enterprises (SMEs). He concludes that SMEs can be classified into five different types in relation to supporting the participation of employees in formalised learning (Hefler, 2010, in Hefler & Markowitsch, 2012b, p. 111). In the best case scenario, SMEs offer 'integrative support'. Employers will strongly support participation, but will also undertake initiatives at the workplace to facilitate training. 'Support in principle' describes a 'medium' instead of high level of organisational support from employers. As barriers to participate in adult lifelong learning are often related to 'time' and 'money', SMEs can undertake a range of strategies to support overcoming these barriers. Examples include adjusting work schedules so that employees have the time to participate, revisiting employees' work packages while in training, providing educational leave to make it possible to devote time to studying and offering partial or full support in covering fees and/or other costs related to the learning activity. Another way to support and motivate employees might be to reward them for successful completion of the course, e.g. through offering a bonus or promotion. Types of 'individualised support' arise when the SME offers a medium level of support and is moderate at offering levels of learning activities within the organisation. The employer will be supportive, but will not necessarily provide the adult learner with financial or time-related support, while they will be supportive in specific circumstances in which they help co-initiate the learning of their employees. The 'acceptance' type characterises SMEs in which there will be an acknowledgment of the employees' interests in participating in learning but the organisation itself will not actively engage in providing or supporting training. Finally, the 'ignorance' type does not deal with training at all; it does not support it, nor does not initiate or organise it. If employees are interested in lifelong learning, then they will have to organise and finance it themselves. This is what I would call the 'worst case

Table 5.1 Elements at the workplace stimulating participation

Supportive manager/supervisor	Knowledge-intensive sector
Expansive environment	Large companies
Innovation	Internal mobility – career opportunities
Organisational flexibility	Training know-how
Funding/economic capacity	Training culture/policy

scenario' and does not show any engagement with current policies for stimulating adults to participate in learning in order to stimulate economic growth and competitiveness.

Going back to the notion of 'reactive' versus 'expansive' cultures, based on case study research on SMEs undertaken as part of the LLL2010 research project, Hefler and Markowitsch classified 44 percent of SMEs having a reactive culture as belonging to the 'ignorance' or 'acceptance' types while only 13 percent of the SMEs with an expansive culture were put in this group. About one third of both reactive and expansive cultures offered 'individualised support'. The types 'support in principle' and 'integrated support' were more present (54 percent) in SMEs with an expansive culture, compared to ones with a reactive culture (26 percent). While it seems clear that SMEs with expansive cultures offer more support, it is important to mention that this research project explored participation in formal adult lifelong learning activities. It might thus be the case that, as Hefler and Markowitsch (2012b) acknowledge, specific SMEs are weak at supporting formal learning, but are good at stimulating and facilitating non-formalised learning.

Having reviewed the role of workplaces as facilitators of adult lifelong learning, Table 5.1 presents a brief summary of factors I want to take forward to my integrative lifelong learning participation theory.

The role of information

Adults can decide to participate based on the characteristics of the course or training event on offer, and as previously explored, be influenced by their psychological, economical and sociological status. However, it is important that potential adult learners receive information about specific courses as an unawareness of educational offers will make it very difficult for the adult learner to reach a positive match between his or her demand and the existing supply.

As mentioned before, Darkenwald and Merriam (1982) add 'lack of information' as a fourth barrier to Cross' typology of barriers, thereby supplementing the situational, dispositional and institutional barriers (Cross, 1981). Research by Boeren (2011), analysing data of the Flemish Adult Education Survey, reveals that the major determinant of participation was previous educational attainment. However, those who did not participate, but who had an intention to participate, were those who had been actively searching for information about adult learning activities. The reason they did not participate, going back to Baert et al.'s intention cycle, was that their educational demand could not be fulfilled because they did not find information about an educational resource matching their demand.

Grotluschen's (2010) research in the German context on interest in adult lifelong learning activities, based on surveys measuring barriers to participation, shows that around 20 percent of adults do not participate because of an information deficit. In understanding what is meant by 'information', there are several ways to reach potential learners (Moore et al., 2013). The easiest way is to maintain a website, but this information is only going to be found by those who are actively searching for information and will not help adults to translate their perceived need into a learning need as they might not be aware of the offer. The distribution of leaflets is another option, but they might not get picked up or might not be understood by the most disadvantaged groups in society. Therefore, it might be more useful for educational providers to undertake partnerships with other services, such as social services, as a channel through which their learning activities can be recommended to potential learners. Outreach work can also be used as a strategy to mobilise potential learners (Hake, in Zarifis & Gravani, 2014, p. 252).

Successful learners can also act themselves as effective and valuable sources of information for new and potential learners through word-of-mouth. However, those who belong to underrepresented groups are less likely to have many peers or contacts in their own circles who have participated in adult lifelong learning activities because participation rates in these communities are rather low. It is therefore important for educational institutions to facilitate interaction between current and potential learners. The remaining question here is whether stronger advertising, marketing and connection-building by educational institutions would be effective in helping adults to recognise that their needs might be fulfilled through participation in an educational activity, so that the 'need' will be translated into an 'educational need' (Baert et al., 2006). More research will have to be undertaken before an answer to this question can be formulated. However, in the field of Higher Education in particular, marketing is a widely recognised tool to attract students into educational institutions. Taylor and Francis publishes the *Journal of Marketing for Higher Education*, which started in 1988 and is edited by the University of Surrey (UK), in order to increase the knowledge base on this topic. Popular articles published in the journal focus on the results of various student satisfaction surveys, the use of online social media such as Twitter, the strengths of university branding and the perception of students as customers in the twenty-first century enterprise university.

Moore et al. (2013) have reviewed the literature on widening participation in higher education for HEFCE and OFFA and argued that 'information, advice and guidance' are important aspects in widening participation processes. In fact, they state that these three separate terms strongly belong together, and in the European context, these strategies are also put forward by the European Commission as ways to mobilise adults and increase adult lifelong learning participation rates (Hake, in Zarifis & Gravani, 2014, p. 255). It is indeed plausible that information in itself might not be effective enough, especially not for potential underrepresented learners who are likely to need additional advice and guidance on starting the participation process. It is not enough to inform future participants of the specific characteristics of the programme, course or activity of their choice. Instead, they should be informed of the expectations from the education or training institutions. Clear information should also be provided about how to overcome other barriers. It is clear that adult learners often feel constrained by time, but also by the financial costs of participation. Information about grants, loans, educational leave and other support mechanisms should therefore be available in an accessible way. One of the most difficult areas in the need for individual guidance and support is that the educational system will have to provide enough staff to undertake these tasks, which is a cost-intensive. However, and in particular for the most underrepresented learners, this outreach approach is likely to be necessary in order to attract people to adult lifelong learning participation. McGivney (2000, 2002), who extensively researched outreach in relation to underrepresented groups, has focused on the need to consult and interact with them, to understand their motivations, to negotiate and network with social partners and to continue supporting learners during participation, as well as follow up with them after participation has ended. It is also important, as Baert et al. (2006) mention, to identify their needs and work towards an educational design able to fulfil these needs.

Going back to the review undertaken by Moore et al. (2013, pp. 33–34), they explored how different groups in higher education deal differently with sources of information, advice and guidance. Some interesting insights can be borrowed from this in relation to understanding the information strategies of adult learners, being that they belong, in any case, to most of the categories in Moore et al.'s overview. Mature learners who want to study at Higher Education Institutions will usually browse institutions' websites, principally in the area in which they live and will likely search for information on how to increase their career chances. Part-time learners will also seek support from educational institutions themselves, although Moore et al. (2013) argue that 'informal information' is very important for these potential learners as well. Knowing friends or family members who started a learning journey and who demonstrate high levels of satisfaction is a good way to positively influence adults' decision-making processes. Those interested in vocational and work-based programmes are most likely to speak directly to tutors offering these types of courses, but also to employers who can recommend training matching the employees' needs. However, Bowes (2008, in Moore et al., 2013, p. 34) finds that it is these adults who are often not aware of what types of lifelong learning activities are available to them. In general, Moore et al. (2013) find that more information, advice and guidance is particularly needed in relation to 'financial support' and 'subject choices'. They also study what choosing a specific subject would mean for future employment prospects in the labour market, information about access requirements and how to apply for places, as well as additional information on support available for learners with disabilities or specific learning needs. Overall, it is clear that information does not only need to be made available, but it is also important that it be made available in a comprehensible way, and that it is regularly updated as rules and regulations can change quickly. Moreover, it is important that information is provided in such a way that it encourages adults to participate, so enhancing their motivation and self-confidence in a healthy way.

Conclusions

This chapter has demonstrated that participation in lifelong learning is more than an individual responsibility. I have discovered many elements that I want to take forward to the following chapters, building towards an integrative theory of lifelong learning participation. Research in previous years has demonstrated that flexible learning environments can facilitate access for adult learners. They need flexible entrance routes, teaching and learning schedules in order to combine learning, work and family. While workplaces are examples of learning environments too, this chapter reiterates the unequal distribution of learning opportunities, influenced by workplace organisations. Finally, I have made clear that high quality information needs to be available but that, especially for the most disadvantaged groups, outreach activities will help in mobilising adults into lifelong learning.

6

Lifelong Learning Participation: Country Level Determinants

Exploring the country level context in relation to lifelong learning participation is very important. In the previous chapters, I demonstrated that psychological, economic and sociological factors determine adults' engagement with lifelong learning activities. It is true that higher-educated adults participate more and that this pattern is found in almost every country. Nevertheless, we have to recognise that participation rates in countries widely vary. In the European context, the latest statistics show much higher participation of adults in Scandinavian countries compared to those living in the Southern Mediterranean countries, such as Spain and Italy. If we want to understand fully why certain adults do and others do not participate in lifelong learning activities, it is important that we understand the underlying mechanisms causing these differences at the country level.

As stated before, differences between countries in relation to adult lifelong learning participation rates have been calculated using various surveys – this is indeed the core focus of Chapter 8. Data is generally available for European countries because of the European Commission's strong involvement in data collection. Amongst various country level surveys, data on rates in non-European countries continue to be collected through the OECD. These surveys are important as they provide a collection of statistics based on a common measurement programme. The OECD has hence created six different groups based on the results of PIAAC's Survey of Adult Skills, (OECD, 2014, p. 392):

- Group 1, with participation rates above 60%, includes Denmark, Finland, the Netherlands, Norway and Sweden.

- Group 2, with participation rates between 55% and 59%, includes Australia, Canada, England/Northern Ireland (UK) and the United States.
- Group 3, with participation rates around the OECD average of 48% to 53%, includes Austria, the Czech Republic, Estonia, Flanders (Belgium), Germany, Ireland and Korea.
- Group 4 consists of two countries with participation rates of between 38% and 47% – Japan and Spain.
- Group 5, with participation rates between 33% and 36%, includes France, Poland and the Slovak Republic.
- Group 6, with participation rates below 25%, consists of Italy and the Russian Federation.

At first glance, one can see some patterns emerging. Based on European data – i.e. that which is gathered within the Labour Force Survey or the Adult Education Survey – I will strive to identify similar patterns. Backed up by numerical evidence, it is generally accepted that participation in adult lifelong learning activities is highest in Nordic countries compared to Southern and Eastern European countries. Various ways of understanding these differences will now be explored.

Macro level determinants of participation

Previous research has explored macro level determinants of adult lifelong learning participation, based on a range of predictors at the level of the initial schooling system. These include the characteristics of the adult education system, the level of innovation of the economy, the structure of the labour market, social security, the strength of labour unions and some general measures such as GDP, and the investment in education, training, research and development as a percentage of this GDP (Desmedt et al., 2006; Dammrich et al., in Blossfeld, 2014, p. 37).

Macro level determinants thus refer to broader structural factors situated and decided at the level of countries or regions' power. They therefore differ from individual factors characterising the potential adult learner. Table 6.1 provides an overview of the research undertaken to understand macro level factors in relation to lifelong learning for the reader's reference. Specific aspects will be analysed below.

Table 6.1   Research on macro level determinants of lifelong learning

Characteristics of the (adult) education system	Wolbers (2005) Groenez et al. (2007) Almeida and Aterido (2008)
Union density	Brunello (2001) Coulombe and Tremblay (2007) Dieckhoff et al. (2007)
Expenditure on research and development (R&D)	Bassanini et al. (2005) Coulombe and Tremblay (2007)
Unemployment rates	Wolbers (2005) Coulombe and Tremblay (2007)
Labour market flexibility	Brunello (2001) Bassanini et al. (2005) Almeida and Aterido (2008)
Wage compression	Coulombe and Tremblay (2007)
Gross Domestic Product (GDP)	Groenez et al. (2007)

Source: Dammrich et al., in Blossfeld, 2014, p. 37.

Initial educational determinants

While there seems to be a relationship between the structure of initial schooling and participation rates in adult lifelong learning participation, it remains unclear what is exactly causing this effect (Groenez et al., 2007). Generally speaking, a distinction has been made between comprehensive and stratified school systems. In comprehensive systems, pupils follow the same track until the end of compulsory education and then choose a specific path afterwards, typically around the age of 15 or 16. In stratified systems, children have to choose between academic and vocational tracks as young as age 10 to 12; this schooling system is therefore often perceived to cause inequalities (Pfeffer, 2008).

European continental countries, including Germany, Belgium and Austria, have high levels of stratification in their initial education systems (Busemeyer, 2015). Scandinavian and Anglo-Saxon countries have low levels of stratification and thus represent stronger forms of comprehensive schooling systems. One hypothesis is that adults who were educated in stratified schooling systems participate less in adult lifelong learning activities because their initial training was already at such a specialised level that further training to develop their working skills is no longer required. On the other hand, it may be argued that those in stratified systems are confronted with selection and failure to a greater extent, a reality which is likely to have a negative impact on their attitudes and self-confidence towards learning. In a previous chapter we explored this as one of the major influential determinants of planning to participate, from a behavioural perspective.

Participation in adult lifelong learning then becomes a matter of either 'compensating' for earlier shortcomings', or as an effect of 'accumulation' where adults build further on the skills they already have. While course offers like Basic Skills Education and Second Chance Education are specifically designed to help low-skilled adults to compensate for previous drop-outs, participation statistics are clear that the highly skilled and highly qualified participate more. The accumulation hypothesis is thus likely to explain persistent inequalities in lifelong learning.

Economic and labour market determinants

At the level of the economy, countries that support high levels of innovation will score higher on participation, often expressed in the percentage of their GDP that they are investing in Research and Development. One of the arguments for stimulating participation in adult lifelong learning activities amongst policy makers is to guarantee competitiveness in the global market, and thus the ability to master continuously the new skills and knowledge needed to fulfil these ambitions. In this respect, the literature often refers to the difference between 'liberal market economies' (LMEs) and 'coordinated market economies' (CMEs) (Hall & Soskice, 2001).

In CMEs, employers are more likely to invest in the human capital of their employees, while in LMEs, it is more the responsibility of the individual to invest in his or her own knowledge and skills. In LMEs, social, employment and income protection is weak, while education systems tend to offer training in generic competences and skills. Within LMEs, the strong focus on individual capability to invest in training is clearly one of the explanations of inequality in participation, as those who cannot afford it will not participate. One example of a CME is Germany, but it is also applicable to Scandinavian countries. The United States and the United Kingdom are examples of LMEs (Busemeyer, 2015). Within the group of CMEs, we find countries with stratified educational systems, such as the German-speaking countries. Germany, along with other Continental countries, is known to have a stronger vocational, work-related system, either in the workplace or through dual learning and working schemes. In countries characterised by LMEs, like the United Kingdom, provision of vocational training tends to be much more market-based.

In relation to the labour market, it is also important to refer to the notion of 'skills equilibrium' and the supply and demand sides of the labour market (Finegold & Soskice, 1988; Crouch et al., 1999; Campbell, 2012, p. 49). Based on Froy and Giguère (2010), Campbell (2012) demonstrates that the supply side of a strong labour market consists of a high quality education and training system in which underrepresented groups receive opportunities to participate in training and in which employers stimulate the skill development of their employees. These systems therefore attract, but also maintain, a highly-skilled workforce with well-developed talents. A strong demand side then refers to employers making effective use of the workforce's skills, through stimulating productivity. This, then, introduces not only new organisational and innovative ways of working, but also the achievement of such objectives through management training.

Labour markets that score high on 'skills supply' and 'skills demand' are referred to as being in a balance or 'high skills equilibrium'. When both 'supply' and 'demand' sides are weak, markets are referred to as being in 'low skills equilibrium'. However, it may also be the case that the demand for skills is high, but the supply is low. This would indicate that there is space for economic growth and that individuals in certain sectors might receive opportunities to improve their skills further because of the skills shortage. However, the opposite can also be true. Labour markets are able to supply high levels of skills, but where the demand for skills is low, a state of recession will follow.

In relation to lifelong learning participation, one can assume that countries with high levels of the population working in knowledge-intensive jobs will have a high proportion of their employees taking part in learning activities. The question is one of how far countries are willing to invest in the regulation of labour markets in order to stimulate better supply and demand for skills. Additionally, for those in unemployment, a return to education and training can also be influenced by factors such as the levels of benefits and the requirement of authorities to have those on benefits participating in courses or learning programmes (Desmedt et al., 2006). Active labour market policies will then help the unemployed to get back into the labour market. Publicly funded employment services not only help adults to find employment that matches their skills, but also to prepare for job interviews and submitting applications. Participation can therefore also be linked with social security and the safety net available to those at risk of exclusion.

Offering training schemes to help the unemployed become more attractive for the labour market is also a characteristic of active labour market policies. Bonoli (2010) argues that active labour market policies can be classified into different types. English-speaking countries tend to target incentives for reinforcement. Examples include lowering benefits or introducing conditions to receiving benefits. These measures are often combined with providing assistance to find employment, also present in Nordic and Continental countries, such as through job centres and counselling services. Continental countries have also developed mechanisms to prevent unemployed people losing their skills or ending up not doing anything with their time. These adults will fairly frequently be put on generic non-job related training activities, or specific employment will be provided for them in the public sector. Finally, Bonoli (2010) refers to active labour market policies targeting investment in human capital, through offers of basic and vocational education and training to the unemployed, which is common in Nordic countries. It can thus be argued that countries differ in the way they deal with activating the unemployed, and that this is likely to be part of the explanation of why participation rates between countries vary.

Financial determinants

Another way of trying to understand the differences that exist between countries is to explore the way in which they deal with financing the adult education and training system (Sohlman, 2011; Busemeyer, 2015). In short, we could argue that there are two main funders of adult lifelong learning activities: private and public investors. On the one hand, adults themselves, or their families as it does not necessarily need to be the specific individual, can make a private investment in their learning. Sohlman (2011) has demonstrated that the willingness of adults to invest in their own learning seems to be higher in countries with high participation rates – such as Denmark – and lower in countries with low participation rates – such as Spain and Portugal.

Private investment can also be made by employers, who decide to pay from company resources for the participation in lifelong learning activities of their employees. In general, this investment will most likely reflect participation in job-related training that will increase knowledge and skills in order to increase the level of work undertaken by the employee. On the other hand, public initiatives could be set up to attract adults into learning activities, without them having to invest themselves financially, although an investment in terms of time might be required, or schemes for study leave may be available, as well as grants, training vouchers or other sources of direct financial support.

Similar to innovation, the investment a country makes is often expressed through the percentage of its GDP that is spent on education and training. Again, it is not surprising that the highest participation rates seem to exist in countries that make the highest investments in education and training. Public investment is also likely to benefit those in unemployment and various countries have systems in place to reduce or waive registration fees for them. Returning to the situation in Europe, Busemeyer (2015) demonstrates that investment in education and training is high in both Anglo-Saxon and Scandinavian countries, but with a major difference that private investment in Anglo-Saxon countries is much higher than public investment. Public investment is the highest in Scandinavia. The relationship between private and public investment in education is thus negatively correlated. Investments in Continental countries are generally low, with the exception of employers and companies choosing to invest in the vocational training of their employees. Unsurprisingly, Busemeyer (2015) also identifies a positive correlation between public investment in education and public investment in other domains of social policy.

The cluster of countries with the lowest overall spending includes Canada, the USA, Australia, the UK and Ireland, while the highest spenders are Denmark, Norway, Sweden and Finland. While financing is often discussed by comparing private and public investments, attention has also been paid to co-financing schemes (OECD, 2004); the importance of the topic is reiterated by Sohlman (in Rubenson, 2011, p. 190) in referring to public-private partnerships. These would enable adults to lower their individual costs, but it would also mean that there is a shared risk between different partners rather than sole individual responsibility.

Determinants at the level of the lifelong learning system

Countries do not only differ in the way initial education systems are organised, but also in how adult lifelong learning systems are structured. Desmedt et al. (2006) have summarised a range of characteristics that influence participation rates in adult lifelong learning, based on empirical findings of previous research. They have stated that it is important that adult learning provisions are easily available to potential adult learners and that a high volume and diversity of offers will give them more choice, although these will need to find a good balance between supply and demand.

Furthermore, they have argued that flexible learning modes will also help in increasing participation rates as adults prefer to learn at their own pace. As explored in the previous chapter, it is important to provide Basic Skills Education and Second Chance Education to raise the skill levels of low-skilled adults. Even the most motivated adults will struggle to participate if the offer of support is not available.

Disappointingly, a diversity of learning activities is not present in every country (Hefler, 2013). Eastern European countries seem to be quite limited in what they have on offer and often lack flexible provision. Countries like Scotland, England and Ireland have a stronger diversification of their learning system, both in terms of what is on offer, as well as the types of provision that are offering courses. Boateng (2009) demonstrated these differences in his analysis of the Adult Education Survey. Participation rates in Hungary are low, but those who do participate spend many hours in education and training. In Anglo-Saxon countries, the participation rates are higher, but the time spent in education and training is much lower. These differences are a reflection of different types of offers being available to potential learners.

Research on the role of institutional barriers in the context of formal adult lifelong learning offered at universities has been conducted by Saar et al. (2014) who published a paper on institutional barriers of higher education for adult learners from a European comparative perspective. Institutional barriers were defined at four levels, including (1) the diversification of course offers, (2) access to courses by means of entrance qualifications or entrance requirements such as entrance examinations, (3) flexibility, operationalised through the availability of distance and online learning opportunities, how many times learners need to attend courses on a weekly basis, and whether students can apply for course exemptions based on the accreditation of prior or prior experiential learning (APL or APEL) and (4) affordability, based on whether learners have to pay fees and whether financial support is available to assist learners to meet the costs of participation.

Based on work conducted by Hefler (2013), Saar et al. (2014) show that levels of diversification significantly differ between countries. Those who have access to a wide variety of institutions offering formal adult education tend to have a highly diverse range of offers in terms of the content and length of their programmes. Based on a set of Anglo-Celtic regions, Continental countries, Norway representing Scandinavia and a set of Eastern European countries, it is argued that the Anglo-Celtic regions (Scotland, England and Ireland) offer most diversity, and that the Eastern European countries remain the weakest providers in terms of diversification of educational supply, potential adult learners having little in the way of choices relating to the courses in which they want to participate.

Institutional barriers relating to access are also the highest in the former communist countries where enrolment conditions seem to be stricter than in the liberal countries such as the United Kingdom. Recognition of prior learning was the strongest in the Continental countries, Austria and Belgium, and low in most of the Eastern European countries. Affordability was found to be the highest in Norway, and tended to be low in Eastern European countries. While affordability was classified as Medium-High in Scotland and England, there is no doubt that the current policy climate strongly reduces financial support for adult learning initiatives.

The interplay of macro level determinants

In understanding the mechanisms behind participation at the level of countries, it is important to discuss concrete examples of projects that have attempted to correlate lifelong learning with other social policies within a country. A specific project that has engaged in this exercise is ELLI, the European Lifelong Learning Index project, as touched upon previously in relation to the outcomes and benefits of lifelong learning participation (Hoskins et al., 2010).

The ELLI index has been correlated with indicators on 'global competitiveness', 'consumer health' and 'corruption', operationalised through the use of available statistics on these topics. It is clear that there is a strong linear relation between the ELLI index and these other indices, which means that strong lifelong learning cultures in countries are associated with higher levels of well-being, health, a strong competitive economy and a well-functioning labour market. The strongest performers were found to be Denmark, Finland, Sweden and The Netherlands, countries with high participation rates in adult lifelong learning activities.

Low performers were Greece, Hungary, Bulgaria and Romania. In general, it is becoming clear that participation in adult lifelong learning is more than an individual choice, but happens in interaction with the structural environment adults live in. Therefore, it is determined by education, training and lifelong learning systems, alongside spending on a wide range of social policies and the structure of the economy and labour market.

Not only participation, but also inequalities in participation have been studied in relation to macro level determinants. Research by Roosmaa and Saar (2010) explores whether there are patterns of inequality in adult lifelong learning, more specifically in non-formal training. Inequality here is defined through comparison of participation rates between high-skilled white-collar employees and low-skilled blue-collar employees. Based on data representing the EU-15 countries, they find that the qualifications background of the population in a country is an important determinant. In a country with a high proportion of highly educated adults and a low proportion of low educated adults, there would appear to be less inequality in the non-formal training system. Strong trade unions, high levels of employment security and active labour market policies will also reduce inequalities. They also found that non-stratified initial education systems tend to generate higher levels of equality in the non-formal system. In general, it can be said that the need for skills for a job and high levels of innovation in the workplace generate a need for lifelong learning participation, and thus higher participation rates. Similarly, research by Desmedt et al. (2006) concludes that active labour market policies generate more equality in lifelong learning participation, based on data from the Labour Force Survey. Innovation, the existence of syndicalism and a high employment rate in a country were all found to have a positive impact on participation rates. In contrast, stratified initial schooling systems were found to have a negative impact on equality in lifelong learning, starting many years before, in fact, through the segregation of pupils in academic and vocational tracks.

While the research examples given above were conducted based on correlating different variables for different countries or by putting a range of variables in regression analysis, it is also important to explore how precisely countries cluster together based on a number of lifelong learning factors. This is what Ragin (1989) would call the difference between variable and case-oriented approaches of comparative research. Below, I will switch from exploring variables to how specific cases of countries show similarities or differences in relation to each other. Particular attention will be paid to lifelong learning as an aspect characterising the specific cases.

The role of country typologies

Much of the recent research conducted in the comparative field of adult lifelong learning has attempted to construct or refine welfare regime typologies. I have witnessed this trend as a member of the LLL2010 consortium, carrying out a lifelong learning research project funded by the European Commission. Work on typologies usually starts by referring to the well-known typology of welfare regimes in Esping-Andersen's work *The three worlds of welfare capitalism*. He distinguishes between Liberal Welfare Regimes, Conservative Welfare Regimes and Social Democratic Welfare Regimes (Esping-Andersen, 1989). His work will first be explored before turning towards a detailed exploration of models specifically presented in the lifelong learning literature. However, it is important to recognise that typologies are also being constructed based on countries not included in Esping-Andersen's typology, i.e. Eastern European, Asian or Latin-American countries.

Furthermore, it is also necessary to understand why typologies are being constructed and why the comparative element is so important.

The difference between policy borrowing and policy learning is important here. Countries can learn from each other to explore the effectiveness of specific systems (Raffe, 2011). However, while it might be tempting to implement other countries' strategies, it is important to analyse whether it would work in the specific context of a country. Moreover, comparing countries and constructing typologies fits into the strategy of the current policy climate in relation to lifelong learning which is built around putting peer pressure on each other in order to increase effectiveness and equality.

Esping-Andersen

While many readers will be familiar with Esping-Andersen's work, it is important to provide a short summary of his work on welfare typologies, as it is key to understanding the new typologies. Countries representing the Liberal Welfare Regime include the United Kingdom and the United States, the label Conservative was chosen to identify the West-European continental countries, and the Social Democratic regimes are represented by the Scandinavian countries, such as Denmark and Sweden.

Esping-Andersen's work has been expanded by other scholars to include the Eastern European countries, especially after the enlargement of the European Union in 2004. However, other typologies also include references to countries outside the Western region, such as those in Asia. Moreover, the European typology has been extended to include Mediterranean countries, being that they differ from other Western European countries.

Explanations of the differences between welfare regimes are usually constructed using the concepts of 'decommodification' and 'stratification' (Fenger, 2007). Esping-Andersen stated that in Liberal Welfare Regimes, there is a strong focus on the individual and the mechanisms of the market, with lower levels of social protection, and thus high levels of stratification. Although benefits exist, they are generally low and not attractive (De Frel, 2009). Conservative regimes are characterised by moderate levels of de-commodification, while protection is the highest for those who are in employment and actively contribute to society, so maintaining levels of stratification. In Social Democratic regimes, there is a high level of de-commodification and a low level of stratification. The benefit system is generous and not dependent on individual contributions, and therefore, social (Fenger, 2007).

One of the limitations of Esping-Andersen's typology is the lack of inclusion of Eastern European countries. After the enlargement of the European Union in 2004 when ten countries joined the EU-15, the need for a further diversification of typologies became more urgent. Fenger (2007) includes a range of Central and Eastern European countries in a new cluster analysis, based on data from the World Development Indicators, the IMF and the World Values Survey. He explores three sets of variables which he labels as: (1) characteristics of governmental programmes, (2) social situation variables and (3) political participation variables (Fenger, 2007, pp. 18–19).

The analysis resulted in six different types of welfare states, including the three well-known ones as defined by Esping-Andersen, the conservative-corporatist states, the social-democratic states and the liberal states. Additionally, Fenger (2007) distinguishes between former-USSR states, having similar characteristics as the conservative-corporatist states but scoring lower on social aspects and political trust. Post-communist European states resemble the former-USSR type but demonstrate higher levels of economic growth with the strongest performance in terms of 'catching up' with the Western European states. Finally, the developing welfare states are those with the poorest social indicators and these include countries that are not yet part of the European Union, such as Georgia and Moldova.

Characteristics of these regions have been studied by various social policy projects, e.g. work by Green et al. (2009) on 'social cohesion regimes'. They refer to 'liberal' countries, including Great Britain, Ireland, the United States, Canada, Australia and New Zealand, 'social market' countries in continental Europe such as Germany, France, Belgium and The Netherlands, and 'social-democratic' countries including Sweden, Denmark, Norway, Finland and Iceland. They also refer to a set of Eastern European countries including Poland, Czech Republic, Slovakia and Hungary, arguing that these might cluster together with some of the mainly German-speaking 'social market' countries. This extra European group has been labelled the 'Romantic conservative' social cohesion regime. Lastly, to include countries outside Europe and the Western world, they refer to an 'East Asian' social cohesion regime representing Japan and South Korea.

In order to understand the specific differences between these types of countries, Green et al. (2009, pp. 94–95) have created a very useful overview of social indicators and how different regimes deal differently with a range of social aspects, such as inequality, wage regulation, employment protection, state involvement, welfare, ethno-racial diversity, crime/disorder, valuing diversity, civic participation, freedom, meritocracy, national identities, ethnic tolerance, social hierarchy and gender equality. Their analysis provides a good overview of strong (+) and weak (–) scores on indicators based on administrative and survey data. Liberal countries are characterised by high levels of inequality, low levels of wage regulation, low levels of employment protection and state involvement. They score low on expenditure on public social domains and have rather high crime rates. These countries have relatively high proportions of people who were born abroad, value freedom above equality and are in favour of financial compensations for more productive employees working at the same level.

Social market systems scored stronger on wage regulation and employment protection, and are characterised by stronger levels of state involvement. In these countries, the crime rate is also known to be lower. Equality is generally perceived to be more important than freedom, but merit and paying people based on their performance is perceived as acceptable. Social democratic countries score high on equality, and have high levels of state involvement through high public spending on social matters. Moreover, they score high on wage regulation and value equality above freedom as in the social market countries.

Social democratic countries differ from social market countries with regard to their values of meritocracy, being that they score negatively on the indicator of paying people more based on performance and prefer a stronger notion of cohesion. Boeren, Holford et al. (2012) have reviewed social indicators in Eastern European countries as part of their motivational analysis in 12 different European countries, which will be explored below. They conclude that the 'slow transforming' Eastern European countries like Lithuania and Bulgaria in particular have significantly lower scores on a number of indicators such as quality of housing, trust in politicians and general well-being. In general, it can be concluded that this type of research has mainly been conducted in Europe, starting with the older EU countries. It is only later that Southern and Eastern European countries have extended these typologies.

Lifelong learning country typologies

In relation to lifelong learning, various separate typologies have been developed in recent years, and there are clear overlaps between generic welfare regime typologies and these specific lifelong learning typologies. Holford et al. (2008) have explored a wide range of country level specific indicators in relation to European education and the labour market as part of the European funded project 'LLL2010 – Towards a Lifelong Learning Society in Europe: the Contribution of the Education System'. Here they identify an Anglo-Celtic cluster (England, Scotland and Ireland), a Conservative cluster (Austria and Belgium) and a Nordic cluster (Norway) similar to Esping-Andersen's work. However, the dataset also includes a range of Eastern European countries, which are clustered together as the 'Catching Up' cluster (Czech Republic, Estonia, Hungary, Bulgaria, Slovenia, Lithuania), a term similarly used by Aiginger and Guger (2006), referring to their status of catching up with capitalist countries having made the transition from being communist societies.

Variables included in the lifelong learning typology reflect participation rates in lifelong learning, specifically for participation in formal and non-formal learning activities. Participation according to work status and educational attainment has been introduced, as well as low, medium or high levels of focus on social and human capital in national policies. Poverty risk and employment protection have been included, along with the percentage of GDP spent on education. A critical note has to be introduced here that this typology has been constructed by the researchers themselves, without statistical testing or validation, e.g. through cluster analysis, which might have broken down the Eastern European countries into two or more sub-clusters. However, the general categorisation of clusters is plausible and shows an overlap with other social policy clustering.

Moving on to work undertaken by other scholars, it is important to reiterate the role of institutional arrangements. Whether adults participate in lifelong learning activities or not might also be dependent on the training offers available to them. I have previously explored the notion of 'institutional barriers'. Simply put, a specific training offer not being available to the adult will result in non-participation. Moreover, in this respect, characteristics at the country level can determine whether a successful match between supply and demand will take place, being that countries differ in their education and training systems, as well as in their skills formation systems.

In relation to 'education and training systems', Saar and Ure (2013) distinguish between five different types, which label as the 'Japanese model', the 'German model', the 'French model', the Swedish model' and the 'UK model'. These models differ in the way in which the labour market is organised, as well as how both secondary schooling and adult education and training are organised. Based on the work of Green (1999, 2006), Saar and Ure (2013, pp. 55–57) constructed a table showing the differences between the systems based on the core variables 'the role of the state', 'management–labour relations', 'labour market structure', 'characteristic features of skill formation', 'education and training system: general organisation and principles', 'compulsory education', 'secondary schools', 'adult education and training', 'relationships between firms and ETS', 'skill formation: level of skills' and 'skill formation: skill polarization'.

While France and Germany are often included in the same cluster of 'Continental countries', it is important to understand there are substantial differences in their education system. The German school system is stratified with opportunities to participate in vocational training, including dual apprenticeships. The French system, however, shares more characteristics with comprehensive schooling systems. In relation to adult learning, German companies have a much stronger commitment to offering training, while employers in France have difficulties organising vocational training in their firms. As in the UK, France is thus more likely to encounter problems of skill polarisation.

At the level of skills formation systems, Saar and Ure (2013, pp. 61–62) distinguish between the 'market model', representing countries like the UK, the USA and Canada; the 'corporatist model', with countries like Germany, Austria, Switzerland and Denmark; the 'developmental state model', representing Asian countries like Japan, Singapore and South Korea; and the 'neo-market model', representing Latin-American countries Chile, Mexico and Brazil. Based on the work by Ashton et al. (2010) they explain the typology in table format based on the variables 'key social characteristics', 'production systems', 'management-labour relations', 'form of interaction between state and market', 'main principles of skill formation', 'skill formation system', 'vocational training system', 'coordination of supply and demand', and 'the role of the state'.

Similarly, Deissinger (in Zhao & Rauner, 2014, p. 102) draws on the work of Busemeyer and Trampusch (2011) to distinguish between a range of skill regimes, labelling the regimes in German-speaking countries as 'collective', those in Anglo-Saxon countries as 'liberal', Scandinavian and European continental systems as 'state run', and the Japanese model as 'segmentalist'. Busemeyer and Thelen (in Eichhorst & Marx, 2015, p. 404) also provide a helpful overview on the understanding of these skill formation systems, based on previous work published by Busemeyer and Trampusch (2012) in their book *The Political Economy of Collective Skill Formation*. They distinguish between two dimensions: 'public commitment to vocational training' and 'involvement of firms in initial vocational training'. The 'collective' systems score high in both dimensions; for instance, the German 'skills machine' (Culpepper & Finegold, 1999). The 'liberal' ones score low on both dimensions.

However, in 'state-run' regimes, public commitment is high but the involvement of firms low. The opposite is true in 'segmentalist' regimes. Green and Green (2012, cited in Campbell, 2012, pp. 17–18) who both work at the LLAKES centre in London have undertaken important research, worthy of considerable discussion, in relation to how countries are dealing with lifelong learning issues. Their insights into skill regimes have been widely published and they identify four different types. Firstly, *'market-oriented systems'* include the typical liberal countries such as the United States and England and participation is mainly determined by the needs of the labour market, driven by competition and meeting the skill needs of employers. Secondly, *'social partner-led co-ordination systems'* refer to the more corporatist-conservative regimes, such as the German-speaking countries on the European continent. In this system, unions, employee representatives and employers themselves play a more active role in regulating the skills system, instead of leaving it completely to the forces of the neo-liberal market. Thirdly, *'state-led social partnership systems'* are found in social democratic systems, such as those of Scandinavia. In addition to the social partners, it is also the state itself that engages in the regulation of the skills system. Fourthly, 'developmental skill systems' characterise the situation in East Asia and South Africa, which enjoy lower levels of involvement of social partners but are primarily directive systems, with the main aim to intervene for the sake of economic development. Comparing the four types as constructed by Green and

Green (2012), it is clear that the first three types are comparable to Esping-Andersen's work on the *Three worlds of welfare capitalism*.

In reference to 'welfare state models', most of this type of research has been developed in Europe, borrowing the concept of 'welfare states' from Esping-Andersen. However, Torres (2013) distinguishes the traditional 'Welfare State Model' from the 'Recruitment Franchisement Model' and the 'Forced Modernisation Model'. All three models adopt an approach that reflects 'instrumental rationality', but while the first model is mainly situated in the modern developed world, the second is used to characterise low income countries that are still in a state of development. The final model also refers to low income developing countries, but the ones that are suffering from dictatorship are usually located in rural and agrarian regions. While development and advancement is a core underpinning of all models, the status of development differs, which is also reflected in the quality of staff members working in the sector. While the 'Welfare State Model' usually employs professionals, although mainly trained as compulsory school teachers, the other two models are based around the engagement of volunteers. In fact, this alternative typology takes the different levels of development across the globe into account, while previous lifelong learning, education and training or skill regime typologies are mainly developed in the Western world.

Another feature of the typologies described above is that they are mainly based on measures of macro level variables. Robert (in Riddell et al., 2012, pp. 87–101) has clustered countries based on individual characteristics of adults, undertaken on the Eurostat Adult Education Survey 2008. He explores participation and non-participation in formal adult lifelong learning activities by adults living in Europe, aged 25 to 64. He undertakes two separate analyses, which he then compares. The first analysis clusters countries based on overrepresentation or underrepresentation of adults with specific demographic characteristics in the formal education system. Anglo-Saxon countries have not been included in the analysis, as data for Ireland was not available and British data contains too many missing values.

The analysis then includes the demographic characteristics 'being a woman', 'aged over 45', having a dependent child between 0 and 3 or between 4 and 5, and residing in a rural area. Countries included in the analysis were divided into four clusters. Bulgaria, Cyprus, France and Hungary were the countries in which these groups are strongly underrepresented in the adult formal system. In Croatia, Czech Republic, Austria, Denmark, Spain and Portugal, they were also underrepresented, but not as strongly as in the first group of countries. In the Baltic countries – Estonia, Lithuania and Latvia, as well as Slovakia – these groups underrepresented nor overrepresented, with the exception of adults living in rural areas, who tend to be overrepresented. Overrepresentation of these groups was found in Belgium, Slovenia and the Scandinavian countries Finland, Sweden and Norway.

A second analysis was conducted on a range of socio-economic variables, including: educational attainment at ISCED level 1–3 representing a maximum of upper secondary schooling; not being labour active; and a set of work-related characteristics, such as being on a fixed-term contract, working part-time or conducting blue-collar manual work. Austria, Denmark and Lithuania are the middle group of three here. Low- and medium-educated adults are underrepresented in formal education, as are those on fixed-term contracts. Other groups are generally underrepresented or overrepresented. Underrepresentation of all these characteristics is very clear in a range of mostly Eastern European countries (Czech Republic, Slovakia, Bulgaria, Latvia, Estonia, Hungary, Croatia, as well as Cyprus and France) with the exception of manual workers in Croatia. Overrepresentation of these groups is the clearest in Belgium, although not significantly for those on temporary contracts. Similar results were found in Norway. Overrepresentation is strong in Finland as well, although part-time workers seem to be strongly underrepresented. Portugal and Spain also belong to this third group, while they belong to a weaker group in relation to the demographic characteristics. Slovenia is also included in this third group, mainly because of the overrepresentation of those on fixed-term contracts and manual workers.

Comparing the result on the two dimensions, Robert (2012) has found that countries succeeding well in attracting underrepresented groups in the formal education system based on individuals' demographic and socio-economic characteristics are Finland, Sweden and Belgium. The case of Belgium, more specifically Flanders, being the odd one out in terms of adult participation in formal education, has been further analysed by Boeren and Nicaise in Saar et al. (2013, pp. 187–204). The countries not succeeding in enrolling these groups in formal education are Hungary, Cyprus, Bulgaria and France. Others are somewhere in between, while Norway and Slovenia are two other countries enjoying a general overrepresentation of these groups.

While comparative lifelong learning research has, in recent years, generated several educational and skills-related country typologies, there is a need to be critical about its use, as spelled out by Saar and Ure (2013). As in other research based on cluster analysis, the outcomes are dependent on the variables included in the analysis, and it is therefore important to consider carefully the aims of the clustering analysis in order to further increase understanding of the field. Typologies are usually generated at the country level and it is important to state that differences within countries can also exist.

Care is therefore advised when investigating education and skill formation systems for entire countries, being that systems within countries can rely on different policies, e.g. education in Scotland is different from education in England; Flanders and Wallonia in Belgium each have their own educational systems too. Furthermore, labour markets in different regions can also vary because of the existence of a specific industry that dominates a region, but not, per se, the entire country.

Riddell and Weedon (in Riddell et al., 2012, pp. 34–35) provide some critical notes in relation to the use of typologies in lifelong learning research. They also refer to the limitations of working with country level variables as governance is also located at regional and transnational levels. Furthermore, it is difficult at this point to reach a sound inclusion about countries that have not been included in typologies before, and more research is needed to understand their characteristics. Finally, Riddell and Weedon (2012) focus on the need for data to be available in a consistent way across countries and state that it is important that this data is reliable. Further critical reflections on the state of current lifelong learning data will be provided in Part III of this book.

Motivational differences across countries

It is not only access to adult learning activities, but also the motivations and reasons why adults participate have been found to show very consistent patterns with existing country typologies (Boeren, Holford et al., 2012). Research shows that adult learners participating in formal adult learning activities in Western European countries score lower on vocationally-oriented motivation compared to adult learners participating in Eastern European countries. The strongest levels of vocational motivation were found in Bulgaria and Lithuania, two of the 'weakest' Eastern European countries in terms of catching up with the Western capitalist markets, having slower transformation processes than other Eastern European countries that already match more closely with traditional capitalist societies.

After checking for sampling effects, Boeren and Holford (2013) found that these country effects are strong and not a representation of uneven characteristics of adult learners in these countries. This means that while it might sound intuitive that men score higher on vocational motivational orientations that women, it is clear from the analysis that women in Eastern European countries score higher in the vocational motivational dimension than men do in Western Europe. These results thus indicate the importance of taking into account country level determinants when analysing lifelong learning aspects. Moreover, the result also indicates the need for policy makers to pay attention to lifelong learning participation as participation decisions and processes clearly go beyond the level of adults' individual choices.

Apart from these interesting findings in relation to formal participation, differences also exist in relation to participation in either formal or non-formal learning activities (Boeren & Nicaise, 2013). As explained in an earlier chapter, formal education refers to those institutionalised activities for which an official qualification will be granted upon successful completion, while non-formal activities are not based on obtaining credentials. In general, participation in non-formal education is higher than in formal education, but some countries differ in this respect. In Europe, participation in formal adult learning is highest in Scandinavian countries, who have the highest overall participation rates. While this overall participation – including both formal and non-formal education – is significantly lower in Flanders (Belgium), participation in adult formal education is as high as in Scandinavian countries. Most notably, in Eastern European countries, participation in formal adult education is very low, with percentages under five percent, measured on a 12 month reference period.

Standardising adult lifelong learning

While countries vary in their lifelong learning policies, it is also important to understand that efforts have been undertaken to standardise several aspects of what is needed to survive in the globalised world. People move around and take up jobs in countries in which they were not educated. They might want to participate in lifelong learning activities in a country other than where they obtained their previous qualifications. In order to make this transition easier, leading players in the field of lifelong learning have worked with countries to implement strategies such as qualification frameworks and credit transfer systems.

Qualification frameworks

The system of qualifications, and the existence of a qualifications framework in a specific country, may have a relationship with participation in adult lifelong learning activities. The OECD (2007) argues that this link is hard to demonstrate and that more research in this area is needed, although it is a strong hypothesis. Qualification systems can help adults to access lifelong learning through the recognition of previous learning elsewhere, to transfer and validate credits and to create alternative routes towards certification (Castejon, 2011).

The portability of qualifications is thus one of the major values of qualification systems. Furthermore, it provides more clarity to both the individual and employers about the level of qualifications obtained in the past, and might help to achieve more consistent qualifications across countries. Castejon (2011) also argues that qualification frameworks are helpful in strengthening educational offers, e.g. through increasing understanding on validated learning outcomes and the usability of qualifications in the labour market. Furthermore, these frameworks might stimulate more efficiency in the teaching and management of adult lifelong learning activities.

However, Young and Allais (2013) warn that while qualification frameworks do, in fact, 'frame' existing opportunities, they fail to place an emphasis on the acquiring of new skills or knowledge. The notion of 'qualifications' is a central concept in these frameworks, and therefore strongly linked to participation in formal learning settings, although Barros (2012) has asserted that current lifelong learning discourses are centred around the acquisition of knowledge and skills. While qualifications frameworks will mainly help to access formal learning activities, they will also be able to provide stronger bridges between formal and non-formal education, which are both measured in relation to participation statistics, as well as informal learning.

The importance of recognising non-formal and informal learning has been reiterated over the past few years (e.g. Singh, 2015). The OECD's 'policy responses' for better lifelong learning strongly focus on qualifications, containing a range of policy recommendations that will be helpful for countries to use to increase the participation rates in their countries OECD, 2007, pp. 12–13: (1) increase flexibility and responsiveness, (2) motivate young people to learn, (3) link education and work, (4) facilitate open access to education, (5) diversify assessment procedures, (6) make qualifications progressive, (7) make the qualifications system transparent, (8) review funding and increase efficiency and (9) improve the way in which the system is managed.

Credit systems

In Europe, credit systems have been developed in order that participation in lifelong learning activities and gaining of knowledge and skills will not be lost once someone moves to another country. At the level of higher education, the European Credit Transfer System (ECTS) helps students to accumulate transferable credits in different countries and is an important aspect of the Bologna process in European Higher Education (Guruz, 2011; Rauhvargers & Rusakova, 2009). However, this is not only in the field of higher education, but also in relation to Vocational Education and Training where a credit system has been developed: the European Credit system for Vocational Education and Training (ECVET) (European Union, 2011; Wilson, 2011). ECVET makes it easier for people to have their work-related skills and knowledge recognised and validated in other countries so that it is clear to new employers in their new country whether or not the prospective employee fits the job criteria. Furthermore, recognition of previous skills will help to meet the access criteria for future participation in adult lifelong learning activities.

Quality indicators

While education and training systems do therefore differ across countries, it is important to recognise that regions in the world do explore the quality of their education systems. Europe has produced a set of 15 'quality indicators' divided into four categories: (A) skills, competencies and attitudes, (B) access and participation, (C) resources for lifelong learning and (D) strategies and system development. Here, a special working group was not only attended by representatives of European members states, but was organised in cooperation with the OECD, UNESCO and a range of other European countries who are non-members of the European Union, such as Albania, Bosnia Herzegovina, Former Yugoslav Republic of Macedonia, Iceland, Liechtenstein, Norway and Turkey. Other European services such as CEDEFOP and Eurydice have also been involved in the development of the quality indicators. One of the core objectives, as outlined in a document presented by the European Commission (2002, p. 4) is *'improving the quality and effectiveness of education and training systems in the EU.'*

An overview of the 15 concrete indicators can be found in Table 6.2. Linked to boosting participation rates based on putting peer pressure on countries, quality indicators provide insight into how good or bad countries perform in maintaining their lifelong learning systems.

Table 6.2   Quality indicators Europe

(A) Skills, competencies and attitudes	1. Literacy
	2. Numeracy
	3. New skills for the learning society
	4. Learning-to-learn skills
	5. Active citizenship, cultural and social Skills
(B) Access and participation	6. Access to lifelong learning
	7. Participation in lifelong learning
(C) Resources for lifelong learning	8. Investment in lifelong learning
	9. Educators and learning
	10. ICT in learning
(D) Strategies and system development	11. Strategies for lifelong learning
	12. Coherence of supply
	13. Guidance and counselling
	14. Accreditation and certification
	15. Quality assurance

Source: European Commission (2002).

While reference has been made to qualification frameworks, credit systems and quality indicators in Europe, it is untrue that other countries or regions in the world have not yet dealt with this issue. CEDEFOP (the European Centre for the Development of Vocational Training) (2013) review qualification frameworks, mechanisms for validation and accreditation in 34 countries. The overview demonstrates that many countries do have specific systems for recognition in place. Interestingly, the United States, Canada and Japan do not have a National Qualifications Framework (CEDOFOP, 2013, p. 34). However, in the context of education and training, mechanisms are in place to judge standards. A range of African countries have explored the equivalencies of basic education, hugely important in regions suffering from high illiteracy rates. South Africa, but also New Zealand and Australia have National Qualification Frameworks in place.

Participation outcomes differ by country

In an earlier chapter in this book, I reflected on the notion of the 'benefits and outcomes' of participation in lifelong learning activities. Although there is optimism that lifelong learning can result in positive outcomes, it is important to understand these benefits across different countries. The outcomes of education are multiple, but previous research by Blossfeld et al. (2014) demonstrates that in relation to participation in formal adult education, countries do not achieve the same outcomes in relation to adults' status in education and in the labour market. Three different outcomes of formal adult learning were distinguished. Firstly, the authors write about 'partial equalisation'. This concept refers to the fact that, in some regions or countries, lower educated adults overtake highly educated adults in terms of participation, and that this is generally perceived as contradictory to what the general statistics on adult lifelong learning participation show.

Research has demonstrated that the occurrence of 'partial equalisation' as a result of adult lifelong learning participation in formal adult learning activities has been a feature of Finland, Russia, Denmark and the USA. Secondly, certain countries show patterns of increased educational inequalities, as those with higher levels of education were more likely to participate, thus enlarging the gap with the low educated adults. However, in these countries, which include Australia, Britain, Spain and Sweden, it was also found that disadvantages in the labour market have in fact stimulated a higher proportion of formal adult learning uptake. Thirdly, in a range of East European countries, including Hungary, Estonia and Czech Republic, disadvantages have increased as a result of formal lifelong learning participation, both in terms of education and labour market positions.

It is interesting to notice that countries belonging to these three clusters are not exactly the same, while clusters identified in other research projects have resulted in adult lifelong learning typologies. One of the reasons might be that this project was based only on formal work-related adult lifelong learning activities. An important recommendation for future research is thus that lifelong learning participation research needs to pay more attention to the different types of learning activities. The lack of data available to make this distinction will be discussed in one of the following chapters. However, our analysis shows that countries do differ in relation to how they manage their lifelong learning systems, and that the inclusion of the country level in lifelong learning participation research is necessary.

Conclusions

This chapter has demonstrated that participation in adult lifelong learning activities is much greater an issue than being merely an individual matter. Countries differ in the way they have structured their education and training systems, the volume of money they invest in education and training and related social policies, as well as in mechanisms like innovation that will increase the demand for a high-skilled workforce. Labour markets and economies are organised differently and safety nets for those in unemployment or inactivity are not equally strong in all countries. In general, it can be said that lifelong learning typologies more or less correlate with existing general welfare regimes – a conclusion drawn from the work of Esping-Andersen (1989). Furthermore, well-structured opportunities to validate and recognise different types of learning are also likely to stimulate access to lifelong learning activities. All these elements will be taken into account when presenting an integrative lifelong learning participation theory.

7
Lifelong Learning Participation: The Need for Integration

The previous chapters in this book have explored why adults participate in lifelong learning activities from different viewpoints, based on insights from policy, psychology, sociology, economy and macro level theories. This chapter attempts to integrate the different disciplinary theories into an interdisciplinary way of thinking. This chapter will refer to existing theories helping to understand the integration of different levels and will focus specifically on integrative approaches as found in relation to adult lifelong learning participation.

Contribution of different disciplines to the understanding of adult lifelong learning participation

Educational research, sociology, psychology, economics and political sciences have been the major contributors to the theorisation of adult lifelong learning participation. Dutch andragogy professor Ten Have described his discipline as a science that relies on a distinct number of basic disciplines (van Gent, 1998). A literate translation from Dutch to English would read as 'a first floor discipline', a discipline that builds on fundamental disciplines located at the ground floor. Ten Have supports this argument through comparing andragogy (the study of teaching adults, introduced by Kapp (1833) as opposed to pedagogy) with medicine. A medical doctor needs to have a basic understanding of different disciplines such as biology, physics and chemistry before he will be able to carry out his profession. A similar mechanism is true for those who want to study andragogy, which has been developed through the lenses of basic disciplines such as psychology, sociology and philosophy. Elias and Vanwing (2002, p. 346) wrote about the 'triangle' of psychology, sociology and philosophy in explaining the adult education degree at the Free University Brussels in Belgium and argued that professionals and scholars in the field should understand the notions of each of these three 'sciences' that inform policy, practice and research. The discussion on the definition of what should be referred to as a separate 'discipline' and when to refer to 'interdisciplinary' is not easy, as a clear definition of the 'discipline' term is lacking (Trowler et al., 2012). Towler et al. (2012, p. 6), based on the work of Krishnan (2009, p. 9), argue that disciplines share 'a body of accumulated specialist knowledge', but mention that this is often not shared with other disciplines. Disciplines are also centred around specific 'theories and concepts' with their own terminologies. While it could be argued that lifelong learning theories have been developed in the past, it is also clear that these have often relied on insights borrowed from other disciplines such as psychology and sociology. I would therefore agree with what Trowler et al. (2012, pp. 13–14) write about interdisciplinarity in relation to lifelong learning:

> Interdisciplinarity can be seen, as Klein (2000) points out, as a methodological approach, a process, a way of thinking, a philosophy and/or as an ideology. It is often adopted as an attempt to solve problems and to avoid the partial, fragmented, understanding of the world that disciplinarity can involve. While multidisciplinarity involves conjoining two or more disciplines in a well-defined way using an aggregative logic that adds the findings from each discipline to those of others, interdisciplinarity and its slight variant transdisciplinarity are often portrayed as 'integrationist and consultative' (Ellis 2009: 7). (Trowler et al., 2012, pp. 13–14)

In this chapter, it is the aim to both integrate findings from different disciplines and to find out how 'consulting' knowledge from different disciplines has helped me in understanding why certain adults do and others do not participate in lifelong learning activities.

In relation to specific adult lifelong learning participation research, Hefler (2013) gives an overview of 11 different theories, linking them back to one of the basic disciplines such as sociology or psychology. Within educational research, he mentioned the construction of motivational typologies, as constructed by Houle (1961) and further validated by Boshier (1973) as explained earlier in the behavioural chapter. The work of Cross (1981) is also classified under the discipline of educational research. I would argue that the psychological dimension of their work is strongly available, but applied to the context of adult learning and participation. Under the discipline of psychology, Hefler (2013) refers to the notion of 'expectancy and value', drawing upon the expectancy valence model developed by Rubenson in the 1970s. Reflections on expectancy and value in this book can be found under the explanation of motivational theories in the behavioural chapter. The psychological dimension of adult lifelong learning participation also includes theories on changes in life, e.g. captured by biographical research such as further developed by scholars in the field like Merrill and West (2009). This dimension also links well to the notion of life cycle approaches as discussed in the behavioural chapter. Sociological theories include references to the work of Bourdieu and the notion of 'class' as explored in the micro-sociological chapter of this book. Hefler (2013) also refers to *'socio-technical requirements and mandatory obligations'* but does not give references to back up this category of participation theory. While Field (2005) is included as a reference for theories on 'social networks', this theory has not been classified within a specific dimension, but it can be argued that discussions on social capital and social networks are likely to be strongly developed within sociology. 'Rational choice theories' have been classified as being developed in both sociology and political economy. Finally, it is interesting to see how Hefler (2013) also refers to the discipline of marketing, based on the work of Tippelt et al. (2008), to reflect on participation as consumption. The role of marketing has also been discussed in the previous chapter on the role of information. While the notion of the different theories is important in order to understand adult lifelong learning participation, it is crucial to explore integrating these theories into a coherent and comprehensive model. It is the aim of this chapter to contribute to this need.

The interplay of structure and individual agency

I start by referring to the general theory on structure and agency approaches as integrative lifelong learning theories are largely related to this idea. Structure and agency approaches reflect on the role of both societal structure and the individual's capabilities and agencies to make decisions in a wide range of life domains. As explored before, participation in adult lifelong learning activities is generally perceived as the result of an underlying decision-making process, which fits with the idea of structure and agency debates.

In fact, the previously explored concept of 'habitus' as widely discussed by Bourdieu (1979) fits in to the structure and agency debate through making reference to his field theory. Bourdieu argues that the habitus is shaped through interaction with the environment and there is thus a relationship between the internal and the external. This notion is important in research into adult lifelong learning participation, especially if we want to better understand the non-participation of disadvantaged groups. Their 'habitus' will often not correspond to the dominant middle class values which are embedded in organisational culture and the adult educators' own backgrounds. The need to include a more integrative perspective has also been critically discussed by experts in biographical research methods:

> ... learning and narration are still conceived as primarily an individual capacity and/or process. Although many life history researchers insist emphatically that their approach is not solely individualistic, the approach nevertheless clearly focuses on the individual's capacity for narrating the own life in such a way as to reflect on their own experiences. (Field et al., 2012, p. 80)

There is thus a recognition that individual experiences are shaped by the culture and environment, and that understanding these perspectives might help to generate more accurate pictures of the situation.

Structure and agency debates in contemporary sociology often draw upon work developed by Giddens, such as his Structuration Theory. Within Giddens' work, the notion of reflexivity is important, referring to the ability of individuals to alter their societal position. In his book *The Third Way*, which has been widely influential in the political landscape, Giddens (1998) focuses on inequalities in society and links this notion with the structure of welfare states. Also, his 1984 work on 'The Constitution of Society' has been an important contribution to the field (Giddens, 1984). Giddens has criticised the duality of 'structure' versus 'agency', arguing that there is strong interconnection, interaction and reciprocal nature between the two. There is no need to create and maintain divisions in the study of structure versus agency as people and social structures are with no doubt linked to each other. While not all human actions are a result of social structures, it is not entirely possible to study human behaviour without exploring structural aspects. Giddens makes the distinction between 'micro' and 'macro' level, referring to 'human agency' and 'social structures'. At the level of human agency, reflexivity and self-identity are the major characteristics as it is important for individuals to understand their own lives. But structure plays an important role as well in producing and/or reproducing behaviour in society.

Structure and agency are terms widely used and developed in the European context, but another way to write about the topic is to refer to the integration of 'microsociology' and 'macrosociology'. The first term refers to the individual level of agency, while the second term refers to the large scale structures in society (Scheff, 1990). In relation to this book, the chapter on country level differences is likely to be classified under 'macrosociology'. While two different terms are used, they are closely connected and preferably studied together in order to understand people's actions and behaviours, as without including both of the levels, it will be impossible to take into account the interactions between the two of them. The integration between micro- and macro-sociological perspectives has been widely discussed, e.g. in Knorr-Centina and Cicourel's edited collection, 'Advances in social theory and methodology' (Knorr-Centina & Cicourel, 2014).

Lewin, born in 1890 and graduating from his doctoral studies in 1916, is often referred to as one of the major scholars in the field of modern social psychology (Youngreen, in Ritzer, 2007). He developed the formula $B = f(P,E)$, which refers to Behaviour being a function of both the Person and his Environment. Kihlstrom published a chapter in The Oxford Handbook of Social Cognition on the 'person-situation interaction' which is based around the work of Lewin, and which provides a good overview on the importance of Lewin's work (Kihlstrom, in Carlston, 2013, pp. 789–805). Applied to the topic of this book, the B reflects participation in lifelong learning activities, the behaviour undertaken by the adult. Lewin is thus arguing that this behaviour is not only the result of forces at the individual level, such as those discussed in the behavioural chapter, e.g. attitudes and motivation, but it is also the result of forces at play in the broader structural environment, including sociocultural aspects and structures that can either encourage or constrain people to perform specific behaviour. While Lewin's work is often placed within the psychological dimension, it integrates a wider structural approach, and is a good example of a multidisplinary approach, incorporating economics, anthropology, sociology, and of course psychology.

Integrative lifelong learning participation theories

Before I provide a critical overview and analysis of a number of integrative models that can be found in the literature, I would like to go back to what Courtney (1992, p. 154) mentioned in the conclusion of 'Why adults learn: towards a theory of participation in adult education':

> Currently, there is no general theory of PAE (Participation in Adult Education) which holds widespread allegiance, and for this reason. A comprehensive theory of PAE would have to do more than deal with reasons for learning as a function of position in the life cycle or motivational orientation. It would have to be more than a decision model. It would have to take account of sociological factors; it would have to recognize learning as a discretionary activity singled out or in competition with other customary and non-customary activities; and it would have to deal with the place of adult education in a capitalist economy, one in which roles and rewards are 'meted out' in accordance with a liberal-conservative ideology of opportunity and individualism. Courtney (1992, p. 154)

Courtney's arguments are reiterated by Merriam et al. (2007, p. 67) who argued that participation studies have relied too much on the *'individual's motivation, attitudes, beliefs, behaviors, position in the life cycle'*, elements that have been introduced in the behavioural chapter of this book. They strongly encourage researchers studying participation to include a 'sociological lens' in their work and to go beyond treating potential adult learners as isolated individuals. Having read Courtney's book and having conducted my own evaluation of existing participation models, my supervisors and I published a paper in 2010 in the International Journal of Lifelong Education on the need for an integrated model (Boeren et al., 2010). I agree with Courtney's argument for the need to integrate psychological and sociological factors, and to include wider societal elements as well. I do think that participation still is the result of an underlying decision-making model, but concur that influencing factors go beyond motivation and stage of life. Hence the importance of developing a model that integrates the different elements touched upon in the previous chapters of this book. What follows is an overview of important integrative work undertaken by scholars in the field.

Bronfenbrenner's ecological system used in adult lifelong learning research

Bronfenbrenner (1979) is widely known for the development of the 'ecological systems theory' in which he distinguishes five levels or subsystems: (1) the microsystem (2) the mesosystem, (3) the exosystem, (4) the macrosystem and (5) the chronosystem. While Bronfenbrenner's work was mainly situated in the field of child development, his work is also of valuable use in other contexts, such as that of adult lifelong learning participation. The theory is mostly based on interactions going from the inner to the outer, starting with the 'individual' as the central agent with core characteristics such as age and gender. The microsystem has been defined by Bronnenbrenner as referring to those groups that are close to the individual's life, such as peers, families, social services and community services. The mesosystem represents the interactions that take place between the individual and the influential systems at the level of the microsystem. The exosystem was described by Weiss and Kreider as *'that level of a developing person's ecology that connects that person's microsystems to other systems not containing that person'*. Specific aspects of life might change because of decisions made in contexts in which family members behave, and although it does not directly relate to the individual, it might change certain patterns. The macrosystem refers to the dominant culture individuals live in which is shaped by its dominant values and ideologies. Finally, the chronosystem refers to events and transitions that occur throughout life and which have the power to impact on the way people develop.

This theory has been used by researchers in the field, such as in Downes' book on *Access to Education in Europe: A Framework and Agenda for System Change* which explores ways to advance Bronfenbrenner's theory in the lifelong learning context (Downes, 2014). He focuses on the importance of Bronfenbrenner's theory in relation to people's transitions across education systems, which are not an individual matter only, but which take place in interaction with the mesolevel, but also between individuals as interactions at the micro-level. However, Downes (2014) also recognises deficits in Bronfenbrenner's work. Firstly, argues Downes, there is a need for a stronger focus on 'time' as systems change, and this is backed up by reference to Sultana (2008, in Downes, 2014, p. 38) who asserts that temporal dimensions need to be included in research on accessing education. Secondly, the ecological system approach does not put enough emphasis on the understanding on how to overcome system blockages, such as institutional barriers. Thirdly, in order to move away from blocked systems, it is crucial to introduce inclusive systems which are supportive of individual agency and can facilitate individual success. While Bronfenbrenner's work is regarded as offering a good 'static' overview of different levels and their interactions, it is important to take into account the evolution of these systems and levels as well, and to update the model regularly in order to avoid losing its value.

Rubenson and Desjardins' focus on Bounded Agency

Rubenson and Desjardins (2009) have made a strong contribution to the field of adult lifelong learning participation from an interdisciplinary point of view through publication of their 'Bounded Agency Model' which explored 'the impact of welfare state regimes' in 2009 in Adult Education Quarterly (Rubenson & Desjardins, 2009). Their model distinguishes between the structural and the individual level. The structural level within the welfare states sets out structural conditions and targeted policy measures, as explored in Chapter 6, but can also create a range of structural barriers in relation to being able to combine participation with job and/or family responsibilities. As mentioned earlier, the institutional structural setting can also create its own barriers. At the level of the individual, Rubenson and Desjardins (2009) focus on the role of the individual's capabilities, defined by the work of Sen (1999), together with the individual's level of consciousness. Dispositional barriers belong to this individual level as well. While the theory presents two different levels, the authors have introduced an interactive element, in which both the structural and individual level 'communicate' with each other, by means of conditioning adults' insights on the available opportunity structures from the structural side, and the dialogue about the subjective perspectives of the opportunity structures from the individuals. The result of participation is therefore 'bounded' as a cooperation between the individual and the available structures.

Feldman and Ng's exploration of Participation in Continuing Education

The *Oxford handbook of lifelong learning*, edited by Manuel London (2011) has a chapter on 'Participation in Continuing Education Programs' (Feldman & Ng, in London, 2011, pp. 180–194). While their chapter focuses on participation in what they call 'continuing education' for those in employment, their work is of relevance to this chapter in terms of the integrative aspect of adult lifelong learning participation as the authors present a comprehensive overview of what they perceive as the 'antecedents' of learning. Unfortunately, the authors did not give their model a specific name (Feldman & Ng, in London, 2011, p. 181). They distinguish three groups of antecedents: (1) individual differences, (2) situational factors and (3) access to Continuing Education opportunities. At the individual level, Feldman and Ng (2011) refer to variables discussed in the behavioural and socio-economic chapter of this book such as age, education, work history and personality. It is positive to see that the authors link individual aspects with 'situational' factors, representing the characteristics of the specific Continuing Education activities on offer. They refer to the notion of 'perceived value' which can be linked to what I have previously discussed regarding attitudes towards learning, researched by Blunt and Yang (1995). In addition, the design of learning activities is mentioned as an important antecedent of participation, as certain types of programmes, their length and mode of delivery have the power to either motivate or discourage adults from participation, which was a central feature in Chapter 5 on institutional barriers. The decision to participate in learning activities will also depend on the support employees receive from their employers or their peers in the work organisation, such as their colleagues. Finally, Feldman and Ng (2011) focus on the role of structural elements likely to play a role in the chances of employees to become a participant or not. Especially in relation to participation in Continuing Education at work, characteristics of the workplace, such as its size, the organisation of its Human Resources, the specific industry in which they are carrying out their work and the economic aspects of the organisation will make it more or less likely that employees will be offered opportunities for participation.

Feldman and Ng's analysis of participation does not end at the level of access. They argue that participation will lead to some outcomes at the individual level such as learning new skills and knowledge, increased levels of self-efficacy and job satisfaction. These positive outcomes will influence their future decisions to participate in lifelong learning activities, but will also have positive effects at the level of the work organisation, such as increased effectiveness of work processes. Interestingly, the authors mention that positive outcomes of participation are more likely to be achieved if the participation process is facilitated by competent trainers and an organisational culture valuing participation. Overall, the model provides some input towards understanding participation from an integrated level, going beyond the level of the individual decision-making process and taking into account important factors at the level of the learning organisation, in this case the workplace.

Baert, De Rick and Van Valckenborgh's exploration of The Learning Climate

Baert et al. (2006) undertook research in order to formulate recommendations on how to boost the learning climate in Flanders. In their review of determinants of participation, they distinguished between the characteristics of the individual (potential) adult learner and the characteristics of adult lifelong learning activities. Baert et al. (2006) connect these two levels through focussing on insights from Fishbein and Ajzen (1980) whose work centres around the concept of 'intention', predicted by attitudinal components. At the level of the individual, the authors of this model constructed four sublevels: (1) socio-demographic characteristics such as age and gender; (2) psychological characteristics including self-confidence and aspirations; (3) characteristics of the live situation referring to adults' financial situations as well as their health, available time and occupational situation; and (4) their educational history, biography, competencies and expectations. The level of lifelong learning activities focuses on three sublevels: (1) the characteristics of the learning process, including the learning content and teaching approaches; (2) the structural and organisational context of the learning activities: where does the activity take place, what does it cost, what information is available about these learning opportunities, who are the adult educators, and so on; and (3) the cultural context which reflects the norms, values, use of language, diversity in life situations and ethnicity of participants. Overall, this model provides a good overview of the interaction of the individual level and the educational institutional level. However, mention of the 'societal context and actors' is rather limited. While the authors state that these characteristics play a determining role as well, specific characteristics have not been analysed in detail.

Boeren, Nicaise and Baert's Comprehensive Lifelong Learning Participation Model

Integrating the different levels and perspectives of adult lifelong learning participation was also part of my own doctoral research (Boeren, 2011). In the first phase, exploring participation models as examined in Courtney's book *Why Adults Learn* and other relevant literature in the field of adult lifelong learning participation, the need for an integrative model was discovered. This analysis resulted in a piece of work which was published in the International Journal of Lifelong Education in 2010 (Boeren et al., 2010). Later on, in my doctoral thesis defended at the Katholieke Universiteit Leuven in Belgium, the newly presented model was named the 'Comprehensive Lifelong Learning Participation Model' (Boeren, 2011).

The model consists of three levels: the individual level, the level representing educational institutions and the country level. At the level of the individual, the model contains a range of specific factors as discussed in previous chapters, such as the individual's socio-economic, socio-demographic, sociocultural and psychological characteristics, but also peers who have the power to influence the individual's decision-making. The institutional level concentrates on the notion of institutional barriers and support mechanisms and is divided into two main sections. The first section refers to the characteristics of the institutions themselves, such as the location and accessibility of the institution, enrolment policies, fee policies etc. But within institutions, specific criteria will often also exist at the level of the programmes on offer, e.g. whether a full-time programme is offered in part-time mode as well. Finally, the country level is defined by a set of characteristics to do with current education policies, levels of social security, structure of the labour market etc.

The Comprehensive Lifelong Learning Participation Model, similar to Bronfenbrenner's and Rubenson's work, needs to be interpreted from an interactive viewpoint in which three levels interact with each other. Individuals' motivations in relation to lifelong learning participation correlate with the country's contextual level (Boeren et al., 2012) although they differ among individuals within a specific country as well. However, adults who are motivated in a specific course that is not on offer will not participate either.

Revisiting participation theories

What are the common features among these theories? Overall, they focus on the need to research adult lifelong learning participation beyond the notion of one simple level. From a statistical point of view, this implies the use of multilevel modelling to explore variance at both the country and individual level when working with surveys like the European Labour Force Survey and the Adult Education Survey. Sociological, economic, psychological and political insights have to be interwoven in order to advance knowledge and to really understand the determinants of participation. Step by step, based on insights generated and discussed in previous chapters, I now intend to bring everything together. A schematic overview is presented in Figure 7.1.

At the individual level, I have discovered that voluntary participation is likely to be the result of an intention to participate. Participants who did not intend to participate were being forced. The intention to participate is influenced by the adult's needs, intentions and attitudes towards learning, as well as their self-confidence and motivation to be more autonomous or to reach a set of expected benefits. However, all of these aspects are likely to change during the lifespan, triggered by life events, or naturally due to growing older. However, apart from time, these aspects are also related to a range of individual sociological characteristics, such as age, gender, employment and occupational status, educational attainment and skill level, social and cultural capital, place of living and race/ethnicity. Adults can experience situational or dispositional barriers. Someone who had negative learning

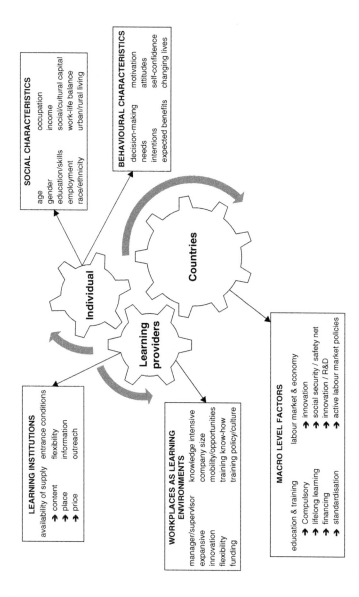

Figure 7.1 Integrative lifelong learning participation model

experiences in the past, who is low-skilled and who lacks confidence is unlikely to participate, as is a young mother with children who is struggling to maintain a satisfying work life balance.

However, educational institutions and workplaces, major providers of adult lifelong learning activities, also have a role to play in facilitating learning, and help adults overcome barriers. Aspects that need to be integrated in the theory are the availability of flexible learning routes, including flexible course modes (e.g. modular or online learning), flexible entrance conditions facilitated by accreditation of previous learning, and the role of information and outreach activities to mobilise potential learners. At the level of the workplace, it became clear that expansive working environments, prioritising long-term thinking and innovation, are better at stimulating learning than restrictive ones. It is clear that offering learning opportunities is largely dependent of the structure and sector of the workplace.

Institutions and workplaces are embedded in society. Participation of adults in lifelong learning activities can be stimulated and constrained by a range of social policy measures. First of all, countries differ in the ways they organise their education and training systems. Initial education systems are either comprehensive or stratified and countries differ in the broadness of their lifelong learning opportunities. Financing systems differ as proportions between public and private investments are not equal in all countries. Furthermore, labour markets' and economies' levels of innovation vary, related to the level of GDP they invest in Research & Development. Social protection and support for unemployed and disadvantaged groups is also unequal. Safety nets for the unemployed and inactive adults will help people (re)integrate in society. These aspects are understood to be linked to participation rates in adult lifelong learning activities.

An attempt to visually present all factors discovered during my reading of participation studies in the field of adult lifelong learning is presented in Figure 7.1. I will label this model the Integrative Lifelong Learning Participation Model. It is important that the three levels interact with each other. Adult lifelong learning participation is therefore perceived as a shared responsibility, but also as a shared risk.

Part III
Advancing Research and Practice

8
Measuring Adult Lifelong Learning Participation

Generating knowledge on the participation of adults in lifelong learning activities is only possible if high quality data are being produced. These data should provide a good measurement of who participates, for what reasons and in what types of education and training activities. But furthermore, it is also crucial that data about education and training opportunities and social policy indicators are available, which can be matched with the individual data, due to the need to study participation as an integrated topic. While we have a wide range of educational data nowadays, Vignoles (2007) argues that much adult learning data have 'serious limitations'. Many research projects tend to be small-scale and those in need of lifelong learning are often hard to reach. Large comparable data have their limitations too. This chapter will explore comparative data available to the scholarly community about participation in adult lifelong learning activities, but also which data sources are being produced and used by policy makers to design their policy interventions to stimulate adult lifelong learning participation with the aim to increase levels of economic competitiveness and social cohesion in society. Because of the strong discourse on benchmarks and indicators, and the 'governance by numbers' approach, it is important to evaluate existing quantitative datasets, but is also necessary to think about alternative research methodologies. I start by discussing the major datasets.

UNESCO-OECD-EUROSTAT

The major agencies collecting data on education are the UNESCO, OECD and the European Commission's statistical office EUROSTAT, who are in fact working together on the UOE joint data collection (Lawn & Grek, 2012). Several data sources are available to calculate participation rates in adult lifelong learning across a range of countries. In the European context, the major data source used for calculating progress towards the benchmark of 15 percent to be obtained by 2020 is calculated based on the Labour Force Survey. However, EUROSTAT is also in charge of the Adult Education Survey, while the OECD is responsible for PIAAC (Desjardins, 2015). These are three major datasets useable for analysis in the field of adult lifelong learning participation (Goglio & Meroni, 2014). Other surveys, like the Continuing Vocational Training Survey include information available to compute lifelong learning statistics as well, but because the data are gathered from the perspective of the employer, and only referring to those in employment, they are not explained in further detail (Kuckulenz, 2007; OECD, 2013d). Codebooks of surveys are usually available on the internet, aggregated data can be found at the Eurostat website or at the OECD Education at a Glance reports, and datasets for detailed statistical analyses can often be obtained from the corresponding agency, based on an application for scientific research, e.g. those in European Framework projects. A summative overview of the three major datasets can be found in Table 8.1.

Labour Force Survey

The Labour Force Survey is a household survey and includes respondents aged 15 and above (Eurostat, 2011). Questions about participation in educational activities use a reference period of four weeks prior to the interview. Calculations of the rate are based on those aged between 25 and 64. The Labour Force Survey (LFS) is the commonly used survey to express adult lifelong learning participation rates by the European Commission. The LFS is a household panel survey which provides information about all sorts of labour market issues and focuses on employees, self-employed persons, job-seekers and inactive persons aged 16 and over. Young people between 16 and 24 are thus excluded from the adult lifelong learning participation rate.

The LFS is a large European survey, which started in 1960 within the six original members of the European Union and in 1995 was enlarged to the EU-15, though separate countries already carried out their own version of the Labour Force Survey, e.g. France, Finland and Sweden organised Labour Force Surveys in the 1950s (Holford &

Table 8.1 Overview of three major surveys measuring adult lifelong learning participation

Survey	Years	Organiser	Type	Reference period	Formal & non-formal learning activities
Labour Force Survey (LFS)	Quarterly Annually	Eurostat (EC) European countries	cross-sectional household survey	4 weeks	Formal education Formal apprenticeship On/off job training Workshops, courses, training, self-learning or leisure activities
Adult Education Survey (AES)	1st: 2005–2008 2nd: 2011–2012 3rd: planned	Eurostat (EC) European countries	cross-sectional household survey	12 months	Formal Education Courses at the workplace Workshops or seminars at the workplace Planned periods of education, instruction or training directly at the workplace Private lessons with the aid of a teacher or tutor
Survey of Adult Skills (PIAAC)	1st: 2008–2013 2nd: 2012–2016 3rd: planned	OECD OECD countries	cross-sectional household survey	12 months	Formal education Open/distance education On-the job training/training by supervisors or co-workers Seminars/workshops Courses/private lessons

Source: Own description.

Mleczko, 2011). Since 2000, the survey took place in Member States and candidate Member States, including the Eastern European countries that joined the Union in 2004. Currently, the Labour Force Survey is a continuous survey that produces four datasets a year, one per quarter. Apart from a core questionnaire, each year, a separate ad hoc module is included. In 2003, this ad hoc module was about lifelong learning. In 2014, the ad hoc module explored the situation of migrants; in 2016, the focus will be on young people, in 2017 on self-employment. The core questionnaire of the LFS contains questions about individual demographics, household characteristics, family characteristics, economic activity, the main and second job, the fact of seeking a job, unemployment, benefit entitlement, the employment situation twelve months previously, education and training, health and injury, and income.

Adult Education Survey

The Eurostat Adult Education Survey was constructed to generate more detailed information on adult lifelong learning topics. The Labour Force Survey is a more general survey focussing on a wide range of work-related aspects, but does not ask detailed questions about participation in educational activities and training (European Commission, 2010; Boeren, 2014). Another difference between the two surveys is that participation in both formal and non-formal learning activities in the Adult Education Survey has been measured in a 12-month reference period prior to interview, not on a four-week reference period as is the case with the Labour Force Survey. The Adult Education Survey only samples adults between the age of 25 and 64, and does not survey young adults under the age of 25 as the Labour Force Survey does, which makes sense as the LFS needs to capture the trends of young adults entering the labour market. Going back to the fieldwork undertaken at the stage of developing the Eurostat AES, the European Commission made extensive reference to its 2001 Communication document 'Making a European Area of Lifelong Learning a Reality'. This document mentioned the need to perceive lifelong learning as a means to strengthen personal fulfilment, active citizenship, social inclusion and employability as a good mix of social and economic objectives, but is now widely criticised as being too focused on the economic aspects of lifelong learning strategies (Boeren, 2014). However, a need was felt to increase knowledge on specific adult lifelong learning themes and thus to develop a specialist survey to measure specific adult lifelong learning variables. The preparatory work for the AES started in June 2003 through a common European Task Force group who provided input to statistical offices at the country level. Finally, specific countries were responsible for data collection among their own citizens (Eurostat, 2007). The first Adult Education Survey was carried out between 2005 and 2008 and is commonly referred to as the Adult Education Survey 2007. In 2011 and 2012, the Adult Education Survey 2011 took place. It is expected that a new wave will be carried out over the next few years.

Looking at the information gathered in the AES, we notice indeed that more detailed data are being gathered on adult lifelong learning topics, compared to the LFS. The core questionnaire of the AES-2007 consisted of 11 sections gathering information about the household, the individual, the individual's participation in education and training, perceived obstacles to participation in education and training, informal learning activities, access to information about learning activities, the use of computer skills and foreign language skills, participation in cultural activities, participation in social activities and the individual's attitude towards learning (Boeren, 2014). Going back to the theoretical aspects of adult lifelong learning, it is clear that many of the individual psychological and sociological aspects can be analysed through use of the AES. However, information about lifelong learning activities is in fact based on what adults themselves have to say about them, and does not reflect on the core characteristics of the education or training institutions they participate in. Because of its international nature, the dataset can be used for European comparisons. However, we have to be careful about the methodological limitations. While the AES-2007 and AES-2011 were carried out in almost all EU countries, with the exception of Ireland and Luxembourg, during the period 2005–2008, and also in the two EFTA countries Norway and Switzerland, as well as candidate countries like Croatia (officially a member of the EU since 2013) and Turkey, survey methodology differed per country. Most Eastern and Southern European respondents had to complete the survey through paper and pencil interview mode (PAPI) (Eurostat, 2010). Other countries used computer aided tools only, or in combination with more traditional ways of interviewing. It is important to acknowledge these differences when analysing the data. As Groves et al. (2009, p. 34) argue 'each aspect of a survey has the potential to affect the results'.

Programme for the International Assessment of Adult Competencies

The main aim of PIAAC – the Programme for the International Assessment of Adult Competencies – is to measure the numeracy and literacy skills of adults, sampling between the ages of 15 and 65, within a specific Survey of Adult Skills (Allen et al., 2013; OECD, 2013c; Desjardins, 2015). The survey is managed by OECD, is often compared to the previous International Adult Literacy Survey (IALS) and is perceived as the PISA survey for adults as the survey collects data from young people and adults from the age of 16, while PISA is undertaken with 15-year-olds. The OECD (2013e, p. 25) summarises the key facts about PIAAC in the following way:

> The Survey of Adult Skills (PIAAC) assesses the proficiency of adults from age 16 onwards in literacy, numeracy and problem solving in technology-rich environments. These skills are 'key information-processing competencies' that are relevant to adults in many social contexts and work situations, and necessary for fully integrating and participating in the labour market, education and training and social and civic life. (OECD, 2013e, p. 25)

In total, 22 OECD countries and two partner countries (Cyprus and Russia) took part in the PIAAC survey during the period 2011–2012, and nine additional countries collected data in 2014, which will be released in 2016. The data collection period in 2011–2012 resulted in responses from 166,000 adults, who were surveyed in the major language of their country of residence (OECD, 2013e). The assessment task consisted of three components – problem solving, literacy and numeracy – but the problem solving assessment and the reading components were not compulsory, although more than 20 countries participated in all modules of the survey. The survey had to be completed together with an interviewer who used Computer Aided Personal Interviewing (CAPI) and respondents were allowed to spend as much time on the assessment task as they wanted, while time had to be recorded.

Data were released in October 2013 and apart from official OECD communication, there are not yet a lot of discussion notes or papers available that refer to the PIAAC results (*International Journal of Lifelong Education Editorial*, 2014), although a few do exist, e.g. Allen et al, 2013; Desjardins, 2015. As with other OECD or Eurostat surveys, the main driver for constructing and conducting the survey was to gather evidence with the aim to influence education policy, and in the case of PIAAC, the aim to map deficiencies in key competencies needed to participate in society at all levels such as the labour market, education and political engagement, in order to understand the relation between skills needed for participation in society and the performance of training systems in specific countries (OECD, 2013c). Based on an analysis of the results, OECD has already formulated several key issues to be considered by policy makers. These include the importance of detecting the skills and training needs of unemployed adults to better integrate them into the labour market, the need to provide accessible information about training opportunities, and the need for employers to make sure relevant and useful training is offered to their employees.

It is also important to explore the added value of working with data from PIAAC's Survey of Adult Skills. While the Adult Education Survey and the Labour Force Survey are typical European household surveys, PIAAC has been conducted in a range of non-European countries as well (in alphabetical order: Australia, Canada, Japan, Korea, Russian Federation, United States). The PIAAC survey collected information about participation in adult lifelong learning activities, similarly to the Adult Education Survey, measured on a 12 months basis, prior to the interview, and thus not on the shorter reference period of four weeks. Furthermore, the added value of PIAAC in addition to AES and LFS is the inclusion of scores on skill assessment tests. The first results of PIAAC's Survey of Adult Skills, as discussed by the OECD (2013c, p. 34), indicated that there is *'a strong positive relationship between participation in adult education and skills proficiency'* ... *'but those whose skills are already weak are less likely to improve their skills through adult education and training.'*

Different surveys: different results?

PIAAC's Survey of Adult Skills, AES and LFS are thus three major comparative lifelong learning surveys. One of the commonalities between these surveys is that they all measure participation in formal and non-formal education through a specific question, an important indicator being used in education policy making.

However, there are differences between the surveys. First of all, in relation to measuring participation, they have different reference periods. Secondly, while a common codebook is usually provided to specific country teams setting out the particular types of variables they have to measure, countries might engage differently with this codebook, might focus differently in the adaptation of turning variables into questions, which might lead to differences in adult lifelong learning participation rankings (Lavrijsen & Nicaise, 2015). Holford and Mleczko (2011) researched the way in which the common codebook of the Labour Force Survey had been translated in different European countries and found that those countries who adopted wide, broad and inclusive definitions of lifelong learning generally ended up with a higher participation rate. But also other methodological aspects vary: participation in the survey – if being sampled – is compulsory in a range of countries but in other countries is not. This might lead to a risk that the main respondents group will consist of specific types of adults as some other groups, e.g. long-term ill people or those living in remote areas, might be hard to reach. Exclusion of these groups might skew the data (Whitley Jr. & Kite, 2012). Non-response is a major problem in survey research, which can thus be worsened through self-selecting mechanisms in non-compulsory surveys.

Goglio and Meroni (2014) analysed the extent to which the different reference periods of surveys (four weeks versus 12 months) impact on lifelong learning rankings and made the following statement:

> Despite the different coverage period AES and LFS rank the 27 European countries in a quite similar way, across different definition of learning (formal and/or informal) and across stratification in different subgroups (age and labour status). Therefore if the interest lies in simply ranking the countries, using one or the other measure does not change dramatically the results. (Goglio & Meroni, 2014, p. 19)

Lavrijsen and Nicaise (2015) made a similar statement, demonstrating that there is no discussion about the fact that Scandinavian countries top all the rankings. However, taking into account the results of the three surveys, it can be said that the strongest differences appear at the level of non-formal participation. Comparing participation rates of younger adults (between the ages of 25 and 34) in non-formal learning, there is only a weak correlation between the results of the LFS and PIAAC's Survey of Adult Skills. The same conclusion has to be drawn for those in employment. General participation rates and those related to formal participation did correlate, and in fact, PIAAC and LFS have a rather strong general correlation, despite using a reference period of 12 months versus four weeks. It can be argued that a 12-month period is preferable as it gives a broader range, able to avoid seasonal effects dependent on the time of the year a respondent has been surveyed (Goglio & Meroni, 2014). Surveys with a 12-months period also generate a larger pool of respondents, which is useful for researchers who want to conduct secondary data analyses on these data sources who will be more confident to run sound statistical models on subgroups of participants, both as a general group, but also in relation to those participating in formal or non-formal education only. However, people might forget about a short induction workshop they attended more than half a year ago, and the advantage of a four-weeks period is that it corresponds to the reference period for other questions in the Labour Force Survey, a survey with a significantly longer history than the Adult Education Survey, which has only been conducted twice so far. PIAAC has only been conducted once. For comparisons over time, it can thus be argued that the four-week period of the LFS is still the best data source to use. The disadvantage of using LFS for time-related research is that it is a cross-sectional survey. While trends in society can be observed over time, it does not follow up on individuals.

Desjardins (2015), who analysed PIAAC data in relation to adult lifelong learning participation, also made some critical notes about the difficulty of comparing adult lifelong learning participation rates because of a range of problems with the different surveys. Similar to the arguments of Holford and Mleczko (2011), this analysis asserts that the wording of survey questions might have an impact on results. However, Desjardins (2015) rightly argues that this is not only a problem in relation to comparing countries, but also in the context of questions being re-formulated in new waves of a specific survey. The results might simply change because of the wording rather than representing a trend. This change in wording is thus an additional problem, on top of the surveys own interpretations of what counts as participation, and the different reference periods. PIAAC, conducted in 2012, is most similar to and often compared to IALS, another OECD survey that was conducted during the period 1994–1998. Desjardins (2015, p. 13) demonstrates that countries that participated both in IALS and PIAAC all show increased participation rates in adult lifelong learning activities. However, exploring trends based on European data – through the Adult Education Survey and the Labour Force Survey – it is clear that this trend is not positive in all countries: e.g. both AES and LFS (adults aged 25–64) show a significant drop in the UK, while the results based on PIAAC (adults aged 25–65) show an increase of around 10 percent. More detailed research about the how and why of these differences ideally needs to be conducted in the near future.

Surveys as research representing the positivist paradigm

The focus on benchmarks and indicators, measured through surveys, needs to be situated in the quantitative research paradigm of positivism (Lincoln & Guba, 1985; Yilmaz, 2013). Robson (2011, p. 21) outlines the characteristics of positivism as a science that generates value-free and objective knowledge or facts. It is a paradigm linked to one of the dominant views in natural sciences, but thus also used in social sciences. Positivist research is mostly done through collection and analysis of quantitative data which are tested against a set of hypotheses. Critics of positivism warn that surveys developed in the positivist tradition often represent dominant male middle-class viewpoints and state that it is unfair to claim the objective nature of these measurement instruments. Furthermore, as surveys are measuring 'facts', it is more difficult to understand the underlying meaning of these data. It could thus be questioned whether it is a good way forward to solely rely on a range of statistics that get monitored year after year against common standards – as is the case in the current lifelong learning policy climate – or whether more interpretivist approaches should be added. Positivist research approaches, such as working large-scale quantitative surveys, usually start from a deductive approach (Creswell, 2009). A theoretical model will be evaluated using a top-down approach and can be refined based on the outcome of the hypothetical model being (partially) rejected. The limitations in doing this are clear (Boeren, 2014). Nowadays, there is no suitable database available to test an interdisciplinary theoretical lifelong learning participation theory or model, and the question remains whether this will be achievable in the future. Furthermore, running the data into a statistical model still leaves us with the need for a more in-depth understanding of why certain mechanisms are happening, as opposed to the simple observation that they are happening. Understanding reality as constructed through the lenses of individuals is a core characteristic of interpretivism, in which the focus is more on contextualisation than generalisability. A combination of both might combine the need for empirical testing of theories, as well as gaining an in-depth understanding of the contexts in which lifelong learning participation is happening. Mixed methods research may also help to understand both the reliability and validity of existing adult lifelong learning participation theories. Using both deductive and inductive approaches would help to complete the research cycle and understand the truth in a more complete way. An example of a qualitative approach to understanding lifelong learning participation that takes into account changes in people's lives is biographical research, as discussed previously (Merrill & West, 2009).

The vagueness of participation

An exploration of journal articles in the field of adult lifelong learning participation research revealed that both quantitative and qualitative approaches are being used by scholars. However, leading research focussing on patterns of adult lifelong learning participation is mainly conducted using quantitative methodologies, mainly through analysis of the leading surveys. Rubenson (2011b) rightly points out that there is a lack of studies exploring participation patterns and barriers to participation from an in-depth qualitative approach. Participation rates as published by the agencies hoping to influence policy, such as 'Progression towards Benchmarks and Indicators – Education and Training' based on Eurostat data, and the OECD's 'Education at a Glance' report, are very meagre in terms of their content. The European Commission's report shows a graph setting out the progress of countries towards the benchmark of

15 percent adult lifelong learning participation, as defined in their core list of benchmarks to be achieved by 2020. The indicator 'adults participating in education and learning' by OECD is also presented using a graph, referring to participation in 'formal and/or non-formal education'. The presentation of these results gives a general picture of how countries are performing towards a general benchmark, but does not demonstrate the characteristics of participation. Detailed analysis of the Adult Education Survey makes clear that while participation in non-formal education among Hungarian adults is low (6.8 percent, compared to 69.4 percent in Sweden), those who do participate spend most hours in training (95 hours spent in education and training in Hungary compared to 24 hours in Sweden) (Mejer & Boateng, 2009). Similar differences in statistics appear when calculating the participation rate in formal learning activities (Hefler & Markowitch, in Brooks et al., 2012b, p. 162). The participation rate in formal education and training in the United Kingdom based on the Adult Education Survey 2007 is 15.1 percent, but exploring the participation rate for those who participate in programmes of more than 200 hours, the participation rate drops to 2 percent. The question is thus not only: do adults participate, but in what type of activities do these adults participate, and actually even more importantly, what levels of knowledge and skills, new competencies, new world views and attitudes do they develop?

The vagueness is problematic in terms of measuring lifelong learning participation, but does in fact correspond well to the dominant view that lifelong learning is not only meant to be 'lifelong' in terms of learning from cradle to grave, but that it is also meant to be life-wide, focussing on a wide range of interests and purposes, such as learning for citizenship, social cohesion and employment. In other terms, lifelong learning is meant to reflect on both 'vertical' and 'horizontal' learning (Ouane, in Jarvis, 2009, p. 302). Vertical refers to learning across the life span, similar to the term lifelong. Horizontal represents the idea of life-wide learning, which takes place in a wide range of life domains such as at work, in the family and the community.

The problem of vagueness is not limited to participation rates. Understanding why adults participate is also vital to generate insight into how policy makers and practitioners can undertake efforts to motivate potential adult learners to enrol for courses. The Labour Force

Survey, however, does not go beyond the dichotomous distinction between either 'job-related motivation' or 'personal motivation', while motivations are likely to interfere with each other and can be of a multidimensional nature or a continuum, as explored earlier.

Alternative scenarios for measuring adult lifelong learning participation

Issues with surveys might also open some avenues for improvement, for additional opportunities to be taken in order to increase the validity and reliability of data, but also in terms of making data a better fit to the needs of researchers who want to empirically validate their theoretical models. One – at first sight – straightforward solution might be to place a stronger focus on the meaning of concepts and definitions, although this might be difficult to achieve, as the meaning and nature of what constitutes an adult learning activity differs among countries. It is thus important to generate a good overview of what is available in the 'supply' side of the education and training market, e.g. starting from deepening structural overviews as provided by Eurydice in Europe. In addition to generating insight on definitions, and the need to design sound sampling and survey methodologies, I would like to focus on two more scenarios.

Firstly, while attrition is generally recognised as one of the major drawbacks of longitudinal research, an alternative scenario for data collection would be to introduce a longitudinal lifelong learning survey, as opposed to purely conducting cross-sectional surveys (Frees, 2004). PIAAC's Survey of Adult Skills, AES and LFS are cross-sectional and might therefore capture changes in society – e.g. mapping the problems of an ageing population – but are thus limited for use in research on the benefits of lifelong learning participation. I would argue that the evidence of benefits is extremely important, as it will provide insights for policy makers and practitioners on specific domains to focus on in their policy making. It is positive that some countries have developed their own longitudinal surveys, usable in lifelong learning participation research, but comparable data are needed as well. In the United Kingdom, the British Household Panel Survey, now included in the Understanding Society Survey has been used in a range of lifelong learning projects (see Macleod & Lambe, 2007; Blanden et al., 2010; Evans et al., 2013). The survey started in 1991. Households are approached and every adult (age 16 and over) in the household is included. The initial sample consisted of 5,500 households in England, Scotland and Wales. Northern Ireland joined the study in 2001. As a general household survey, respondents answer a wide range of questions in relation to health, income, financial issues, work and employment, but also education and training. As the same households are followed up, the survey makes a great resource for exploring people's patterns over time and how changes in participation are linked to changes in other life domains.

Secondly, I would argue that there is a lot of data available, but that it is fragmented. Data linkage or data matching might partly solve the issue of the need for integrative data (Christen, 2012). Census data, data from educational institutions, employment registers and adult lifelong learning providers are all available in one way or another. However, for data protection reasons, as well as because of the absence of unique identifiers, it is often impossible to link records together. A few countries have already mode progress: e.g. in The Netherlands, every person will have his or her unique number which will be entered every time they participate in a survey. If an adult participated in the Labour Force Survey at a specific point, but also participates in the Adult Education Survey (or basically in every other official survey gathered at the national level), records can be matched. Matching educational surveys with other surveys would help in assessing the impact lifelong learning is having (Tuijnman, 2003). In an ideal world, data sharing and linkages would provide a much better basis for undertaking research, both for fundamental and conceptual research and for extracting evidence to be used in arguments in policy making.

Conclusions

This chapter has provided short descriptions of the major comparative surveys measuring adult lifelong learning participation: PIAAC's Survey of Adult Skills, the Adult Education Survey and the Labour Force Survey. While general trends in participation extracted from the different surveys are comparable, trends in participation in non-formal education and training activities tend to differ for younger adults and those in employment. Survey limitations include the use of different definitions and differences in sampling and data collection methods across the countries involved. In relation to comparing the results of the three surveys, different reference periods for participation are being used, causing confusion. Future measurement of participation should ideally be supported by additional in-depth interviews to generate better understanding of the context of participation. It is recommended to introduce a longitudinal lifelong learning survey and to explore opportunities to match surveys with other databases.

9
Implications for Policy, Practice and Research

The final chapter of this book aims to reflect on the future. Previous chapters of the book have referred to insights on why adults do or do not participate in adult lifelong learning activities and how these differences can be explained by different levels of analysis relating to the individual, the lifelong learning education and training providers and the role of countries' various social policies. The need for an integrative approach has been presented and discussed. With all this knowledge now presented, what recommendations do I want to make for use of my work in both policy and practice, but also as a starting point for the development of future research projects exploring the role of lifelong learning in contributing to both society and individuals' lives?

Recommendations for policy

In formulating recommendations for policy, a feeling of sadness often overcomes me. I mention this because when exploring the recommendations of previous research undertaken years ago, often similar recommendations remain valid, which indicates the slow progress that is being made. Exploring the recommendations made by Desjardins et al. (2006), based on work undertaken about inequalities in adult lifelong learning participation, it has to be said that many of their recommendations could be repeated here. Their first recommendation, *'basis for public intervention in the planning of Adult Education and Training provision'*, still makes sense. If people, especially those who want to participate, do not participate because

166

of course offers not being available, it is important that this situation undergoes an evaluation. Equally, I agree with the recommendation on co-financing participation. Given the different players involved in participation, it is recommended that different parties explore the contributions they can make, including governments who can spend on public provision, but also firms and organisations offering private provision, and the adult learners themselves who are the participants. Furthermore, I agree with Desjardin et al.'s recommendation about the *'interplay between the private and public sectors'* and would link this to *'the need for integration of policies across policy sectors'*. One of the aims of this book has been to demonstrate and further understand the complexity of lifelong learning participation. It is so much more than an individual who returns to the education system; it relates to a much wider range of aspects influenced by the employment sector in which the adult is working, the benefit system available to them, the geographical area in which they live ... on top of all the individual psychological and sociological factors. It is thus extremely important that these different players understand each other, and cooperate, in order to create chances for everyone to benefit from participation in lifelong learning activities. While individuals and public providers have a role to play as well, I would like to reiterate the role of public funding as a means to stimulate and help, especially those from the most disadvantaged groups. Nowadays, there is a trend that governments cut their spending on education and training instead of investing in it, and it is important that society does not lose the public player which results in reinforcing the idea that lifelong learning is an individual, not collective, matter.

Apart from recommendations for policy made previously, which I have confirmed, I would like to formulate a range of additional ones.

Invest in longitudinal data collection

The current focus on benchmarks and indicators across the globe has seen the development of a number of relevant datasets in the field of lifelong learning, including the European Adult Education Survey in the beginning of the 2000s and the OECD's work on PIAAC. However, longitudinal datasets measuring participation will be more useful to fully understand the benefits compared to cross-sectional datasets as respondents will be followed over time. In cross-sectional datasets, a proportion of the population is included in different rounds, but these respondents are not the same. Cross-sectional data are suitable for understanding changes in society, but there is no doubt that longitudinal data would add valuable insights. Currently, some longitudinal datasets are available, e.g. the British Household Panel Study, now called Understanding Society, but good quality longitudinal data are not available everywhere. My recommendation therefore would be to stimulate policy makers to develop a longitudinal survey instead of releasing another cross-sectional survey like AES or PIAAC.

Provide a clear overview of the institutional architecture of the adult lifelong learning system

It has now become clear that participation in adult lifelong learning activities cannot take place if there is no offer available to fulfil the potential learner's need. However, it is important that there is an increased understanding of the availability of courses and programmes available to adults. In Europe, Eurydice provides data on the different types of institutions available in the countries of the European Union. However, in many countries, it is hard to find a strong overview of courses available to adults and it would be good to have a website in place to show the existence of educational initiatives on a country's map and to provide insight into the structure of the available systems.

Provide teacher education specifically for adult educators

In Chapter 6, I mentioned that many countries suffer from a lack of well-trained adult educators. Especially in developing countries, adult educators are often volunteers who did not undertake any teacher training. In developed countries, like the modern welfare states, educators are mostly trained as primary or secondary school teachers, but did not automatically receive training to cope with the demands of the adult learning sector. It is therefore important that policy makers create opportunities to provide specific training and professional development activities for those working in the adult lifelong learning sector.

Pay attention to mature and part-time learners instead of solely focussing on young learners

The term lifelong learning refers to learning 'from cradle to grave'. However, education policies tend to focus on the role of initial education, including the transition to higher education for younger learners. Attention to mature and part-time students is weaker. A clear example of this situation is happening in England where cuts have led to a significant drop in the number of part-time learners in Higher and Further Education. It is important for policy makers to recognise that a knowledge-based society needs to focus on learning in adult life as well. It is therefore recommended that they keep on supporting adult lifelong learning and publicly fund this domain in order to provide a range of activities and lower existing barriers to participation.

Stimulate innovation through adequate investment in Research and Development

Participation in lifelong learning activities will increase the skill and knowledge base of the workforce, but as stated before, countries have to take care that highly educated adults do not see their work being outsourced to other low income countries. It is therefore important that governments keep on investing in Research and Development to stimulate innovation in the workplace in order to optimise the workforce's skills, and thus create a 'high skills equilibrium', instead of ending up with an under-skilled population unable to perform work tasks, or an over-skilled population for which there is no work because of a lack of innovative working processes.

Provide initiatives that stimulate intergenerational learning

Especially within the chapters focussing on individual levels of participation, it became clear that it is important to develop a good range of psychological attributes such as a positive attitude towards learning, a strong self-determined motivation and high levels of self-efficacy and confidence. Discussions were provided on the role of social class and social mobility and the role of the 'habitus'. Instead of solely focussing on the role of initial education to create a better future for children, it is also important that policy makers think about initiatives to stimulate intergenerational learning. Parents with low educational attainment would profit from increasing their knowledge and skills because it is likely to have a positive effect on their children in terms of their attitudes towards education and learning. Learning starts indeed from the 'cradle', but providing adequate support during development is important as well.

Recommendations for practice

Previous research has provided a number of recommendations for practice. Feldman and Ng (in London, 2011, pp. 190–191) formulated a range of recommendations in relation to continuing education in the workplace. I agree with their comments on not forcing employees into too many learning activities if they do not want them. As explained in this book, participation is the result of an underlying decision-making process based on the formulation of an intention to participate. If this intention is lacking, one could question the usefulness of participation at all; this can be explained by going back to the motivational theories explored in one of the previous chapters: e.g. the self-determination theory asserts that those with very controlled, instrumental motivation are more likely to be engaged in surface learning, which is not something that should be stimulated. Feldman and Ng also focus on how employers can increase the smoothness of the participation process of their employees, which I would like to link back to the exploration in the chapter on institutional barriers. It does not make sense to ask employees to participate in training but not give them the time to do so. As an organisation offering lifelong learning activities, it is important to undertake efforts to lower institutional barriers.

In terms of work to be undertaken by practitioners, both in the public and private lifelong learning sectors, I would like to make additional recommendations.

Build partnerships with other social providers

Participation will not happen unless potential adult learners are aware of educational offers that will be able to fulfil their needs. It is thus extremely important that information reaches the right target groups and those in need of further learning. Especially for disadvantaged adults, it will be important to work together with other services in the community as they are unlikely to find detailed information themselves and are likely to need advice and guidance in their decision-making process to become an adult lifelong learning participant. Partnerships can also be built between different educational institutions offering lifelong learning activities at different levels in order to let learners experience a smooth transition.

Apply flexible entrance conditions through recognition of previous credentials, experience and learning

For those adults who did not obtain any qualifications in the past, it can be difficult to start participating in adult lifelong learning activities, especially in formal education activities, as they will have to start at the bottom of the ladder. However, several adults might have higher levels of skills and knowledge than their qualification record demonstrates, e.g. if they have gained these skills during work experience or because they have participated in non-formal non-credential based lifelong learning activities. It is therefore important that educational managers consider exploring alternative access routes into their programmes. If not, they will deprive a group of adults from developing themselves further.

Reserve part of the budget to facilitate access of underrepresented groups

From a social justice perspective, it is recommended that educational institutions undertake an effort to attract a wide range of learners, not only those with the strongest socio-economic profiles. It is therefore recommended that learning providers reserve part of their budget to attract underrepresented groups actively through providing them with adequate information, but also to offer them advice and guidance where needed.

Offer courses in flexible modes

Adult learners have multiple identities and often have to combine participation in adult lifelong learning activities with duties related to work and family. It is therefore important to organise learning activities at convenient times and to offer learners opportunities to participate during their preferred time and at their own pace. Several options are possible here. Institutions can consider moving towards more online and distance learning provisions, but they can also offer more extensive courses or programmes in shorter blocks and modules that can be taken separately. While more and more Higher Education Institutions are working with credit transfer systems and while many universities nowadays have distance learning activities in place, it is unclear, and probably unlikely, whether this would work for the most disadvantaged learners who have little or no previous (positive) learning experiences. For these learners, it is important to offer courses in such a way that they will be able to cope and persist in their efforts.

Put positive learning experiences from participants in the picture

Provision of information from educational providers does not only need to focus on the practical aspects of the learning activity; it is also important that potential learners have the motivation to undertake courses and that they have confidence in their own abilities to participate in learning activities successfully. Providing examples from adults who experienced a satisfactory learning experience is a good way to prepare the adult learner mentally for his or her learning journey.

Stimulate learners to provide informal promotion based on their own learning experiences

The literature points out that learners gather information through informational sources other than and in addition to existing websites or leaflets containing facts and figures about existing lifelong learning activities. Especially, disadvantaged groups seem to be sensitive to informal information and insights. It is therefore important that practitioners stimulate a positive learning experience among their learners, but that they also stimulate their peers to consider participating themselves.

Develop new programmes in areas where specific offers are not available

Various chapters in this book refer to the importance of the availability of educational offers. Adults will not participate in lifelong learning activities if a suitable learning activity does not exist, despite strong levels of motivation, confidence and positive attitudes towards learning. Those who have the highest odds to become an adult learner – based on their strong socio-economic and psychological background – will fail to finalise their decision-making process (see Baert et al., 2006) if a matching offer is lacking. Therefore, it is important that educational providers are sensitive to the needs of the community they serve. They can consider offering their learning activities in different locations, develop new non-existing programmes or widening their target groups through implementing online and distance learning provisions. This will help adults living in remote areas or in areas of high social deprivation which are known to have low adult lifelong learning participation statistics.

Courtney (1992) devotes the last chapter of his *Why Adults Learn* book to exploring some implications for practice. He focuses on the role of adult educators and how they can use knowledge of adult lifelong learning participation within their day-to-day practice. I would like to focus here again on what I have said in relation to motivating adult learners who are already participating in specific activities. Teaching and learning approaches and the creation of a positive classroom environment will help generate higher levels of satisfaction. Previous research has demonstrated this is strongly linked with stimulating autonomy among learners, while providing clear guidance on final learning objectives. It is important that adult educators generate knowledge about learning practices in adult learning activities on top of their general training.

Recommendations for future research

Ten years' ago, Desjardins et al. (2006) also formulated a range of recommendations for research. Their first point *'improving the information base'* is still very valid and some of my own recommendations below, as well as my decision to devote an entire chapter to 'measuring participation', demonstrate that there is still a lot of room for improvement, both at the level of data available for secondary analyses, as well as in terms of applying a range of research methods to answer participation related research questions. While Desjardins et al. (2006) also recommend undertaking more research linking country level institutional factors to the distribution of adult learning across these countries, it has to be said that research during the past ten years has evolved into this direction. The work undertaken by the Sixth European Framework project 'LLL2010: Towards a Lifelong Learning Society – the Contribution of the Education System' has led to a range of publications taking into account the country level. Also, another European project led by Blossfeld has increased knowledge in this area, alongside work undertaken by the London based LLAKES centre. What might be needed more in the next few years, is research that tries to incorporate the various factors into one single analytical model, using techniques like multilevel analysis.

Based on my own insights into adult lifelong learning participation, I would like to formulate the following recommendations for research.

Supplement the monitoring of indicators and benchmarks with in-depth qualitative research

At the policy level, the focus is on monitoring benchmarks and indicators towards specific targets, e.g. 15 percent adult lifelong learning participation in Europe by 2020. Research reports comparing lifelong learning participation across countries or regions are thus often based on quantitative analysis of survey or administrative data. However, it is recommended that more qualitative research in this area is undertaken in the near future, especially to gain more in-depth information on how adults perceive barriers and how adult learners have overcome these barriers. While statistics are very helpful to generate a clear bird's eye view, it is difficult to generate meaning from these findings. A mixed methods approach, supplementing survey and administrative data, would profit from the strengths of both quantitative and qualitative research approaches and would partly eliminate the weaknesses of using one single method.

Undertake multilevel research

Research often focuses on a single aspect, often the individual, or in more recent research on the level of countries in order to understand how lifelong learning policy aspects cluster together with other social policy characteristics. However, it is important to integrate different levels as decisions to participate in adult lifelong learning activities are shaped through interaction between the individual, the educational institution and the characteristics of the country's education and labour market policies. Statistical datasets are therefore best analysed using multilevel approaches in order to estimate how much of the variation in participation can be assigned to the country level or to the individual level. But also in qualitative research, it is recommended that scholars integrate the different levels in a comprehensible way to generate more in-depth insight into the interaction between the different agents.

Work together with specialists in social geographical research

It has been articulated many times that an educational offer needs to exist before a potential adult learner will be able to participate in an educational activity. How far are adult learners willing to travel to take part in learning activities? What about learners who live in deprived areas and who seem to be least likely to fulfil their learning intentions, even when they are highly educated? Research indicates that those who formulated an intention to participate but who did not participate in the end, were likely not to do so because the activity of their interest was simply not available to them. From higher education research, we know that learners from stronger socio-economic backgrounds are more likely to move away from home to attend a prestigious university compared to those who come from lower socio-economic classes, but who also obtained good results. In order to understand these mechanisms better in relation to adult learning, it is important to undertake extra research in this area.

Undertake extra (longitudinal) research on the economic and financial benefits of adult lifelong learning

An overview on the benefits of lifelong learning demonstrated that these can be positive, negative or non-significant. Field (2012) argued that we can feel fairly optimistic that lifelong learning participation results in positive benefits, both at the economic and the social level, although he admitted that effects size tend to be relatively small. However, there is still no clear agreement on the economic and financial benefits of learning and several research findings seem to contradict each other. It is important that additional research in this area is undertaken, ideally on longitudinal datasets. It is therefore important to encourage policy makers to make an investment in the development of longitudinal surveys in the area as these will provide the field with an added value on top of the existing cross-sectional datasets.

Undertake research about the participation in adult lifelong learning activities of people living in developing countries

Trends in adult lifelong learning participation demonstrate that the focus of lifelong learning programmes in developing countries is mainly on literacy training. However, it is difficult to generate a strong picture on the determinants of lifelong learning participation as research in these region tends to be poorly developed. Good quality data are also lacking. It is therefore recommended that scholars in the developed world work together with organisations in developing countries to understand their problems and challenges, with the aim to make the system more accessible and efficient for everyone, including women, who tend to have higher chances of remaining illiterate during adulthood.

Provide better understanding about how decision-making processes differ in relation to different types of learning activities.

As mentioned in the section on 'the vagueness of participation', it is important to understand that certain factors in the decision-making process might differ because of different needs that the adult is looking to fulfil. For policy makers, it is useful to generate insight about the best strategies to attract potential learners. While some of the underlying mechanisms, such as the availability of an offer, the learners' need for time and resources to pay for the course, will work in a wide range of scenarios; we can all feel that those interested in a knitting course will differ from those wanting to undertake an MBA programme. However, in the general European benchmark, they would fit within the same category: participants. More diversification is needed.

Final conclusions

To conclude this book, I would like to go back to the notion of the 'changing policy context', a core part of the title of this study. As explained in Part I, the focus of lifelong learning has evolved to a situation in which individual agency for taking part in learning, and individual initiative to increase one's skills and knowledge has become vital. Nowadays, we have to 'tame our own horses' and find our ways in a world that has become much more global and unstructured than it used to be. While I agree with the importance of individual agency and the need for people to undertake actions, I hope this book has demonstrated that participation in adult lifelong learning activities is much more than an outcome of motivational forces within the individual. I hope that people involved in policy making and those practising in the field realise that the individual is an important part in understanding the participation puzzle, but that education and training institutions, as well as governing bodies, can help in lowering barriers and stimulating access. Participation generates benefits for the individual as well as for society and it is therefore recommended to treat it as a shared responsibility between the state and its inhabitants. Additionally, I hope this book has been a helpful tool for my colleagues and students interested in improving their knowledge of adult lifelong learning participation theories.

References

Abell, P. (2000). Sociological theory and rational choice theory. In B. Turner (Ed.), *The Blackwell companion to social theory* (pp. 223–224). Oxford: Blackwell.

Ahmed, M. (2009). *The state and development of adult learning and education in Asia and the Pacific Regional synthesis report.* Hamburg: UNESCO Institute for Lifelong Learning.

Aiginger, K., & Guger, A. (2006). The European social model: from obstruction to advantage. *Progressive Politics, 4*(3), 1–5.

Aitchison, J., & Alidou, H. (2009). *The state and development of adult learning and education in Subsaharan Africa Regional synthesis report.* Hamburg: UNESCO Institute for Lifelong Learning.

Albasheer, A., Khasawneh, S., Abu Nabah, A., & Hailat, S. (2008). Perceptions of student teachers towards the effectiveness of co-operating teachers, school principals and university supervisors participating in the teacher education program in Jordan. *International Journal of Lifelong Education, 27*(6), 693–705.

Albrecht, J., van der Berg, G., & Vroman, S. (2007). *The aggregate labor market effects of the Swedish Knowledge Life programme.* Uppsala: Institute for Labour Market Policy Evaluation.

Aldridge, F., & Lavender, P. (2000). *The impact of learning on health.* Leicester: National Institute of Adult Continuing Education.

Allen, J., Levels, M., & van der Velden, R. (2013). *Skill mismatch and use in developed countries: evidence from the PIAAC study.* Maastricht: Maastricht University School of Business and Economics.

Allingham, M. (2002). *Choice theory: a very short introduction.* Oxford: Oxford University Press.

Almeida, R., & Aterido, R. (2008). *The incentives to invest in job training: do strict labor codes influence this decision? SP Discussion Paper No 0832.* Washington, D.C.: World Bank.

Ananiadou, K., Jenkins, A., & Wolf, A. (2003). *The benefits to employers of raising workplace basic skills levels: a literature review.* London: National Research and Development Centre.

Appelbaum, R., & Chambliss, W. (1997). *Sociology: a brief introduction.* New York: Longman.

Ashton, D., Brown, P., & Lauder, H. (2010). Skill webs and international human resource management: lessons from a study of the global skill strategies of transnational companies. *International Journal of Human Resource Management, 21*(6), 836–850.

Australian Bureau of Statistics. (2007). *Adult learning, Australia, 2006–07.* Canberra: Australian Bureau of Statistics.

Babchuk, W. A., & Courtney, S. (1995). Toward a sociology of participation in adult education programmes. *International Journal of Lifelong Education, 14*(5), 391–404.

Baert, H., De Rick, K., & Van Valckenborgh, K. (2006). Towards the conceptualisation of learning climate. In R. Vieira de Castro, A. V. Sancho & V. Guimaraes (Eds.), *Adult education: new routes new landscapes* (pp. 87–111). Braga: University de Minho.

Bandura, A. (1977). Self-efficacy: toward a unifying theory of behavioral change. *Psychological Review, 84*(2), 191–215.

Barros, R. (2012). From lifelong education to lifelong learning: discussion of some effects of today's neoliberal policies. *European Journal for Research on the Education and Learning of Adults, 3*(2), 119–134.

Basham, R. E., & Buchanan, F. R. (2009). A survey comparison of career motivations of social work and business students. *Journal of Social Work Education, 45*(2), 187–208.

Bassanini, A., Booth, A., Brunello, G., De Paola, M., & Leuven, E. (2005). *Workplace training in Europe – IZA Discussion Paper 1640.* Bonn: Institute for the Study of Labour.

Bassot, B., Barnes, A., & Chant A. (2014) *A practical guide to career learning and development.* London: Routledge.

Beck, U. (1992). *Risk society: towards a new modernity.* Thousand Oaks: Sage.

Becker, E. A., & Gibson, C. C. (1998). Fishbein and Ajzen's theory of reasoned action: accurate prediction of behavioral intentions for enrolling in distance education courses. *Adult Education Quarterly, 49*(1), 43–55.

Becker, G. S. (1964). *Human capital: a theoretical and empirical analysis, with special reference to education.* Chicago: University of Chicago Press.

Beckett, D., & Hager, P. (2002). *Life, work and learning: practice in postmodernity.* London: Routledge.

Bell, D. (1973). *The coming of post-industrial society. a venture in social forecasting.* New York: Basic Books.

Benavot, A., Huang, J., & Cervero, R. M. (1993). An analysis of structural factors associated with participation in state-funded adult basic education programmes. *International Journal of Lifelong Education, 12*(1), 17–25.

Berggren, C. (2011). The education–occupation match, seen from an educational perspective. *Scandinavian Journal of Educational Research, 55*(2), 105–120.

Bernardi, F., & Ballarino, G. (2014). Participation, equality of opportunity and returns to tertiary education in contemporary Europe. *European Societies, 16*(2), 422–442.

Bialostok, S., & Withman, R. (2012). Education and the risk society: an introduction. In S. Bialostok, R. Whitman & W. Bradley (Eds.), *Education and the risk society: theories, discourse and risk identities in education contexts* (pp. 1–34). Rotterdam: Sense Publishers.

Biesta, G. J. J. (2006). *Beyond learning: democratic education for a human future.* Boulder: Paradigm Publishers.

Billett, S. (2001). *Learning in the workplace: strategies for effective practice.* Crows Nest: Allen & Unwin.

Billett, S. (2002). Toward a workplace pedagogy: guidance, participation, and engagement. *Adult Education Quarterly, 53*(1), 27–43.

Birch, E. R., Le, A., & Miller, P. (2009). *Household divisions of labour: teamwork, gender and time*. Basingstoke: Palgrave Macmillan.

Blanden, J., Buscha, F., Sturgis, P., & Urwin, P. J. (2010). *Measuring the returns to lifelong learning*. London: Centre for the Economics of Education.

Blaschke, L. M. (2012). Heutagogy and lifelong learning: a review of heutagogical practice and self-determined learning. *The International Review of Research in Open and Distributed Learning, 13*(1), 56–71.

Blaxter, L., & Tight, M. (1995). Life transitions and educational participation by adults. *International Journal of Lifelong Education, 14*(3), 231–246.

Blossfeld, H. P., Kilpi-Jakonen, E., Vono de Vilhena, D., & Buchholz, S. (2014). *Adult learning in modern societies: an international comparison from a life-course perspective*. Cheltenham: Edward Elgar.

Blundell, R., Dearden, L., & Meghir, C. (1996). *The determinants and effects of work related training in Britain*. London: Institute for Fiscal Studies.

Blunt, A., & Yang, B. (1995). *An examination of the validity of the Education Participation Scale (EPS) and the Adult Attitudes towards Continuing Education Scale (AACES)*. Alberta: Adult Education Research Conference.

Blunt, A., & Yang, B. (2002). Factor structure of the adult attitudes toward adult and continuing education scale and its capacity to predict participation behavior: evidence for adoption of a revised scale. *Adult Education Quarterly, 52*(4), 299–314.

Boateng, S. K. (2009). *Significant country differences in adult learning*. Luxembourg: Eurostat.

Bobbitt-Zeher, D. (2007). The gender income gap and the role of education. *American Sociological Association, 80*(1), 1–22.

Boeren, E. (2011). *Participation in adult education: a bounded agency approach*. Leuven: Katholieke Universiteit Leuven.

Boeren, E. (2014). Evidence-based policy-making: the usability of the Eurostat Adult Education Survey. *International Journal of Lifelong Education, 33*(3), 275–289.

Boeren, E., & Holford, J. (2013). *Vocationalism varies a lot: motivational patterns of adult learners in 12 European countries*. Paper Presented at the ECS Seminar.

Boeren, E., Holford, J., Nicaise, I., & Baert, H. (2012). Why do adults learn? Developing a motivational typology across 12 European countries. *Globalisation, Societies and Education, 10*(2), 247–269.

Boeren, E., & Nicaise, I. (2013). Flemish formal adult education: (g)rowing against the stream? In E. Saar, O. B. Ure & J. Holford (Eds.), *Lifelong learning in Europe: national patterns and challenges* (pp. 187–205). Cheltenham: Edward Elgar.

Boeren, E., Nicaise, I., & Baert, H. (2010). Theoretical models of participation in adult education: the need for an integrated model. *International Journal of Lifelong Education, 29*(1), 45–61.

Boeren, E., Nicaise, I., Roosmaa, E. -L., & Saar, E. (2012). Formal adult education in the spotlight: profiles, motivations and experiences of participants in 12 European countries. In S. Riddell, J. Markowitsch & E. Weedon (Eds.), *Lifelong learning in Europe: equity and efficiency in the balance* (pp. 63–85). Bristol: Policy Press.

Bohman, J. (1992). The limits of rational choice theory. In J. Coleman & T. Fararo (Eds.), *Rational choice theory: advocacy and criticism* (pp. 207–228). Thousand Oaks: Sage.

Bonal, X., & Tarabini, A. (2013). The role of PISA in shaping hegemonic educational discourses, policies and practices: the case of Spain. *Research in Comparative and International Education, 8*(3), 335–341.

Bonoli, G. (2010). *The political economy of active labour market policy.* Edinburgh: Reconciliation of Work and Welfare in Europe RECWOWE.

Borowsky, A. (2013). *Monitoring adult learning policies: a theoretical framework and indicators EDU Working Paper 88.* Paris: OECD.

Boshier, R. (1971). Motivational orientations of adult education participants: a factor analytic exploration of Houle's typology. *Adult Education, 21*(2), 3–26.

Boshier, R. (1973). Educational participation and dropout: a theoretical model. *Adult Education, 4,* 282–288.

Boshier, R. (1998). Edgar Faure after 25 years: down but not out. In J. Holford, P. Jarvis & C. Griffin (Eds.), *International perspectives on lifelong learning* (pp. 3–20). London: Kogan Page.

Boshier, R., & Collins, J. B. (1985). The Houle typology after twenty-two years: a large-scale empirical test. *Adult Education Quarterly, 35*(3), 113–130.

Boudard, E., & Rubenson, K. (2003). Revisiting major determinants of participation in adult education with a direct measure of literacy skills. *International Journal of Educational Research, 39*(3), 265–281.

Bourdieu, P. (1984). *Distinction: a social critique of the judgement of taste.* London: Routledge.

Bourdieu, P. (1986). The forms of capital. In J. Richardson (Ed.), *Handbook of theory and research for the sociology of education* (pp. 241–258). New York: Greenwood.

Bowes, L. (2008). *Mapping information, advice and guidance (IAG) and learner support for vocational and work-based learners in Birmingham, the Black Country and Solihull.* Birmingham: Black Country and Solihull Lifelong Learning Network.

Breakspear, S. (2012). *The policy impact of PISA: an exploration of normative effects of international benchmarking in school system performance – OECD working paper.* Paris: OECD.

Brockett, R. G., & Hiemstra, R. (1991). *Self-direction in adult learning: perspectives on theory, research and practice.* London: Routledge.

Broek, S., & Hake, B. (2012). Increasing participation of adults in higher education: factors for successful policies. *International Journal of Lifelong Education, 31*(4), 397–417.

Bronfenbrenner, U. (1979). *The ecology of human development: experiments by nature and design.* Cambridge, MA: Harvard University Press.

Brookfield, S. (2010). Theoretical frameworks for understanding the field. In C. E. Kasworm, A. D. Rose & J. M. Ross-Gordon (Eds.), *Handbook of adult and continuing education* (pp. 71–82). Thousand Oaks: Sage.

Brown, B. A., & Duku, N. S. (2008). Participation politics: African parents' negotiation of social identities in school governance and its policy implications. *International Journal of Lifelong Education, 27*(4), 413–429.

Brown, P. (2013). Education, opportunity and the prospects for social mobility. *British Journal of Sociology of Education, 34*(5–6), 678–700.

Brown, P., Lauder, H., & Ashton, D. (2011). *The global auction the broken promises of education, jobs and incomes.* Oxford: Oxford University Press.

Brunello, G. (2001). On the complementarity between education and training in Europe. Padova: University of Padova.

Brunello, G., Garibaldi, P., & Wasmer, E. (2007). *Education and training in Europe.* Oxford: Oxford University Press.

Busemeyer, M. (2015). *Skills and inequality. Partisan politics and the political economy of education reforms in Western welfare states.* Cambridge: Cambridge University Press.

Busemeyer, M., & Thelen, K. (2015). Non-standard employment and systems of skill formation in European countries. In W. Eichhorst & P. Marx (Eds.), *Non-standard employment in post-industrial labour markets: an occupational perspective* (pp. 401–430). Cheltenham: Edward Elgar.

Busemeyer, M., & Trampusch, C. (2011). *The comparative political economy of collective skill formation systems.* Oxford: Oxford University Press.

Butterwick, S., & Egan, J. P. (2010). Sociology of adult and continuing education: some key understandings for the field of practice. In C. E. Kasworm, A. D. Rose & J. M. Ross-Gordon (Eds.), *Handbook of adult and continuing education* (pp. 113–122). Thousand Oaks: Sage.

Byrd, S. R. (1990). *Perceptions and barriers to undergraduate education by nontraditional students at selected non-public, liberal arts institutions in the mid-south.* Paper Presented at the Annual Conference of the Mid-South Educational Research Association.

Callender, C. (2011). Widening participation, social justice and injustice: part-time students in higher education in England. *International Journal of Lifelong Education, 30*(4), 469–487.

Callender, C. (2013). Widening participation, social justice and injustice: part-time students in higher education in England. In S. Jackson (Ed.), *Challenges and inequalities in lifelong learning and social justice* (pp. 39–58). London: Routledge.

Campbell, M. (2012). *Skills for prosperity? A review of OECD and partner country skill strategies.* London: Centre for Learning and Life Chances in Knowledge Economies and Societies.

Canadian Council on Learning. (2010). *Composite Learning Index.* Ottawa: Canadian Council on Learning.

Carp, A., Petersen, R., & Roelfs, P. (1973). *Learning interests and experiences of adult Americans.* Berkley: Educational Testing Service.

Castejon, J. M. (2011). *Developing qualifications frameworks in EU partner countries.* London: Anthem Press.

CEDEFOP. (2013). *Global national qualifications framework inventory.* Thessaloniki: CEDEFOP.

Chapman, J., Cartwright, P., & McGilp, J. (2006). *Lifelong learning, participation and equity*. Dordrecht: Springer.

Chapman, J., McGilp, J. E., Cartwright, P., De Souza, M., & Toomey, R. (2006). Overcoming barriers that impede participation in lifelong learning. In J. Chapman, P. Cartwright & J. E. McGilp (Eds.), *Lifelong learning, participation and equity* (pp. 151–174). Dordrecht: Springer.

Chauhan, C. P. S. (2009). Lifelong learning on the Indian subcontinent: policies, programmes and progress. In P. Jarvis (Ed.), *The Routledge international handbook of lifelong learning* (pp. 491–501). London: Routledge.

Chickering, A. W., & Havighurst, R. J. (1981). The life cycle. In A. W. Chickering (Ed.), *The modern American college: responding to the new realities of diverse students and a changing society* (pp. 16–50). San Francisco: Jossey-Bass.

Christen, P. (2012). *Data matching: concepts and techniques for record linkage, entity resolution, and duplicate detection*. Heidelberg: Springer.

Cohn, S. (1999). *Race, gender, and discrimination at work*. New York: Perseus.

Colley, H., Hodkinson, P., & Malcolm, J. (2003). *Informality and formality in learning*. London: Learning and Skills Research Centre.

Cook, B., & King, J. E. (2004). *Low-income adults in profile: improving lives through higher education*. Washington, D.C.: American Council on Education.

Cookson, P. S. (1983). *Determinants of adult educational participation*. Paper Presented at the Twenty-Fourth Annual Adult Education Research Conference, Montreal.

Cookson, P. S. (1986). A framework for theory and research on adult education participation. *Adult Education Quarterly, 36*(3), 130–141.

Coulombe, S., & Tremblay, J. -F. (2007). Explaining cross-country differences in job-related training: macroeconomic evidence from OECD countries. *Économie internationale, 110*(1), 5–29.

Courtney, S. (1992). *Why do adults learn? Towards a theory of participation in adult education*. London: Routledge.

Cranton, P. (2006). *Understanding and promoting transformative learning*. San Francisco: Jossey-Bass.

Creswell, J. W. (2009). *Research design: qualitative, quantitative and mixed approaches: 3rd edition*. Thousand Oaks: Sage.

Cross, K. P. (1981). *Adults as learners*. San Francisco: Jossey-Bass.

Crouch, C., Finegold, D., & Sako, M. (1999). *Are skills the answer? The political economy of skill creation in advanced industrial societies*. Oxford: Oxford University Press.

Culpepper, P., & Finegold, D. (1999). *The German skills machine: sustaining comparative advantage in a global economy*. Berghahn Books: New York.

Dammrich, J., Vono de Vilhena, D., & Reichart, E. (2014). Participation in adult learning in Europe: the impact of country-level and individual characteristics. In H. P. Blossfeld, E. Kilpi-Jakonen, D. Vono de Vilhena, S. Buchholz (Eds.), *Adult learning in modern societies: an international comparison from a life-course perspective* (pp. 29–55). Cheltenham: Edward Elgar.

Darkenwald, G. G., & Merriam, S. (1982). *Adult education: foundations to practice*. New York: Harper & Row.

Darkenwald, G. G., & Valentine, T. (1985). Factor structure of deterrents to public participation in adult education. *Adult Education Quarterly, 35*(4), 177–193.

Darkenwald, G. G., & Valentine, T. (1986). *Measuring the social environment of adult education classrooms.* Paper Presented at the Adult Education Research Conference, Syracuse University.

De Coulon, A., Marcenaro-Gutierrez, F., & Vignoles, A. (2007). *The value of basic skills in the British labour market.* London: Centre for the Economics of Education, London School of Economics.

De Coulon, A., & Vignoles, A. (2008). *An analysis of the benefit of NVQ2 qualifications acquired at age 26–34.* London: Centre for the Economics of Education, London School of Economics.

De Frel, J. (2009). *Welfare state classification: the development of Central Eastern European welfare states.* Rotterdam: University of Rotterdam.

Deci, E. L., & Ryan, R. M. (2013). *Handbook of self-determination research.* Rochester: University of Rochester Press.

Dehmel, A. (2006). Making a European area of lifelong learning a reality? Some critical reflections on the European Union's lifelong learning policies. *Comparative Education, 42*(1), 46–62.

Deissinger, T. (2014). TVET system research. In Z. Zhao & F. Rauner (Eds.), *Areas of vocational education research* (pp. 91–108). Berlin: Springer.

Delors, J., UNESCO., & International Commission on Education for the Twenty-First Century. (1996). *Learning: the treasure within : report to UNESCO of the International Commission on Education for the Twenty-First Century.* Paris: United Nations Educational, Scientific and Cultural Organization.

Dench, S., & Regan, J. (1999). *Learning in later life: motivation and impact.* London: Department for Education and Employment.

Department of Education, Employment and Work Relations (2009). *The development and state of the art of adult learning and education (ALE) national report of Australia.* Canberra: Department of Education, Employment and Workplace Relations.

Descy, P. (2006). Review of European and international statistics. In T. Tikkanen & B. Nyhan (Eds.), *Promoting lifelong learning for older workers: an international overview* (pp. 68–89). Luxembourg: Office for Official Publications of the European Communities.

Desjardins, R. (2015). *Participation in adult education opportunities: evidence from PIAAC and policy trends in selected countries – background paper prepared for the Education for All Global Monitoring Report 2015.* Los Angeles: University of California.

Desjardins, R., & Rubenson, K. (2011). *An analysis of skill mismatch using direct measures of skills.* Paris: OECD.

Desjardins, R., Rubenson, K., & Milana, M. (2006). *Unequal chances to participate in adult learning: international perspectives.* Paris: UNESCO.

Desmedt, E., Groenez, S., & Van den Broeck, G. (2006). *Onderzoek naar de systeemkenmerken die de participatie aan levenslang leren in de EU-15 beïnvloeden.* Leuven: Katholieke Universiteit Leuven.

Dieckhoff, M., Jungblut, J. M., & O'Connell, P. J. (2007). Job-related training: do institutions matter? In D. Gallie (Ed.), *Employment regimes and the quality of work* (pp. 77–103). Oxford: Oxford University Press.

Dobele, A. R., Rundle-Thiele, S., & Kopanidis, F. (2014). The cracked glass ceiling: equal work but unequal status. *Higher Education Research & Development, 33*(3), 456–468.

Dorsett, R., Liu, S., & Weale, M. (2010). *Economic benefits of lifelong learning.* London: National Institute of Economic and Social Research.

Downes, P. (2014). *Access to education in Europe: a framework and agenda for system change.* Dordrecht: Springer.

Ekström, E. (2003). *Earnings effects of adult secondary education in Sweden.* Uppsala: Institute for Labour Market Policy Evaluation.

Elias, W., & Vanwing, T. (2002). *De opleiding sociale en culturele agogiek aan de Vrije Universiteit Brussel.* Leuven/Apeldoorn: Garant.

Engel, L. C. (2015). Steering the national: exploring the education policy uses of PISA in Spain. *European Education, 47*(2), 100–116.

Engel, L. C., & Frizzell, M. (2015). Competitive comparison and PISA bragging rights: sub-national uses of the OECD's PISA in Canada and the USA. *Discourse: Studies in the Cultural Politics of Education, 36*(5), 665–682.

Eraut, M. (2000). Non-formal learning, implicit learning and tacit knowledge. In F. Coffield (Ed.), *The necessity of informal learning* (pp. 12–31). Bristol: Policy Press.

Eraut, M., Alderton, J., Cole, G., & Senker, P. (1998). Learning from other people at work. In F. Coffield (Ed.), *Learning at work* (pp. 37–48). Bristol: Policy Press.

Eraut, M., & Hirsch, W. (2009). *The significance of workplace learning for individuals, groups and organisations.* Oxford: SKOPE.

Erikson, E. (1982). *The life cycle completed.* New York: Norton.

Erikson, R., & Goldthorpe, J. H. (1992). *The constant flux: a study of class mobility in industrial societies.* Oxford: Oxford University Press.

Erikson, R., & Goldthorpe, J. H. (2010). Has social mobility in Britain decreased? Reconciling divergent findings on income and class mobility. *The British Journal of Sociology, 61*(2), 211–230.

Ertl, H. (2006). Educational standards and the changing discourse on education: the reception and consequences of the PISA study in Germany. *Oxford Review of Education, 32*(5), 619–634.

Esping-Andersen, G. (1989). *The three worlds of welfare capitalism.* Cambridge: Polity Press.

European Commission (2001). *Making a European area of lifelong learning a reality.* Brussels: European Commission.

European Commission (2002). *European report on quality indicators of lifelong learning: fifteen quality indicators.* Brussels: European Commission.

European Commission (2009). *Strategic framework for education and training.* Brussels: European Commission.

European Commission (2010). *Europe 2020. A European strategy for smart, sustainable and inclusive growth.* Brussels: European Commission.

European Union. (2011). *The European Credit System for Vocational Education and Training (ECVET): get to know ECVET better, questions and answers.* Brussels: European Union.

Eurostat. (2007). *Task force report on Adult Education Survey.* Luxembourg: Eurostat.

Eurostat. (2010). *Synthesis quality report Adult Education Survey.* Luxembourg: Eurostat.

Eurostat. (2011). *Labour Force Survey in the EU, Candidate and EFTA countries: main characteristics of the national surveys: 2004.* Luxembourg: Eurostat.

Eurostudent. (2009). *Social and economic conditions of student life in Europe.* Bielefeld: Eurostudent.

Evans, K., Schoon, I., & Weale, M. (2013). Can lifelong learning reshape life chances? *British Journal of Educational Studies, 61*(1), 25–47.

Feinstein, L., & Hammond, C. (2004). The contribution of adult learning to health and social capital. *Oxford Review of Education, 30*(2), 199–221.

Fejes, A., & Nylander, E. (2014). The Anglophone international(e): a bibliometric analysis of three adult education journals, 2005–2012. *Adult Education Quarterly, 64*, 222–239.

Feldman, D. C., & Ng, T. W. H. (2011). Participation in continuing education programs: antecedents, consequences and implications. In M. London (Ed.), *The Oxford handbook of lifelong learning* (pp. 180–194). Oxford: Oxford University Press.

Fenger, H. (2007). Welfare regimes in Central and Eastern Europe: incorporating post-communist countries in welfare regime typology. *Contemporary Issues and Ideas in Social Sciences, 3*(2), 1–30.

Field, J. (2005). *Social capital and lifelong learning.* Bristol: Policy Press.

Field, J. (2012). Is lifelong learning making a difference? Research-based evidence on the impact of adult learning. In D. Aspin, J. Chapman, K. Evans & R. Bagnall (Eds.), *Second international handbook of lifelong learning* (pp. 887–897). Dordrecht: Springer.

Field, J., Merrill, B., & West, L. (2012). Life history approaches to access and retention of non-traditional students in higher education: a cross-European approach. *European Journal for Research on the Education and Learning of Adults, 3*(1), 77–89.

Findsen, B., & Formosa, M. (2011). *Lifelong learning in later life.* Dordrecht: Springer.

Finegold, D., & Soskice, D. (1988). The failure of training in Britain: analysis and prescription. *Oxford Review of Economic Policy, 4*(3), 21–53.

Finger, M. (1989). The biographical method in adult education research. *Studies in Continuing Education, 11*(1), 33–42.

Finnegan, F., Merrill, B., & Thunborg, C. (2014). *Student voices on inequalities in European higher education: challenges for theory, policy and practice in a time of change.* London: Routledge.

Fishbein, M., & Ajzen, I. (1980). *Understanding attitudes and predicting social behavior.* Englewood Cliffs, NJ: Prentice Hall.

Frees, E. W. (2004). *Longitudinal and panel data: analysis and applications in the social sciences*. Cambridge: Cambridge University Press.

Freire, P. (1970). *Pedagogy of the oppressed*. New York: The Seabury Press.

Froy, F., & Giguère, S. (2010). *Putting in place jobs that last*. Paris: OECD.

Fujita-Starck, P. J. (1996). Motivations and characteristics of adult students: factor stability and construct validity of the educational participation scale. *Adult Education Quarterly, 47*(1), 29–40.

Fuller, A., & Unwin, L. (2011). Workplace learning and the organization. In M. Malloch, L. Cairns, K. Evans & B. N. O'Connor (Eds.), *The SAGE handbook of workplace learning*. Thousand Oaks: Sage.

Gaillard, M., & Desmette, D. (2010). (In)validating stereotypes about older workers influences their intentions to retire early and to learn and develop. *Basic and Applied Social Psychology, 32*(1), 86–98.

Gershuny, J. (2000). *Changing times: work and leisure in postindustrial society*. Oxford: Oxford University Press.

Giddens, A. (1984). *The constitution of society: outline of the theory of structuration*. Cambridge: Polity Press.

Giddens, A. (1998). *The third way: the renewal of social democracy*. Cambridge: Polity Press.

Gilligan, C. (1986). *In a different voice*. Cambridge, MA: Harvard University Press.

Ginsberg, M. B. (2004). *Motivation matters: a workbook for school change*. San Francisco: Jossey-Bass.

Ginsberg, M. B., & Wlodkowski, R. J. (2010). Access and participation. In C. E. Kasworm, A. D. Rose & J. M. Ross-Gordon (Eds.), *Handbook of adult and continuing education* (pp. 25–34). Thousand Oaks: SAGE.

Goglio, V., & Meroni, E. C. (2014). *Adult participation in lifelong learning. The impact of using a 12-months or 4-weeks reference period. Technical briefing*. Ispra: Joint Research Centre of the European Commission.

Goldthorpe, J. H., & Jackson, M. (2007). Intergenerational class mobility in contemporary Britain: political concerns and empirical findings. *The British Journal of Sociology, 58*(4), 525–546.

Gorard, S. (2009). The potential lifelong impact of schooling. In P. Jarvis (Ed.), *The Routledge international handbook of lifelong learning* (pp. 91–101). London: Routledge.

Gorard, S., & Smith, E. (2006). Beyond the 'learning society': what have we learnt from widening participation research? *International Journal of Lifelong Education, 25*(6), 575–594.

Gould, R. L. (1990). Clinical lessons from adult development. In A. Nemiroff & C. A. Colarusso (Eds.), *New dimensions in adult development* (pp. 345–370). New York: Basic Books.

Green, A. (1999). Education and globalization in Europe and Asia: convergent and divergent trends. *Journal of Education Policy, 14*(1), 55–71.

Green, A. (2006). Models of lifelong learning and the 'knowledge society'. *Compare, 36*(3), 307–325.

Green, A., & Green, F. (2012). *A proposed framework for the OECD skills strategy. Conceptual report written for OECD.* London: LLAKES.

Green, A., Janmaat, G., & Han, C. (2009). *Regimes of social cohesion.* London: Centre for Learning and Life Chances in Knowledge Economies and Societies.

Green, C. L. (1998). *An investigation of the perceived barriers to undergraduate education for nontraditional students at Montana State University Northern.* Montana: Montana State University.

Grek, S. (2008). From symbols to numbers: the shifting technologies of education governance in Europe. *European Education Research Journal, 7*(2), 208–218.

Grek, S. (2009). Governing by numbers: the PISA effect in Europe. *Journal of Education Policy, 24*(1), 23–37.

Grek, S., & Ozga, J. (2010). Governing education: England, Scotland the contrasting uses of 'Europe'. *British Educational Research Journal, 36*(6), 937–952.

Greller, M., & Strohl, L. (2004). Making the most of 'late-career' for employers and workers themselves: becoming elders not relics. *Organizational Dynamics, 33*(2), 202–212.

Griffin, C. (2010). Policy and lifelong learning. In P. Jarvis (Ed.), *The Routledge international handbook of lifelong learning* (pp. 261–270). London: Routledge.

Griffith, W. S. (1991). Cyril O. Houle. In P. Jarvis (Ed.), *Twentieth century thinkers in adult education* (pp. 147–168). London: Routledge.

Groenez, S., Desmedt, E., & Nicaise, I. (2007). *Participation in lifelong learning in the EU-15: the role of macro-level determinants.* Paper Presented at the European Conference for Education Research.

Grotelueschen, A.D., & Caulley, D.N. (1977). A model for studying determinants of intention to participate in continuing education. *Adult Education, 28*, 22-37.

Grotluschen, A. (2010). *Erneuerung der interessetheorie: die genese von interesse an erwachsenen- und weiterbildung.* Wiesbaden: VS Verlag fur Sozialwissenschaften.

Groves, R. M., Fowler, Jr. F. J., Couper, M. P., Lepkowski, J. M., Singer, E., & Tourangeau, R. (2009). *Survey methodology.* Hoboken, NJ: John Wiley & Sons.

Guruz, K. (2011). *Higher education and international student mobility in the global knowledge economy.* New York: State University of New York Press.

Hake, B. J. (2014). 'Bringing learning closer to home': understanding 'outreach work' as a mobilisation strategy to increase participation in adult learning. In G. K. Zarifis & M. N. Gravani (Eds.), *Challenging the 'European Area of Lifelong Learning': a critical response.* Dordrecht: Springer.

Hall, P. A., & Soskice, D. (2001). An introduction to varieties of capitalism. In P. A. Hall & D. Soskice (Eds.), *Varieties of capitalism: the institutional foundations of comparative advantage* (pp. 1–68). Oxford: Oxford University Press.

Hammond, C., & Feinstein, L. (2006). *Are those who flourished at school healthier adults? What role for adult education? Research report 17.* London: Centre for Research on the Wider Benefits of Learning.

Hansen, H. (2012). Review Symposium: Phillip Brown, Hugh Lauder and David Ashton, the global auction: the broken promises of education, jobs, and incomes. *Socio-Economic Review, 10*(4), 784.

Harkness, S. (2009). The household division of labour: changes in families' allocation of paid and unpaid work. In J. L. Scott, S. Dex & H. Joshi (Eds.), *Women and employment: changing lives and new challenges* (pp. 234–267). Cheltenham: Edward Elgar.

Hase, S. & Kenyon, C. (2000). *From andragogy to heutagogy.* Melbourne: Royal Melbourne Institute of Technology.

Heath, B. A., & Payne, C. (1999). *Twentieth century trend in social mobility in Britain. Working paper No. 70.* Oxford: Centre for Research into Elections and Social Trends University of Oxford.

Hefler, G. (2010). *The qualification supporting company: the significance of formal adult education in small and medium organisations. Comparative report LLL2010 Subproject 4.* Krems: Danube University.

Hefler, G. (2013). *Taking steps. Formal adult education in private and organisational life: a comparative overview.* Vienna: Lit Verlag.

Hefler, G., & Markowitsch, J. (2008). To train or not to train: explaining differences in average enterprises' training performance in Europe – a framework approach. In J. Markowitsch & G. Hefler (Eds.), *Enterprise training in Europe: comparative studies on cultures, markets and public support initiatives* (pp. 24–63). Vienna: Lit Verlag.

Hefler, G., & Markowitsch, J. (2010). Formal adult learning and working in Europe: a new typology of participation patterns. *Journal of Workplace Learning, 22*(1), 79–93.

Hefler, G., & Markowitsch, J. (2012a). Bridging institutional divides: linking education, careers and work in 'organizational space' and 'skill space' dominated employment systems. In R. Brooks, A. Fuller & J. Waters (Eds.), *Changing spaces of education: new perspectives on the nature of learning* (pp. 160–181). London: Routledge.

Hefler, G., & Markowitsch, J. (2012b). The qualification-providing enterprise? Support for formal adult education in small and medium-sized enterprises. In S. Riddell, J. Markowitsch & E. Weedon (Eds.), *Lifelong learning in Europe: equity and efficiency in the balance* (pp. 103–124). Bristol: Policy Press.

Henry, M., Lingard, B., Rizvi, F., & Taylor, S. (2001). *The OECD, globalisation and education policy.* Amsterdam: Pergamon.

Hodkinson, P., & Hodkinson, H. (2001). *Problems of measuring learning and attainment in the workplace: complexity, reflexivity and the localised nature of understanding.* Paper Presented at the Conference on Context, Power and Perspective: Confronting the Challenges to Improving Attainment in Learning at Work.

Hodkinson, P., Sparkes, A. C., & Hodkinson, H. (1996). *Triumphs and tears: young people, markets and the transition from school to work.* London: David Fulton.

Hofstede, G. (1984). The cultural relativity of the quality of life concept. *The Academy of Management Review, 9*(3), 389–398.

Holford, J., & Mleczko, A. (2011). *The European indicator of adult participation in lifelong learning: the significance of interview questions.* Paper Presented at the 41th Annual SCUTREA Conference.

Holford, J., Riddell, S., Weedon, E., Litjens, J., & Hannan, G. (2008). *Patterns of lifelong learning, policy and practice in an expanding Europe.* Vienna: Lit Verlag.

Holford, J., & Mohorčič-Špolar, V. A. (2012). Neoliberal and inclusive themes in European lifelong learning policy. In S. Riddell, J. Markowitsch & E. Weedon (Eds.), *Lifelong learning in Europe: equity and efficiency in the balance* (pp. 39–61). Bristol: Policy Press.

Holmes, T. H., & Rahe, R. H. (1967). The social readjustment rating scale. *Journal of Psychosomatic Research, 11*(2), 213–221.

Hoskins, B., Cartwright, F., & Schoof, U. (2010). *Making lifelong learning tangible: the ELLI index Europe 2010.* Gutersloh: Bertelsmann Stiftung.

Houle, C. O. (1940). *The coordination of adult education at the state level. Doctoral dissertation.* Chicago: University of Chicago.

Houle, C. (1960). *The effective board.* New York: National Board of Young Men's Christian Association.

Houle, C. O. (1961). *The inquiring mind.* Wisconsin: University of Wisconsin Press.

Houle, C. O. (1964). *Continuing your education.* New York: McGraw-Hill.

Houle, C. O. (1972). *The design of education.* San Francisco: Jossey-Bass.

Houle, C. O. (1973). *The external degree.* San Francisco: Jossey-Bass.

Houle, C. O. (1980). *Continuing learning in the professions.* San Francisco: Jossey-Bass.

Houle, C. O. (1984). *Patterns of learning: new perspectives on life-span education.* San Francisco: Jossey-Bass.

Hudson, L., Bhandari, R., Peter, K., & Bills, D. B. (2005). *Labor force participation in formal work-related education in 2000–01 statistical analysis report.* Washington, D.C.: National Center for Education Statistics.

Hunt, D. M. (1986). *Formal vs informal mentoring: towards a framework.* Paper Presented at the First International Conference on Mentoring.

Hurtz, G. M., & Williams, K. J. (2009). Attitudinal and motivational antecedents of participation in voluntary employee development activities. *Journal of Applied Psychology, 94*(3), 635–653.

Iannelli, C., & Paterson, L. (2005). *Does education promote social mobility? CES Briefing 35.* Edinburgh: Centre for Educational Sociology University of Edinburgh.

Illeris, K. (2009). Lifelong learning as a psychological process. In P. Jarvis (Ed.), *The Routledge international handbook of lifelong learning* (pp. 401–410). London: Routledge.

Ioannidou, A. (2007). A comparative analysis of new governance instruments in the transnational educational space: a shift to knowledge-based instruments? *European Educational Research Journal, 6*(4), 336–347.

James, K. (2004). *Winning hearts and minds: how to promote health and well-being through participation in adult learning.* Leicester: National Institute of Adult Continuing Education.

Jarvis, P. (1991). *Twentieth century thinkers in adult education.* London: Routledge.

Jarvis, P. (2010). *The Routledge international handbook of lifelong learning.* London: Routledge.

Jauhiainen, A., Nori, H., & AlhoMalmelin, M. (2007). Various portraits of Finnish Open University students. *Scandinavian Journal of Educational Research, 51*(1), 23–39.

Jenkins, A., Vignoles, A., Wolf, A., & Galindo-Rueda, F. (2003). The determinants and labour market effects of lifelong learning. *Applied Economics, 35,* 1711–1721.

Johnstone, J. W., & Rivera, R. J. (1965). *Volunteers for learning.* Chicago: Aldine.

Jung, J.-C., & Cervero, R. M. (2002). The social, economic and political contexts of adults' participation in undergraduate programmes: a state-level analysis. *International Journal of Lifelong Education, 21*(4), 305–320.

Kapp, A. (1833). *Platon's Erziehungslehre, als Paedagogik für die Einzelnen und als Staatspaedagogik.* Minden und Leipzig: Ferdinand Essmann.

Kasworm, C., Rose, A., & Ross-Gordon, J. (2010). *The handbook of adult and continuing education.* Thousand Oaks: Sage.

Kaufmann, K. (2015). *AES from a research perspective.* Paper Presented at the DwB-Training Course: Working with Data from Official Statistics in Europe Particularly the Adult Education Survey (2011).

Kaufmann, K., & Widany, S. (2013). Berufliche Weiterbildung – Gelegenheits- und Teilnahmestrukturen. *Zeitschrift für Erziehungswissenschaft, 16*(1), 29–54.

Keller, J. M. (1987). Strategies for stimulating the motivation to learn. *Performance and Instruction, 26*(8), 1–7.

Kihlstrom, J. F. (2013). The person-situation interaction. In D. Carlston (Ed.), *Oxford handbook of social cognition* (pp. 789–805). Oxford: Oxford University Press.

Klein, J. (2000). A conceptual vocabulary of interdisciplinary Science. In P. Weingart & N. Stehr (Eds.), *Practising interdisciplinarity* (pp. 3–24). Toronto: Toronto University Press.

Knipprath, H., & De Rick, K. (2015). How social and human capital predict participation in lifelong learning: a longitudinal data analysis. *Adult Education Quarterly, 65*(1), 50–66.

Knorr-Cetina, K., & Cicourel, A. V. (2014). *Advances in social theory and methodology: towards an integration of micro- and macro-sociologies.* London: Routledge.

Knowles, M. S. (1975). *Self-directed learning: a guide for learners and teachers.* Englewood Cliffs: Prentice Hall.

Koch, J., Polnick, B., & Irby, B. (2013). *Girls and women in stem: a never ending story.* Charlotte, NC: Information Age Publishing.

Kuckulenz, A. (2007). *Studies on continuing vocational training in Germany: an empirical assessment.* Heidelberg: Physica-Verlag.

Kyndt, E., & Baert, H. (2013). Antecedents of employees' involvement in work-related learning: a systematic review. *Review of Educational Research, 83*(2), 273–313.

Kyndt, E., Dochy, F., & Nijs, H. (2009). Learning conditions for non-formal and informal workplace learning. *Journal of Workplace Learning, 21*(5), 369–383.

Kyndt, E., Govaerts, N., Claes, T., De La Marche, J., & Dochy, F. (2013). What motivates low-qualified employees to participate in training and development? A mixed-method study on their learning intentions. *Studies in Continuing Education, 35*(3), 315–336.

Kyndt, E., Michielsen, M., van Nooten, L., Nijs, S., & Baert, H. (2011). Learning in the second half of the career: stimulating and prohibiting reasons for participation in formal learning activities. *International Journal of Lifelong Education, 30*(5), 681–699.

Laal, M., & Salamati, P. (2012). Lifelong learning; why do we need it? *Procedia – Social and Behavioral Sciences, 31*(2012), 399–403.

Landers, M. R., McWhorter, J. W., Krum, L. L., & Glovinsky, D. (2005). Mandatory continuing education in physical therapy: survey of physical therapists in states with and states without a mandate. *Physical Therapy, 85*(9), 861–871.

Lave, J., & Wenger, E. (1991). *Situated learning: legitimate peripheral participation.* Cambridge: Cambridge University Press.

Lavrijsen, J., & Nicaise, I. (2015). *Patterns in life-long learning participation. A descriptive analysis using the LFS, the AES and PIAAC.* Leuven: Steunpunt Studie- en Schoolloopbanen.

Lawn, M., & Grek, S. (2012). *Europeanizing education: governing a new policy space.* Oxford: Symposium Books.

Lee, M., Thayer, T., & Madyun, N. (2008). The evolution of the European Union's lifelong learning policies: an institutional learning perspective. *Comparative Education, 44*(4), 445–463.

Levinson, D. (1986). A conception of adult development. *American Psychologist, 41*(1), 3–13.

Liang, J., & Wu, S. (2010). Nurses' motivations for web based learning and the role of Internet self-efficacy. *Innovations in Education and Teaching International, 47*(1), 25–37.

Lincoln, Y. S., & Guba, E. G. (1985). *Naturalistic inquiry.* Newbury Park: Sage.

Lindeman, E. C. (1926). *The meaning of adult education.* New York: New Republic.

Livingstone, D. W. (2001). *Adults' informal learning: definitions, findings, gaps and future research. NALL Working Paper No 21.* Toronto: University of Toronto.

Livneh, C., & Livneh, H. (1999). Continuing professional education among educators: predictors of participation in learning activities. *Adult Education Quarterly, 49*(2), 91–106.

Loevinger, J. (1976). *Ego development.* San Francisco: Jossey-Bass.

London, J., Wenkert, R., & Hagstrom, W. O. (1963). *Adult education and social class.* Berkeley: University of California.

London, M. (2011). *The Oxford handbook of lifelong learning.* Oxford: Oxford University Press.

Lowenthal, M. F., Thurnher, M., & Chiriboga, D. (1977). *Four stages of life.* San Francisco: Jossey-Bass.

Macionis, J. J. (2013). *Sociology.* Cambridge: Pearson Publishers.

Macleod, F., & Lambe, P. (2007). Patterns and trends in part-time adult education participation in relation to UK nation, class, place of participation, gender, age and disability 1998–2003. *International Journal of Lifelong Education, 26*(4), 399–418.

Manninen, J., & Merilainen, M. (2011). *Benefits of lifelong learning: BeLL survey results.* Joensuu: University of Eastern Finland.

Martens, K., & Jakobi, A. J. (2010). Expanding and intensifying governance: the OECD in education policy. In K. Martens & A. J. Jakobi (Eds.), *Mechanisms of OECD governance: international incentives for national policy-making?* (pp. 163–179). Oxford: Oxford University Press.

Maruatona, T. (2006). Lifelong learning for facilitating democratic participation in Africa. *International Journal of Lifelong Education, 25*(6), 547–560.

Maslow, A. H. (1943). A theory of human motivation. *Psychological Review, 50*, 370–396.

Maurer, T. J., Weiss, E., & Barbeite, F. (2003). A model of involvement in work-related learning and development activity: the effects of individual, situational, motivational, and age variables. *Journal of Applied Psychology, 88*(4), 707–724.

McDonald, J. C. (2003). *Barriers to participation in educational programs as perceived by first-time enrolling freshmen in higher education. Doctoral dissertation.* Louisiana: Louisiana State University.

McGivney, V. (1999). *Informal learning in the community: a trigger for change and development.* Leicester: NIACE.

McGivney, V. (2000). *Working with excluded groups: guidelines on good practice for providers and policy-makers in working with groups under-represented in adult learning.* Leicester: NIACE.

McGivney, V. (2002). *Spreading the word, reaching out to new learners.* Leicester: NIACE.

McIntosh, S., & Vignoles, A. (2001). Measuring and assessing the impact of basic skills on labour market outcomes. *Oxford Economic Papers, 53*(3), 453–481.

Meissner, M. (1971). The long arm of the job: a study of work and leisure. *Industrial Relations, 10*(3), 239–260.

Mejer, L., & Boateng, S. K. *The EU Adult Education Survey: history and latest developments.* Luxembourg: Eurostat.

Merizow, J. (1991). *Transformative dimensions in adult learning.* San Francisco: Jossey-Bass.

Merriam, S., Caffarella, R., & Baumgartner, L. (2007). *Learning in adulthood: a comprehensive guide.* San Francisco: Jossey-Bass.

Merrill, B. (2014). Determined to stay or determined to leave? A tale of learner identities, biographies and adult students in higher education. *Studies in Higher Education, 40*(10), 1859–1871.

Merrill, B., & West, L. (2009). *Using biographical methods in social research.* Thousand Oaks: Sage.

Milana, M. (2012). Political globalization and the shift from adult education to lifelong learning. *European Journal for Research on the Education and Learning of Adults, 3*(2), 103–117.

Milana, M., & McBain, L. (2014). Adult education in the United States of America: a critical examination of national policy (1998–2014). *ENCYCLOPAIDEIA, XVIII*(40), 34–52.

Milana, M., & Holford, J. (2014). *Adult education policy and the European Union: theoretical and methodological perspectives* Rotterdam: Sense Publishers.

Milburn, A. (2012). *University challenge: how higher education can advance social mobility a progress report by the independent reviewer on social mobility and child poverty.* London: Cabinet Office.

Miller, H. (1967). *Participation of adults in education: a force-field analysis.* Boston: Center for the Study of Liberal Education for Adults.

Ministry of Human Resource Development (1986). *National policy on education.* New Delhi: Ministry of Human Resource Development.

Moore, J., Sanders, J., & Higham, L. (2013). *Literature review of research into widening participation to higher education.* London: HEFCE.

Morgan-Klein, B., & Osborne, M. (2007). *The concepts and practices of lifelong learning.* London: Routledge.

Mulenga, D., & Liang, J. -S. (2008). Motivations for older adults' participation in distance education: a study at the National Open University of Taiwan. *International Journal of Lifelong Education, 27*(3), 289–314.

Nesbit, T. (2005a). *Class concerns: adult education and social class.* San Francisco: Jossey-Bass.

Nesbit, T. (2005b). Social class and adult education. *New Directions for Adult and Continuing Education, 2005*(106), 5–14.

Nielsen, P. (2004). *Personale i vidensokonomien.* Aalborg: Aalborg Universitetsforlag.

Nilsson, A., & Wrench, J. (2009). Ethnic inequality and discrimination in the labour market. In K. Kraal, J. Roosblad & J. Wrench (Eds.), *Equal opportunities and ethnic inequality in European labour markets: discrimination, gender and policies of diversity* (pp. 23–46). Amsterdam: Amsterdam University Press.

O'Donnell, V. L., & Tobbell, J. (2007). The transition of adult students to higher education: legitimate peripheral participation in a community of practice? *Adult Education Quarterly, 57*(4), 312–328.

OECD. (2004). *Co-financing lifelong learning: towards a systematic approach.* Paris: OECD.

OECD. (2007). *Qualifications systems: bridges to lifelong learning.* Paris: OECD.

OECD. (2010). Equity and equality of opportunity. In OECD (Ed.), *Education today 2010: the OECD perspective* (pp. 67–77). Paris: OECD.

OECD. (2012). *Assessment of higher education learning outcomes feasibility study report volume 1 design and implementation.* Paris: OECD.

OECD. (2013a). *Assessment of higher education learning outcomes feasibility study report volume 2 data analysis and national experiences.* Paris: OECD.

OECD. (2013b). *Assessment of higher education learning outcomes feasibility study report volume 3 further insights.* Paris: OECD.

OECD. (2013c). *OECD Skills Outlook 2013: first results from the survey of adult skills.* Paris: OECD.

OECD. (2013d). *OECD skills studies skills development and training in SMEs.* Paris: OECD.

OECD. (2013e). *Technical report of the OECD Survey of Adult Skills (PIAAC)*. Paris: OECD.

OECD. (2014). *Education at a Glance 2014 OECD indicators*. Paris: OECD.

Óhidy, A. (2008). *Lifelong learning interpretations of an education policy in Europe*. Wiesbaden: Springer VS.

Oplatka, I., & Tevel, T. (2006). Liberation and revitalization: the choice and meaning of higher education among Israeli female students in midlife. *Adult Education Quarterly, 57*(1), 62–84.

Osborne, M. (2003). Policy and practice in widening participation: a six country comparative study of access as flexibility. *International Journal of Lifelong Education, 22*(1), 43–58.

Ouane, A. (2009). UNESCO's drive for lifelong learning. In P. Jarvis (Ed.), *The Routledge international handbook of lifelong learning* (pp. 302–311). London: Routledge.

Ozga, J. (2012). Governing knowledge: data, inspection and education policy in Europe. *Globalisation, Societies and Education, 10*(4), 439–455.

Parsons, T. (1942). Age and sex in the social structure of the United States. *American Sociological Review, 7*(5), 604–616.

Paterson, L., & Iannelli, C. (2007). Social class and educational attainment: a comparative study of England, Wales, and Scotland. *Sociology of Education, 80*(4), 330–358.

Paulson, K., & Boeke, M. (2006). *Adult learners in the United States: a national profile*. Washington, D.C.: American Council on Education.

Pfeffer, F. T. (2008). Persistent inequality in educational attainment and its institutional context. *European Sociological Review, 24*(5), 543–565.

Pont, B. (2004). Improving access to and participation in adult learning in OECD countries. *European Journal of Education, 39*(1), 31–45.

Prins, E. (2006). Relieving isolation, avoiding vices: the social purposes of participation in a Salvadoran literacy program. *Adult Education Quarterly, 57*(1), 5–25.

Puhani, P. A., & Sonderhof, K. (2011). The effects of parental leave extension on training for young women. *Journal of Population Economics, 24*(2), 731–760.

Putnam, R. (2000). *Bowling alone: the collapse and revival of American community*. New York: Simon & Schuster.

Putnam, R. (2004). *Democracies in flux: the evolution of social capital in contemporary society*. Oxford: Oxford University Press.

Raey, D. (2010). Sociology, social class and education. In M. Apple, S. Ball & L. A. Gandin (Eds.), *The Routledge handbook of the sociology of education* (pp. 396–404). London: Routledge.

Raffe, D. (2011). *Policy borrowing or policy learning? How (not) to improve education systems – Briefing 57*. Edinburgh: Centre for Educational Sociology.

Ragin, C. C. (1989). *The comparative method: moving beyond qualitative and quantitative strategies*. Berkeley: University of California Press.

Rathus, S. (2012). *Psychology: concepts and connections*. Belmont: Wadsworth Cengage Learning.

Rauhvargers, A., & Rusakova, A. (2009). *Improving recognition in the European Higher Education Area: an analysis of national action plans.* Strasbourg: Council of Europe Publishing.

Reeves, F. W., Fansler, T., & Houle, C. O. (1938). *Adult education: the Regents' Inquiry into the character and cost of public education in the State of New York.* New York: McGraw-Hill.

Rhodes, C. M. (2013). *Culturally responsive teaching practices of adult education English for speakers of other languages and English for academic purposes teachers. Doctoral dissertation.* Tampa: University of South Florida.

Richards, M., & Sacker, A. (2003). *Lifetime antecedents of cognitive reserve. Journal of Clinical and Experimental Neuropsychology, 25,* 614–624.

Riddell, S., Edward, S., Boeren, E., & Weedon, E. (2013). *Widening access to higher education: does anyone know what works?* Edinburgh: Universities Scotland.

Riddell, S., Markowitsch, J., & Weedon, E. (2012). *Lifelong learning in Europe: equity and efficiency in the balance.* Bristol: Policy Press.

Riddell, S., & Weedon, E. (2012). Lifelong learning and the wider European socioeconomic context. In S. Riddell, J. Markowitsch & E. Weedon (Eds.), *Lifelong learning in Europe: equity and efficiency in the balance* (pp. 17–38). Bristol: Policy Press.

Riley, M. W., Foner, A., & Waring, J. (1972). *Ageing and society volume 3: a sociology of age stratification.* New York: Russell Sage.

Robert, P. (2012). The socio-demographic obstacles to participation in lifelong learning across Europe. In S. Riddell, J. Markowitsch & E. Weedon (Eds.), *Lifelong learning in Europe: equity and efficiency in the balance* (pp. 87–101). Bristol: Policy Press.

Robson, C. (2011). *Real world research.* Chichester: John Wiley & Sons.

Robson, S. M., Hansson, R. O., Abalos, A., & Booth, M. (2006). Successful aging: criteria for aging well in the workplace. *Journal of Career Development, 33*(2), 156–177.

Rokeach, M. (1968). *Beliefs, attitudes, and values: a theory of organization and change.* San Francisco: Jossey-Bass.

Roosmaa, E.-L., & Saar, E. (2010). Participating in non-formal learning: patterns of inequality in EU-15 and the new EU-8 member countries. *Journal of Education and Work, 23*(3), 179–206.

Roosmaa, E.-L., & Saar, E. (2012). Participation in non-formal learning in EU-15 and EU-8 countries: demand and supply side factors. *International Journal of Lifelong Education, 31*(4), 477–501.

Rubenson, K. (1977). *Participation in recurrent education: a research review.* Paper Presented at the Meeting of National delegates on Developments in Recurrent Education.

Rubenson, K. (1998). Adults' readiness to learn: questioning lifelong learning for all. In Proceedings of the Adult Education Research Conference, No. 39 (pp. 257–262). San Antonio: University of the IncarnateWord and Texas A & M University.

Rubenson, K. (2006). Constructing the lifelong learning paradigm: competing visions from the OECD and UNESCO. In S. Ehlers (Ed.), *Milestones towards lifelong learning systems* (pp. 151–170). Copenhagen: Danish School of Education.

Rubenson, K., Desjardins, R. & Milana, M. (2006). *Unequal chances to participate in adult learning: international perspectives.* Paris: UNESCO.

Rubenson, K. (2009). OECD educational policies and world hegemon. In R. Mahon & S. McBride (Eds.), *The OECD and transnational governance* (pp. 96–116). Vancouver: UBC Press.

Rubenson, K. (2011a). *Adult learning and education.* Oxford: Elsevier.

Rubenson, K. (2011b). Barriers to participation in adult education. In K. Rubenson (Ed.), *Adult learning and education* (pp. 216–223). Oxford: Elsevier.

Rubenson, K., & Desjardins, R. (2009). The impact of welfare state regimes on barriers to participation in adult education: a bounded agency Model. *Adult Education Quarterly, 59*(3), 187–207.

Rubenson, K., Desjardins, R., & Yoon, E.-S. (2007). *Adult learning in Canada: a comparative perspective results from the Adult Literacy and Life Skills Survey.* Ottawa: Statistics Canada.

Saar, E., Taht, K., & Roosalu, T. (2014). Institutional barriers for adults' participation in higher education in thirteen European countries. *Higher Education, 68*(5), 691–710.

Saar, E., & Ure, O.-B. (2013). Lifelong learning systems: overview and extension of different typologies. In E. Saar, O.-B. Ure & J. Holford (Eds.), *Lifelong learning in Europe: national patterns and challenges* (pp. 46–81). Cheltenham: Edward Elgar.

Saar, E., Ure, O. B., & Holford, J. (2013). *Lifelong learning in Europe: national patterns and challenges.* Cheltenham: Edward Elgar.

Sabates, R., & Feinstein, L. (2006). Education and the take-up of preventative health care. *Social Science & Medicine, 62*, 2998–3010.

Sabates, R., & Hammond, C. (2008). *The impact of lifelong learning on happiness and well-being.* Leicester: National Institute for Adult and Continuing Education.

Sahu, F. M., & Sageeta, R. (2004). Self-efficacy and well-being in working and non-working women: the moderating role of involvement. *Psychology and Developing Societies, 15*, 187–200.

Savage, M., & Bennett, T. (2005). Editors' introduction: cultural capital and social inequality. *The British Journal of Sociology, 56*(1), 1–12.

Scanlan, C. L., & Darkenwald, G. G. (1984). Identifying deterrents to participation in continuing education. *Adult Education Quarterly, 34*(3), 155–166.

Scheff, T. J. (1990). *Microsociology: discourse, emotion, and social structure.* Chicago: The University of Chicago Press.

Schmidt-Hertha, B., Jelenc Krasovec, S., & Formosa, M. (2014). *Learning across generations. Contemporary issues in older adult education.* Rotterdam: Sense Publishers.

Schuetze, H. G. (2006). International concepts and agendas of lifelong learning. *Compare: A Journal of Comparative and International Education, 36*(3), 289–306.

Schuetze, H. G., & Slowey, M. (2002). Participation and exclusion: a comparative analysis of non-traditional students and lifelong learners in higher education. *Higher Education, 44*(3–4), 309–327.

Schuller, T. (2010). The OECD and lifelong learning. In P. Jarvis (Ed.), *The Routledge international handbook of lifelong learning*. London: Routledge.

Schuller, T., Preston, J., Hammond, C., Brassett-Grundy, A., & Bynner, J. (2004). *The benefits of learning: the impact of education on health, family life and social capital*. London: Routledge.

Schuller, T. & Watson, D. (2009). *Learning through life: inquiry into the future for lifelong learning*. Leicester: NIACE.

Scott, C., Burns, A., & Cooney, G. (1998). Motivation for return to study as a predictor of completion degree amongst female mature students with children. *Higher Education, 35*(2), 221–239.

Sellar, S., & Lingard, B. (2014). The OECD and the expansion of PISA: new global modes of governance in education. *British Educational Research Journal, 40*(6), 917–936.

Sen, A. K. (1999). *Development as freedom*. Oxford: Oxford University Press.

Shauman, K. A. (2006). Occupational sex segregation and the earnings of occupations: what causes the link among college-educated workers? *Social Science Research, 35*, 577–619.

Sheared, V., Johnson-Bailey, J., Colin, S. A. J., Peterson, E., & Brookfield, S. D. (2010). *The handbook of race and adult education: a resource for dialogue on racism*. San Francisco: Jossey-Bass.

Simola, H., Ozga, J., Segerholm, C., & Varjo, J. (2011). Governing by numbers: the rise of data in education. In J. Ozga, Dahler-Larsen, C. Segerholm & H. Simola (Eds.), *Fabricating quality in education: data and governance in Europe* (pp. 96–100). London: Routledge.

Simpson, T. (1997). The initial motivation of students enrolling in an adult and workplace education programme. *Asia-Pacific Journal of Teacher Education, 25*(1), 67–77.

Singh, M. (2015). *Global perspectives on recognising non-formal and informal learning: why recognition matters*. Dordrecht: Springer.

Skilbeck, M. (2006). Participation in learning: why, what, where and how do people learn? In J. D. Chapman, P. Cartwright & J. McGilp (Eds.), *Lifelong learning, participation and equity* (pp. 47–78). Dordrecht: Springer.

Skilton-Sylvester, E. (2002). Should I stay or should I go? Investigating Cambodian Women's participation and investment in adult ESL programs. *Adult Education Quarterly, 53*(1), 9–26.

Smith, C. A., Cohen-Callow, A., Dia, D. A., Bliss, D. L., Gantt, A., Cornelius, L. J., et al. (2006). Staying current in a changing profession: evaluating perceived change resulting from continuing professional education. *Journal of Social Work Education, 42*(3), 465–482.

Smith, E. (2008). *Using secondary data in educational and social research*. Maidenhead: Open University Press.

Smith, M. K. (1999). Learning theory. Retrieved from http://infed.org/mobi/learning-theory-models-product-and-process/.

Smith, R. (2012). Clarifying the subject centred approach to vocational learning theory: negotiated participation. *Studies in Continuing Education, 34*(2), 159–174.

Sniehotta, F. F., Scholz, U., & Schwarzer, R. (2005). Bridging the intention–behaviour gap: planning, self-efficacy, and action control in the adoption and maintenance of physical exercise. *Psychology & Health, 20*(2), 143–160.

Sohlman, A. (2011). Financing of adult and lifelong learning. In K. Rubenson (Ed.), *Adult learning and education* (pp. 186–191). London: Elsevier.

Sørensen, J. H. (2008). Like the chicken and the egg? Relationship between innovation activity and training activities in enterprises – a critical assessment. In J. Markowitsch & G. Hefler (Eds.), *Enterprise training in Europe: comparative studies on cultures, markets and public support initiatives* (pp. 210–237). Vienna: Lit Verlag.

Stern, Y. (2006). *Cognitive reserve: theory and application.* New York, NY: Taylor and Francis, Inc.

Stern, Y. (2009). Cognitive reserve. *Neuropsychologia, 47*(10), 20105–2028.

Stern, E., Sommerlad, L., Institute of Personnel and Development, & International Federation of Training and Development Organizations. (1999). *Workplace learning, culture and performance.* London: Institute of Personnel & Development.

Stine-Morrow, E. L., & Parisi, J. M. (2011). The adult development of cognition and learning. In K. Rubenson (Ed.), *Adult Learning and Education.* Oxford: Elsevier.

Sullivan, A. (2002). Bourdieu and education: how useful is Bourdieu's theory for researchers? *The Netherlands' Journal for Social Sciences, 38*(2), 144–166.

Sultana, R. G. (2008). *The challenge of policy implementation: a comparative Analysis of VET school reforms in Albania, Kosovo and Turkey.* Turin: European Training Foundation.

Takayama, K. (2009). Politics of externalization in reflexive times: reinventing Japanese education reform discourses through 'Finnish PISA success'. *Comparative Education Review, 54*(1), 51–75.

Tamassia, C., Lennon, M., Yamamoto, K., & Kirsch, I. (2007). *Adult education in America: a first look at results from the Adult Education Program and Learner Surveys.* Princeton, NJ: Educational Testing Service.

Tennant, M. (1997). *Psychology and adult learning.* London: Routledge.

Tennant, M., & Pogson, P. (2002). *Learning and change in the adult years: a developmental perspective.* San Francisco: Jossey-Bass.

Thomas, L. (2000). 'Bums on Seats'; or 'Listening to Voices': evaluating widening participation initiatives using participatory action research. *Studies in Continuing Education, 22*(1), 95–113.

Thomas, L. (2005). *Widening participation in post-compulsory education.* London/ New York: Continuum.

Tippelt, R., Jutta, H., von Hippel, A., Barz, H., & Baum, D. (2008). *Weiterbildung und soziale Milieus in Deutschland - Band 3: Milieumarketing implementieren.* Bielefeld: Bertelsmann Verlag.

Torres, C. A. (2013). *Political sociology of adult education.* Rotterdam: Sense Publishers.

Trowler, P., Saunders, M., & Bamber, V. (2012). *Tribes and territories in the 21st-century: rethinking the significance of disciplines in higher education.* London: Routledge.

Tuijnman, A. (1991). Lifelong education: a test of the accumulation hypothesis. *International Journal of Lifelong Education, 10*(4), 275–285.

Tuijnman, A. (2003). Measuring lifelong learning for the new economy. *Compare, 33*(4), 471–482.

UNESCO. (1979). *Terminology of adult education.* Paris: UNESCO.

UNESCO. (2006). *The Executive Board of the United Nations Educational, Scientific and Cultural Organization.* Paris: UNESCO.

UNESCO. (2013). *Global report on adult learning and education.* Paris: UNESCO.

UNESCO. (2014). *Joint proposal of the EFA Steering Committee on education post-15.* Paris: UNESCO.

UNESCO. (2015). *Education for all global monitoring report.* Paris: UNESCO.

Vaillant, G. E. (1977). *Adaptation to life.* Boston: Little Brown.

Valentine, T., & Darkenwald, G. G. (1990). Deterrents to participation in adult education: profiles of potential learners. *Adult Education Quarterly, 41*(1), 29–42.

van Gent, B. (1998). T.T. ten Have; architect van de andragologie. In J. Goudsblom, P. de Rooy & J. Wieten (Eds.), *In de zevende; de eerste lichting hoogleraren aan de Politiek-Sociale Faculteit in Amsterdam* (pp. 66–80). Amsterdam: Het Spinhuis.

Vansteenkiste, M., Niemiec, C., & Soenens, B. (2010). The development of the five mini-theories of self-determination theory: An historical overview, emerging trends, and future directions. In T. Urdan & S. Karabenick (Eds.), *Advances in Motivation and Achievement, vol. 16: the decade ahead* (pp. 105–166). UK: Emerald Publishing.

Vermeersch, L., Vandenbroucke, A., & Boeren, E. (2009). *Het leren zoals het is ... bij volwassenen met een geletterdheidsrisico.* Leuven: Research Institute for Work and Society.

Vignoles, A. (2007). *The use of large scale data-sets in educational research.* London: Teaching and Learning Programme.

Vroom, V. H. (1964). *Work and motivation.* New York: Wiley & Sons.

Wacquant, L. (2004). Habitus. In J. Beckert & M. Zafirovski (Eds.), *International encyclopedia of economic sociology* (pp. 315–319). London: Routledge.

Wainwright, E., Marandet, E., Buckingham, S., & Smith, F. (2011). The training-to-work trajectory: pressures for and subversions to participation in the neoliberal learning market in the UK. *Gender, Place & Culture: A Journal of Feminist Geography, 18*(5), 635–654.

Walter, P. (2004). Through a gender lens: explaining North-Eastern Thai women's participation in adult literacy education. *International Journal of Lifelong Education, 23*(5), 423–441.

Walters, M. (2000). The mature students' three Rs. *British Journal of Guidance & Counselling, 28*(2), 267–278.

Wang, Q. (2008). *Individuals' perceptions of lifelong learning and the labour market competition – a case study in Shanghai, China. Doctoral thesis.* Bath: University of Bath.

Weedon, E., & Riddell, S. (2012). Reducing or reinforcing inequality: assessing the impact of European policy on widening access to higher education. In S. Riddell, J. Markowitsch & E. Weedon (Eds.), *Lifelong learning in Europe: equity and efficiency in the balance* (pp. 125–150). Bristol: Policy Press.

West, L. (1996). Beyond fragments: adults, motivation and higher education. *Studies in the Education of Adults, 27*(2), 133–156.

White, P. (2012). Modelling the 'learning divide': predicting participation in adult learning and future learning intentions 2002 to 2010. *British Educational Research Journal, 38*(1), 153–175.

Whitley Jr., B. E., & Kite, M. E. (2012). *Principles of research in behavioral science: third edition.* New York: Routledge.

Williams, T., & LeMire, S. D. (2011). Air Force commanders and barriers to entry into a doctoral business program. *Journal of Education for Business, 86*(3), 140–147.

Willis, E. (1984). Radical feminism and feminist radicalism. *Social Text, 1984*(9/10), 91–118.

Wilson, A. L., & Hayes, E. R. (2000). *Handbook of adult and continuing education.* San Francisco: Jossey-Bass.

Wilson, J. P. (2011). *The Routledge encyclopaedia of UK education, training and employment: from the earliest statutes to the present day.* London: Routledge.

Wiseman, A. (2010). The uses of evidence for educational policymaking: global contexts and international trends. *Review of Research in Education, 34*(1), 1–24.

Wlodkowski, R. J., & Ginsberg, M. B. (1995). *Diversity and motivation: culturally responsive teaching.* San Francisco: Jossey-Bass.

Wolbers, M. H. J. (2005). Initial and further education: substitutes or complements? Differences in continuing education and training over the life-course of European workers. *International Review of Education, 51*(5–6), 459–478.

World Bank (2003). *Lifelong learning in the global knowledge economy: challenges for developing countries.* Washington, D.C.: World Bank.

Xu, Y. (2015). Focusing on women in STeM: a longitudinal examination of gender based earning gap of college graduates. *The Journal of Higher Education, 86*(4), 489–523.

Yang, B. (1998). Longitudinal study of participation in adult education: a theoretical formulation and empirical investigation. *International Journal of Lifelong Education, 17*(4), 247–259.

Yeaxlee, B. (1929). *Lifelong education: a sketch of the range and significance of the adult education movement.* London: Cassell and Company.

Yilmaz, K. (2013). Comparison of quantitative and qualitative research traditions: epistemological, theoretical, and methodological differences. *European Journal of Education, 48*(2), 311–325.

Young, M., & Allais, S. (2013). *Implementing national qualifications frameworks across five continents.* London: Routledge.

Youngreen, R. (2007). Kurt Lewin. In G. Ritzer (Ed.), *Encyclopedia of sociology* (pp. 2615–2618). Hoboken: Blackwell.

Yousif, A. A. (2009). *The state and development of adult learning and education in the Arab States Regional synthesis report.* Hamburg: UNESCO Institute for Lifelong Learning.

Zhang, X., & Palameta, B. (2006). *Participation in adult schooling and its earnings impact in Canada.* Ottawa: Statistics Canada.

Index

Lightning Source UK Ltd.
Milton Keynes UK
UKOW06n1527311016

286541UK00001B/2/P

9 781137 441829